Camp-Fire And Cotton-Field
Southern Adventure In Time Of War

by

Thomas W. Knox

Double 9
BOOKS

Camp-Fire And Cotton-Field
Southern Adventure In Time Of War
by Thomas W. Knox

ISBN: 978-93-60465-07-0

Published by

DOUBLE 9 BOOKS

2/13-B, Ansari Road
Daryaganj, New Delhi – 110002
info@double9books.com
www.double9books.com
Tel. 011-40042856

ABOUT THE AUTHOR

Journalist, novelist, and globe traveler Thomas Wallace Knox is most remembered for his work as a New York Herald correspondent during the American Civil War. Knox was a prolific writer who authored more than 45 books, including a well-liked line of adventure trip books for boys. Knox gained notoriety for his written critiques of William Tecumseh Sherman and his Union soldiers, which brought up the question of Sherman's sanity once more in public discourse. Because he provided crucial information on the Vicksburg Campaign, his work was controversial. Although Knox was found guilty of defying orders, he was cleared of spying accusations. Born in 1835 in Pembroke, New Hampshire, Thomas Wallace Knox attended the local schools. After training as a teacher, he relocated to Kingston, New York State, and established an institution there. Knox traveled west in 1860, when he was twenty-five years old, to participate in the Colorado gold rush. He began working for the Denver Daily News shortly after. Knox joined the California Volunteers at the start of the Civil War and was commissioned as a lieutenant colonel. After being hurt in a skirmish in Missouri, he was released. At that point, Knox went back to work for the New York Herald as a correspondent.

CONTENTS

CHAPTER I
ANTE BELLUM 9

CHAPTER II
MISSOURI IN THE EARLY DAYS 14

CHAPTER III
THE BEGINNING OF HOSTILITIES 21

CHAPTER IV
THE FIRST BATTLE IN MISSOURI 26

CHAPTER V
TO SPRINGFIELD AND BEYOND 31

CHAPTER VI
THE BATTLE OF WILSON CREEK 38

CHAPTER VII
THE RETREAT FROM SPRINGFIELD 46

CHAPTER VIII
GENERAL FREMONT'S PURSUIT OF PRICE 53

CHAPTER IX
THE SECOND CAMPAIGN TO SPRINGFIELD 59

CHAPTER X
TWO MONTHS OF IDLENESS 65

CHAPTER XI
ANOTHER CAMPAIGN IN MISSOURI 70

CHAPTER XII

THE FLIGHT AND THE PURSUIT..74

CHAPTER XIII

THE BATTLE OF PEA RIDGE 80

CHAPTER XIV

UP THE TENNESSEE AND AT PITTSBURG LANDING....................86

CHAPTER XV

SHILOH AND THE SIEGE OF CORINTH...92

CHAPTER XVI

CAPTURE OF FORT PILLOW AND

BATTLE OF MEMPHIS...99

CHAPTER XVII

IN MEMPHIS AND UNDER THE FLAG.. 105

CHAPTER XVIII

SUPERVISING A REBEL JOURNAL 111

CHAPTER XIX

THE FIRST SIEGE OF VICKSBURG... 116

CHAPTER XX

THE MARCH THROUGH ARKANSAS.--

THE SIEGE OF CINCINNATI 121

CHAPTER XXI

THE BATTLE OF CORINTH.. 126

CHAPTER XXII

THE CAMPAIGN FROM CORINTH.. 130

CHAPTER XXIII

GRANT'S OCCUPATION OF MISSISSIPPI....................................... 138

CHAPTER XXIV

THE BATTLE OF CHICKASAW BAYOU 144

CHAPTER XXV

BEFORE VICKSBURG... 150

CHAPTER XXVI
KANSAS IN WAR-TIME 155

CHAPTER XXVII
GETTYSBURG 164

CHAPTER XXVIII
IN THE NORTHWEST 173

CHAPTER XXIX
INAUGURATION OF A GREAT ENTERPRISE 182

CHAPTER XXX
COTTON-PLANTING IN 1863 187

CHAPTER XXXI
AMONG THE OFFICIALS 193

CHAPTER XXXII
A JOURNEY OUTSIDE THE LINES 198

CHAPTER XXXIII
OH THE PLANTATION 204

CHAPTER XXXIV
RULES AND REGULATIONS UNDER THE OLD
AND NEW SYSTEMS 212

CHAPTER XXXV
OUR FREE-LABOR ENTERPRISE IN PROGRESS 228

CHAPTER XXXVI
WAR AND AGRICULTURE 234

CHAPTER XXXVII
IN THE COTTON MARKET 240

CHAPTER XXXVIII
SOME FEATURES OF PLANTATION LIFE 249

CHAPTER XXXIX
VISITED BY GUERRILLAS 256

CHAPTER XL
PECULIARITIES OF PLANTATION LABOR 261

CHAPTER XLI
THE NEGROES AT A MILITARY POST.................................. 266

CHAPTER XLII
THE END OF THE EXPERIMENT 271

CHAPTER XLIII
THE MISSISSIPPI AND ITS PECULIARITIES....................... 281

CHAPTER XLIV
STEAMBOATING ON THE MISSISSIPPI IN
PEACE AND WAR... 287

CHAPTER XLV
THE ARMY CORRESPONDENT 295

CHAPTER XLVI
THE PRESENT CONDITION OF THE SOUTH 303

CHAPTER XLVII
HOW DISADVANTAGES MAY BE OVERCOME.............. 309

CHAPTER XLVIII
THE RESOURCES OF THE SOUTHERN STATES.............. 313

CHAPTER I
ANTE BELLUM

I passed the summer and autumn of 1860 in the Rocky Mountain Gold Region. At that time the population of the young Territory was composed of emigrants from Northern and Southern States, those from the colder regions being in the majority. When the Presidential election took place, there was much angry discussion of the great questions of the day, and there were threats of violence on the part of the friends of the "institution." The residents of the Gold Region were unable to cast their votes for the men of their choice, but their anxiety to know the result was very great.

When it was announced that the Republican candidate had triumphed, there were speedy signs of discontent. Some of the more impulsive Southerners departed at once for their native States, predicting a separation of Dixie from the North before the end of the year. Some went to New Mexico, and others to Texas, while many remained to press their favorite theories upon their neighbors. The friends of the Union were slow to believe that any serious difficulty would take place. Long after the secession of South Carolina they were confident our differences could be healed without an appeal to arms.

My visit to the Rocky Mountains was a professional one. During my stay in that region I supplied several Eastern journals with letters from Colorado and New Mexico. One after another, the editors of these journals informed me that letters from the Territories had lost their interest, owing to the troubles growing out of the election. Wishing to take part in the drama about to be enacted, I essayed a midwinter journey across the plains, and, early in February, stood in the editorial room of *The Herald*.

I announced my readiness to proceed to any point between the Poles, wherever *The Herald* desired a correspondent. The editor-in-chief was busy over a long letter from some point in the South, but his response was promptly given. Half reading, half pausing over the letter, he briefly said:--

"A long and bloody war is upon us, in which the whole country will be engaged. We shall desire you to take the field; probably in the West. It may be several weeks before we need you, but the war cannot be long delayed."

At that time few persons in the North looked upon the situation with any fears of trouble. There were some who thought a hostile collision was among the possibilities, but these persons were generally in the minority. Many believed the secession movement was only the hasty work of political leaders, that would be soon undone when the people of the South came to their senses.

That the South would deliberately plunge the country into civil war was difficult to comprehend, even after the first steps had been taken. The majority of the Northern people were hoping and believing, day by day, that something might transpire to quell the excitement and adjust the difficulties threatening to disturb the country.

Before leaving the Rocky Mountains I did not believe that war was certain to ensue, though I considered it quite probable. As I passed through Missouri, the only slave State that lay in my route, I found every thing comparatively quiet. In St. Joseph, on the day of my arrival, the election for delegates to the State Convention was being held. There was no disorder, more than is usual on election days in small cities. Little knots of people were engaged in discussion, but the discussions partook of no extraordinary bitterness. The vote of the city was decidedly in favor of keeping the State in the Union.

Between the 7th of December and the 12th of April, the Northern blood warmed slowly. The first gun at Sumter quickened its pulsations. When the President issued his call for seventy-five thousand men for three months, to put down insurrection, the North woke to action. Everywhere the response was prompt, earnest, patriotic. In the Northern cities the recruiting offices were densely thronged. New York and Massachusetts were first to send their favorite regiments to the front, but they were not long in the advance. Had the call been for four times seventy-five thousand, and for a service of three years, there is little doubt the people would have responded without hesitation.

For a short time after my arrival at the East, I remained in a small town in Southern New Hampshire. A few days after the first call was issued, a friend invited me to a seat in his carriage for a ride to Portsmouth, the sea-port of the State. On reaching the city we found the war spirit fully aroused. Two companies of infantry were drilling in the public square, and the citizens were in a state of great excitement. In the course of the afternoon my friend and myself were arrested, by a committee of respectable citizens, who suspected us of being Southern emissaries. It was with great difficulty we convinced them they had made a slight mistake. We referred them to the only acquaintances we had in the city. They refused to consider the truth established in the mouths of two witnesses, and were not induced to give us our liberty until all convenient proof of our identity had been adduced.

To be arrested within twenty miles of home, on suspicion of being delegated from Charleston or Montgomery, was one of my most amusing experiences of the war. The gentleman who accompanied me was a very earnest believer in coercion. His business in Portsmouth on that occasion was to offer his services in a regiment then being formed. A few months later he received a commission in the army, but did not obtain it through any of our temporary acquaintances at Portsmouth.

Our captors were the solid men of the city, any one of whom could have sat for the portrait of Mr. Turveydrop without the slightest alteration. On taking us into custody, they stated the grounds on which they arrested us. Our dark complexions and long beards had aroused suspicions concerning the places of our nativity. Suspicion was reduced to a certainty when one of them heard me mention my presence in Missouri on the day of choosing candidates for the Convention. Our purpose was divined when I asked if there was any activity at the Navy Yard. We were Rebel emissaries, who designed to lay their Navy Yard in ashes!

On our release and departure we were followed to our homes, that the correctness of our representations might be ascertained. This little occurrence, in the center of New England, where the people claim to be thoroughly quiet and law-abiding, indicated that the war spirit in that part of the North was more than momentary.

The West was not behind the Eastern States in the determination to subdue the Rebellion. Volunteers were gathering at Cairo, and threatening to occupy points further down the Mississippi. At St. Louis the struggle was active between the Unionists and the Secessionists.

A collision was a mere question of time, and of short time at the best.

As I visited *The Herald* office for final instructions, I found that the managing editor had determined upon a vigorous campaign. Every point of interest was to be covered, so that the operations of our armies would be fully recorded from day to day. The war correspondents had gone to their posts, or were just taking their departure. One correspondent was already on the way to Cairo. I was instructed to watch the military movements in Missouri, and hastened to St. Louis as fast as steam could bear me.

Detained twelve hours at Niagara, by reason of missing a railway train, I found that the opening war gave promise of affecting that locality. The hotel-keepers were gloomy at the prospect of losing their Southern patronage, and half feared they would be obliged to close their establishments. There were but few visitors, and even these were not of the class which scatters its money profusely. The village around the Falls displayed positive signs of dullness, and the inhabitants had personal as well as patriotic interest in wishing there was no war. The Great Cataract was unchanged in its beauty and grandeur. The flood from the Lakes was not diminished, and the precipice over which the water plunged was none the less steep. The opening war had no effect upon this wonder of the New World.

In Chicago, business was prostrated on account of the outbreak of hostilities. Most of the banks in Illinois had been holding State bonds as securities for the redemption of their circulation. As these bonds were nearly all of Southern origin, the beginning of the war had materially affected their value. The banks found their securities rapidly becoming insecure, and hence there was a depreciation in the currency. This was not uniform, but varied from five to sixty per cent., according to the value of the bonds the respective banks were holding. Each morning and evening bulletins were issued stating the value of the notes of the various banking-houses. Such a currency was very inconvenient to handle, as the payment of any considerable sum required a calculation to establish the worth of each note.

Many rumors were in circulation concerning the insecurity of a Northern visitor in St. Louis, but none of the stories were very alarming. Of one thing all were certain--the star of the Union was in the ascendant. On arriving in St. Louis I found the city far from quiet, though there was nothing to lead a stranger to consider his personal safety in danger. I had ample material for entering at once upon my professional duties, in chronicling the disordered and threatening state of affairs.

On the day of my arrival, I met a gentleman I had known in the Rocky Mountains, six months before. I knew his courage was beyond question, having seen him in several disturbances incident to the Gold Regions; but I was not aware which side of the great cause he had espoused. After our first greetings, I ventured to ask how he stood.

"I am a Union man," was his emphatic response.

"What kind of a Union man are you?"

"I am this kind of a Union man," and he threw open his coat, and showed me a huge revolver, strapped to his waist.

There were many loyal men in St. Louis, whose sympathies were evinced in a similar manner. Revolvers were at a premium.

Some of the Secessionists ordered a quantity of revolvers from New York, to be forwarded by express. To prevent interference by the Union authorities, they caused the case to be directed to "Colonel Francis P. Blair, Jr., care of ----." They thought Colonel Blair's name would secure the property from seizure. The person in whose care the revolvers were sent was a noted Secessionist, who dealt extensively in fire-arms.

Colonel Blair learned of the shipment, and met the box at the station. Fifty revolvers of the finest quality, bought and paid for by the Secessionists, were distributed among the friends of Colonel Blair, and were highly prized by the recipients.

CHAPTER II
MISSOURI IN THE EARLY DAYS

The Border States were not prompt to follow the example of the States on the Gulf and South Atlantic coast. Missouri and Kentucky were loyal, if the voice of the majority is to be considered the voice of the population. Many of the wealthier inhabitants were, at the outset, as they have always been, in favor of the establishment of an independent Southern Government. Few of them desired an appeal to arms, as they well knew the Border States would form the front of the Confederacy, and thus become the battle-field of the Rebellion. The greater part of the population of those States was radically opposed to the secession movement, but became powerless under the noisy, political leaders who assumed the control. Many of these men, who were Unionists in the beginning, were drawn into the Rebel ranks on the plea that it would be treason to refuse to do what their State Government had decided upon.

The delegates to the Missouri State Convention were elected in February, 1861, and assembled at St. Louis in the following April. Sterling Price, afterward a Rebel general, was president of this Convention, and spoke in favor of keeping the State in the Union. The Convention thought it injudicious for Missouri to secede, at least at that time, and therefore she was not taken out. This discomfited the prime movers of the secession schemes, as they had counted upon the Convention doing the desired work. In the language of one of their own number, "they had called a Convention to take the State out of the Union, and she must be taken out at all hazards." Therefore a new line of policy was adopted.

The Governor of Missouri was one of the most active and unscrupulous Secessionists. After the failure of the Convention to unite Missouri with the Confederacy, Governor Jackson overhauled the militia laws, and, under their sanction, issued a call for a muster of militia near St. Louis. This militia assembled at Lindell Grove, in the suburbs of St. Louis, and a military camp was established, under the name of "Camp Jackson." Though ostensibly an innocent affair, this camp was intended to be the nucleus of the army to hoist the Rebel flag in the State. The officers in command were known Secessionists, and every thing about the place was indicative of its character.

The Governor of Louisiana sent, from the arsenal at Baton Rouge, a quantity of guns and munitions of war, to be used by the insurgent forces in Missouri. These reached St. Louis without hinderance, and were promptly conveyed to the embryonic Rebel camp. Captain Lyon, in command of the St. Louis Arsenal, was informed that he must confine his men to the limits of the United States property, under penalty of the arrest of all who stepped outside. Governor Jackson several times visited the grounds overlooking the arsenal, and selected spots for planting his guns. Every thing was in preparation for active hostility.

The Union people were by no means idle. Captain Lyon had foreseen the danger menacing the public property in the arsenal, and besought the Government for permission to remove it. Twenty thousand stand of arms were, in a single night, loaded upon a steamer and sent to Alton, Illinois. They were conveyed thence by rail to the Illinois State Arsenal at Springfield. Authority was obtained for the formation of volunteer regiments, and they were rapidly mustered into the service.

While Camp Jackson was being formed, the Union men of St. Louis were arming and drilling with such secrecy that the Secessionists were not generally aware of their movements. Before the close of the day Captain Lyon received permission for mustering volunteers; he placed more than six hundred men into the service. Regiments were organized under the name of "Home Guards," and by the 9th of May there were six thousand armed Union men in St. Louis, who were sworn to uphold the national honor.

Colonel Francis P. Blair, Jr., commanded the First Regiment of Missouri Volunteers, and stood faithfully by Captain Lyon in all those early and dangerous days. The larger portion of the forces then available in St. Louis was made up of the German element, which was always thoroughly loyal. This fact caused the Missouri Secessionists to feel great indignation toward the Germans. They always declared they would have seized St. Louis and held possession of the larger portion of the State, had it not been for the earnest loyalty of "the Dutch."

In the interior of Missouri the Secessionists were generally in the ascendant. It was the misfortune of the time that the Unionists were usually passive, while their enemies were active. In certain counties where the Unionists were four times the number of the Secessionists, it was often the case that the latter were the ruling party. The Union people were quiet and law-abiding; the Secessionists active and unscrupulous. "Peaceably if we can, forcibly if we must," was the motto of the enemies of the Republic.

In some localities the Union men asserted themselves, but they did not generally do so until after the first blows were struck at St. Louis. When they did come out in earnest, the loyal element in Missouri became fully apparent.

To assure the friends of the Union, and save Missouri from the domination of the insurgents, it was necessary for Captain Lyon to assume the offensive. This was done on the 10th of May, resulting in the famous capture of "Camp Jackson."

On the night of the 9th, loyal parties in St. Louis supplied a sufficient number of horses to move the light artillery necessary to accomplish the desired object. On the morning of the 10th, Captain Lyon's command moved from various points, so as to surround the Rebel camp at three o'clock in the afternoon. At that hour General Frost, the Rebel commander, was surprised at the appearance of an overpowering force on the hills surrounding his position. A demand for surrender gave half an hour for deliberation. At the end of that time General Frost concluded to capitulate. The prisoners, less than a thousand in number, were marched to the arsenal and safely secured.

This achievement destroyed Camp Jackson, and established the United States authority in full force over St. Louis. An unfortunate collision occurred between the soldiers and the crowd outside. Provoked by insults terminating in an assault with fire-arms, a portion of the German troops fired upon the multitude. Upward of thirty persons were killed or wounded in the affair. With the exception of this unhappy collision, the capture was bloodless.

General Harney arrived at St. Louis soon after this event, and assumed command in Missouri. The agreement known as "the Price-Harney truce" was immediately made. Under an assurance from Governor Jackson that the State troops should be disbanded, General Harney promised that no hostilities should be undertaken, and attempted to cause the dispersal of the Union volunteers. The status of the latter had been so fixed that General Harney was not empowered to disarm them, and he so informed, the State authorities. His message announcing this read nearly as follows:--

"I have ascertained that I have no control over the Home Guards.
"W. S. HARNEY, *Brig.-Gen.*"

This message was received at the Police Head-Quarters in St. Louis, on the morning of Sunday, May 15th. It was misunderstood by the parties who read it. They inferred, from the tenor of the dispatch, that General Harney was unable to restrain the Union volunteers.

The most frightful stories had been circulated concerning the blood-thirsty character of these soldiers, particularly the German portion. Visions of murder, pillage, house-burning, and all the accompanying outrages committed by an unrestrained army, flitted through the minds of the Secessionists. The story spread, and gained intensity with each repetition. "The Dutch are rising; we shall all be slain in cold blood!" was the cry, echoed from house to house. Not less than five thousand people fled from the city on that day, and as many more within the succeeding twenty-four hours. Carriages, wagons, drays, every thing that could transport persons or valuables, commanded exorbitant prices. Steamboats were chartered as ferries to the Illinois shore or to go to points of safety, either up or down the river. Many persons abandoned their houses, taking with them only a few articles of value or necessity, while others carried away nothing, in their haste to escape.

In a few days the excitement subsided and nearly all the refugees returned, but there are some who have never been in St. Louis since their remarkable hegira. In their determination to obtain their "rights," they entered the Rebel army and followed its checkered fortunes. Less than half of these persons are now alive.

For a time after the appearance of General Harney's proclamation, there were no hostile demonstrations on either side. Governor Jackson had promised to disband the small force of militia at Jefferson City, but he failed to do so. The Rebel flag was flying in Jefferson City, from a staff in front of the Governor's mansion, and over the head-quarters of the Missouri State Guard. Missouri, through her State officers, was in favor of an armed neutrality, which really meant nothing less than armed secession.

The Secessionists were quietly but earnestly at work to effect their object. They did not heed their promise to remain inactive. The Union authorities observed theirs to the letter. The Camp Jackson prisoners were paroled and restored to liberty. A portion of them observed the parole, but many did not. General Frost remained on his farm and took no part in the Rebellion until relieved from his parole, several months later. It is proper to add, that he was of very little account to the Rebels when he finally entered the field.

While watching the progress of affairs in St. Louis, I determined upon a visit to Jefferson City. Though the Rebel flag was flying over the State Capitol, and the nucleus of the Missouri State Guard (Rebel) had its camp in the suburbs, the communication by railroad had not been interrupted. Taking the morning train from St. Louis, on the 27th of May, I found myself, at three o'clock of the afternoon, under the secession banner. The searching of the train for articles contraband of war was then a new feature.

In the early days only the outside of a package was examined. If the "marks" indicated nothing suspicious, the goods were allowed to pass. Under this regulation, a large number of boxes marked "soap" were shipped on a steamboat for Lexington. So much soap going into Missouri was decidedly suspicious, as the people of the interior do not make extensive use of the article. An examination disclosed canisters of powder instead of bars of soap. The discovery was followed by the promulgation of an order requiring a rigid examination of all packages that might be of doubtful character. This order, with various modifications, was kept in force for a long time.

In starting from St. Louis, I left a company of Union volunteers at the railway station. At Jefferson City I found the depot filled with the Rebel soldiers, or "neutrals," as Governor Jackson persisted in calling them. The particular duty they were performing I was unable to ascertain, but they bore unmistakable signs of being something more than a "neutral" body of men. Their camp was just in rear of the city. The Rebel flag, which floated above the camp, was recognized as the emblem of their neutrality.

The proprietor of the hotel where I stopped held the reputation of an earnest friend of the Union, ready to Suffer any thing rather than sink his principles. He introduced me to several citizens, most of them, like himself, thoroughly loyal. We discussed freely the condition of affairs in Missouri.

It was evident the State authorities intended war, as soon as the necessary preparations could be made. They were not quite ready to strike their first blow, but when they should be prepared, they would not hesitate a moment. Governor Jackson was exerting himself to the utmost to accumulate arms and military stores at various points in the State, where they would be of most value. In defiance of the truce between Generals Price and Harney, companies were being formed throughout the State, and were drilling for service in the field. Time was of great importance to the Rebels, and this they had secured by means of the truce.

During my stay at Jefferson City, I met the three, men most prominent in bringing war upon Missouri. These were Governor Jackson, General Sterling Price, and Jeff. Thompson. Governor Jackson was elected in the previous December, before it was thought any serious trouble would grow out of Mr. Lincoln's election. He was not looked upon as a man of great ability, but no one doubted his desire to promote the best interests of the State. Those who knew him said his strength lay more in a public than in a private direction. He had few, if any, personal friends, and was considered dangerous when his passions were roused. Some said he was cold and treacherous, giving all around him a feeling of aversion. Even among the Secessionists, and those who should have been his ardent supporters, he was never mentioned with enthusiasm.

Within two weeks from the day I saw him, Governor Jackson, by his own act, was a fugitive from the State capital. He never returned. After wandering in Arkansas and Louisiana, during the early part of the war, he died at Little Rock, in 1863, in a condition of extreme poverty.

Of General Price, I heard many praises, even from those who opposed his course. He was said to be a man of warm friendship, of fair abilities, and quite popular among the masses of the inhabitants. He possessed much personal pride, and his ambition for public honor was very great. At the outset he deprecated secession, and prophesied a devastating war as the result. He was inclined to be loyal, but his ambition was greater than his patriotism. The offer of a high position in the Rebel service touched his weakest point, and carried him with the insurgents.

In the Rebel service he never obtained much distinction. His principal successes were in saving his army after defeat. He displayed a capacity for annoying the Union armies without doing great damage. Though his oft-repeated promise of victory was never fulfilled, it served to keep many Missourians in the Rebel ranks. He was constantly expected to capture St. Louis. Some of the Rebel residents fully believed he would do so, and kept their wine-cellars ready for the event. Until the official announcement of the surrender of all forces west of the Mississippi, they did not abandon hope. General Price had given his promise, and, as they argued, was sure to keep it.

Of Jeff. Thompson little can be said. Previous to that time he had been known as the mayor of St. Joseph, and a politician of some little importance in Northwest Missouri. He was famous for much gasconading, and a fondness for whisky and other material things. I could never learn that he commanded much respect. During the war the Rebels never trusted him with any command of importance. He made a very fair guerrilla, and, in 1861, gave our forces at Cairo and Bird's Point considerable annoyance. History is not likely to give him a very prominent place in the roll of distinguished military heroes.

At this time Cairo was the most southerly point on the Mississippi in possession of the National forces. We could have occupied Columbus or Hickman, Kentucky, had not the sacredness of the soil prevented. Kentucky was neutral, and declared that neither party must set foot within her limits. Her declaration of neutrality was much like that issued by the Governor of Missouri. The United States forces were under great restrictions, while the Rebels could do pretty much as they pleased. General Prentiss sent a small expedition down the Mississippi, some sixty miles below Cairo. The Kentuckians were greatly enraged because our forces landed at Hickman and tore down a Rebel flag which the citizens had hoisted. It was an invasion of their soil, for which they demanded apology. A few weeks later the Rebels occupied both Hickman and Columbus, without any objection on the part of the neutrals.

Columbus was made very strong by the Rebel engineers, and supplied with many heavy guns for its protection. At the same time, General Prentiss pushed forward the defenses of Cairo, in readiness for any attack by the Rebel gun-boats. For more than half a year Columbus was the northern limit of the Rebel domination of the Great River. On assuming command there, General Polk announced that Columbus was the throat of the Mississippi, and must be held at all hazards. The Rebels repeatedly urged the capture of Cairo, but it was never attempted.

CHAPTER III
THE BEGINNING OF HOSTILITIES

On the first of June an order was received from Washington, relieving General Harney from command in Missouri. Captain Lyon had been promoted to the rank of a brigadier-general of volunteers, and was assigned to duty in General Harney's stead. On the 5th of June, General Price issued a proclamation, calling for the State Guard to be in readiness to defend Missouri against all enemies. The appearance of this proclamation was not altogether unexpected. It was far more satisfactory to the friends of the Union than to the Secessionists, as it showed the hostile position of Governor Jackson and his abettors, and gave an opportunity for proceeding actively against them. It demonstrated very clearly that the Secessionists were determined to make their actions correspond to their words.

It was ascertained that, a few days before the publication of Price's proclamation, Governor Jackson was in consultation with an agent of the Rebel Government, who promised twenty-five thousand men, and arms and ammunition for fifty thousand more, if the State were fairly and unequivocally out of the Union. He had also conferred with an agent from the Indian Nation, with a view to putting several thousand Indians into the field on the side of the Rebels. General Lyon wanted an "overt act" on the part of the Rebels, before commencing actual hostilities. Price's proclamation was the thing desired.

The troops in and around St. Louis were drilled as thoroughly as possible. Every day added to their effectiveness. Recruiting was pushed, trade with the interior was suspended, and boats passing down the river were made subject to stoppage and search at the arsenal. Every thing was assuming a warlike appearance. The Government was very tardy in supplying General Lyon's wants. In many cases it did not authorize him to do what was needed. Much of the money for outfitting the troops for the field was voluntarily contributed in the Eastern cities, or by patriotic men in St. Louis. In several things, General Lyon acted upon his own responsibility, under the advice and co-operation of Colonel Blair.

On the 9th of June, Governor Jackson and General Price asked General Lyon to give them a safeguard to visit St. Louis. They wished to confer with General Lyon and Colonel Blair, upon the best means of bringing peace to the State and making an end of hostilities. The safeguard was granted, and, on the 11th of June, Jackson and Price reached St. Louis, and signified their readiness for the proposed conference. The meeting took place at the Planters' House, Governor Jackson declining to trust himself inside the walls of the arsenal, where General Lyon had invited him to be his guest. The interview began with many professions of goodwill on the part of Governor Jackson, and the assurance of his earnest desire for peace. He promised to disband the State troops, if General Lyon would first remove all United States troops from the limits of Missouri, and agree not to bring them back under any consideration. Of course, this proposition could not be entertained. A conversation then took place between General Lyon and General Price, but all to no purpose. Price and Jackson would do nothing, unless the United States troops were first sent out of Missouri. Lyon and Blair would not consent to any thing of the kind, and so the conference ended.

Jackson and Price left St. Louis on a special train for Jefferson City, on the afternoon of the 11th. On the way up the road, they set fire to the bridges over the Gasconade and Osage Rivers, the former thirty-five miles from Jefferson City, and ninety from St. Louis, and the latter within nine miles of Jefferson City. If the conduct of these men had been neutral up to that time, this act made an end of their neutrality.

General Lyon left the conference fully satisfied there was no longer any reason for hesitation. The course he should pursue was plain before him.

Early in the forenoon of the 12th, he learned of the destruction of the bridges over the Gasconade and Osage Rivers. He immediately ordered a force to proceed up the road, and protect as much of it as possible from further damage. Within four hours of the reception of the order to move, the troops were on their way. On the next day, three steamers, with about two thousand men, left St. Louis for Jefferson City. General Lyon knew the importance of time, and was determined to give Governor Jackson very little opportunity for preparation.

My first experience of a military campaign was on the expedition up the Missouri. I had seen something of Indian troubles on the Plains, in which white men were concerned, but I had never witnessed civilized warfare where white men fought against white men. A residence of several weeks in St. Louis had somewhat familiarized me with the appearance of troops at the arsenal and at the various camps in the city, but the preparations to take the field were full of novelty.

I was on the boat which carried the First Missouri Infantry, and which General Lyon had selected for his head-quarters. The young officers were full of enthusiasm, and eagerly anticipating their first encounter with the Rebel battalions. Colonel Blair was less demonstrative than the officers of his regiment, but was evidently much elated at the prospect of doing something aggressive. General Lyon was in the cabin, quiet, reserved, and thoughtful. With Colonel Blair he conversed long and freely. Few others approached him. Outside the cabin the soldiers were ardently discussing the coming campaign, and wishing an early opportunity for winning glory in battle.

To one who travels for the first time by steamboat from St. Louis in a northerly direction, a curious picture is presented. The water in the Mississippi above the mouth of the Missouri is quite clear and transparent. That from the Missouri is of a dirty yellow color, derived from the large quantity of earthy matter which it holds in solution. For several miles below the junction of the streams, the two currents remain separated, the line between them being plainly perceptible. The pilots usually endeavor to keep on the dividing line, so that one can look from the opposite sides of a boat and imagine himself sailing upon two rivers of different character at the same moment.

Sometimes this distinctive line continues for fifteen or twenty miles, but usually less than ten. A soldier wittily remarked, that the water from the Upper Mississippi derived its transparency from the free States, from whence it came, while the Missouri, emerging from a slave State, was, consequently, of a repulsive hue. As Missouri is now a free State, the soldier's remark is not applicable.

Steaming up the Missouri toward the State capital, we found the sentiment along the banks of the river strongly in favor of the Union. Home Guard organizations had been hastily formed, and were doing their best for the protection of the railway. Most of the villages along the Lower Missouri contained a strong German element, which needs no question of its loyalty. The railway bridges were thoroughly guarded, and each town had a small garrison to suppress any rising of the Secessionists. The conduct of the people in these villages was quite different from the course of those residing above Jefferson City. Where the inhabitants possessed no slaves, there was outspoken loyalty. In the most populous slave districts it was the reverse. Slaveholders declared that their interest lay in secession. There were a few exceptions, but they were very far in a minority.

Our triumphal entry into Jefferson City was not marked by any noteworthy event. The Capitol was deserted. The Governor and most of the State officials had departed the previous day, in the direction of Booneville. We marched through the principal streets, and found many of the people delighted at our coming. We occupied the State House, and, of course, unfurled our flag from its cupola. A steamboat, seized at the landing, was pressed into our service for use further up the stream. An encounter with the Rebels was eagerly desired.

We left a full regiment, a large force in those days, to retain possession of the place, and then pushed on in pursuit. The Rebels had disabled the railway, taking off nearly all the rolling stock and destroying a large bridge four miles west of the city. As the point where they had fled lay upon the river, we pursued them by water. At noon, on the 16th, General Lyon left Jefferson City for Booneville. Within twenty-four hours he fought his first battle in Missouri.

It is slow work to proceed with a steamboat where one's way must be felt. Though we had only fifty miles to move, we advanced less than thirty before nightfall. Touching at a landing on the left bank of the river, fifteen miles below Booneville, a scout from the enemy's camp came easily into our hands. From being a scout of the enemy he became our scout, as he revealed in his fright all we wished to know. The enemy, confident of an easy victory, was waiting our approach, and expressed the most lively intention of destroying us all in the twinkling of an eye.

Experience had not then demonstrated that there is little difference in the bravery of Americans, when well officered. Each side cherished the delusion that it had a monopoly of courage and endurance. One Southern man was thought equal to five Northern men in a fair contest, and if the former were given the advantage of a defensive position, any odds of numbers would be taken. There was nearly, though not quite, as much boasting on the part of our own press and people. The first severe battles made an end of the greater part of this gasconading.

It is said the most trying moment on shipboard is when the deck, previous to an engagement, is sprinkled with saw-dust to receive the blood yet unshed. No man can know whose blood will be first to moisten that dust, or whose life will be passed away before the action is over. So on the eve of that first battle in Missouri, as I reclined in the cabin of our flag-boat, and saw the surgeons busy with their preparations for the coming day; as I saw them bring to light all the dreadful implements of their trade, and arrange them in readiness for sudden use--a coldness crept over me, and I fully realized we had earnest work before us. Since that time I have witnessed many a battle, many a scene of preparation and of bloody work with knife and saw and bandage, but I have never experienced a chill like that I felt on that early day of the Rebellion.

The war has made us familiar with horrors. That which once touched us to the heart is now passed over with scarce a moment's thought. Our nerves have been hardened, our sensibilities blunted, our hearts steeled against suffering, in the terrible school through which we have passed.

CHAPTER IV
THE FIRST BATTLE IN MISSOURI

Daybreak on the 17th found us slowly moving up the river toward Booneville. General Lyon sat forward of the steamer's cabin, closely scanning both banks of the stream. Four miles below the town his glass sought out two pieces of artillery, partially concealed in a clump of trees, and trained upon the channel by which we were to pass. At once our engines were reversed, and the boats moved back to a landing about eight miles below Booneville. A little before seven o'clock we were on shore, and our column of fifteen hundred men began its advance upon the Rebel camp.

It was the story that has found its repetition in many a battle since that time. The enemy's pickets were driven in. The enemy, in line of battle, was discovered on a long ridge, and our own line was formed on a ridge parallel to it. Then we opened fire with our artillery (one battery was all we possessed), and received no response, save by a desultory discharge of small-arms. Next our infantry added its tenor notes to the bass of the field-guns; the Rebel forces melted steadily away, and the field was in our possession, twenty minutes after the opening shot had been fired.

Once in retreat, the Rebels did not halt until out of harm's reach. Their camp lay in the line of retreat, but they made no stop in passing it. Following in the rear of our column, I entered the camp, and found many signs of a hasty departure. I found the fires burning, and dozens of coffee-pots and frying-pans filled with the materials for breakfast. Here was a pan full of meat fried to a crisp, from the neglect of the cook to remove it before his sudden exodus. A few feet distant lay a ham, with a knife sticking in a half-severed slice. A rude camp-table was spread with plates and their accessories, and a portion of the articles of food were carefully arranged. The seats for the breakfast party were in position, two of them being overturned. I could not help fancying the haste with which that table had been abandoned, only a few moments before. The tents were standing, and in some the blankets were lying on the ground, as if they had been very suddenly vacated. In one tent was a side-saddle, a neat pair of gaiters, and a hoop-skirt. The proper connection of those articles with the battle-field I was unable to ascertain.

In that camp was a fine lot of provisions, arms, equipments, and ammunition. Saddles were numerous, but there were no horses. It was evident that, the hasty evacuation left no time for the simple process of saddling.

Early in the day I had come into possession of a horse with a very poor outfit. Once in camp, I was not slow to avail myself of the privilege of supply. I went into battle on foot, carrying only a knapsack containing a note-book and two pieces of bread. When the fight was over, I was the possessor of a horse and all the equipments for a campaign. I had an overcoat, a roll of fine blankets, and a pair of saddle-bags. The latter were well filled from the trunk of some one I had not the pleasure of knowing, but who was evidently "just my size." Mr. Barnes, of the Missouri *Democrat*, was my companion on that occasion. He was equally careful to provide himself from the enemy's stores, but wasted, time in becoming sentimental over two love-letters and a photograph of a young woman.

The flags captured in this affair were excellent illustrations of the policy of the leading Secessionists. There was one Rebel flag with the arms of the State of Missouri filling the field. There was a State flag, with only fifteen stars surrounding the coat of arms. There was a. Rebel flag, with the State arms in the center, and there was one Rebel flag of the regular pattern. The rallying-cry at that time was in behalf of the State, and the people were told they must act for Missouri, without regard to any thing else. In no part of the country was the "State Rights" theory more freely used. All the changes were rung upon the sovereignty of States, the right of Missouri to exclude United States soldiers from her soil, the illegality of the formation of Union regiments, and the tyranny of the General Government.

The flags under which Missouri soldiers were gathered clearly blended the interests of the State with secession.

Our troops entered Booneville amid demonstrations of delight from one portion of the inhabitants, and the frowns and muttered indignation of the other. The Rebels had fled, a part of them by land, and the balance on a steamboat, toward Lexington. Quiet possession obtained, there was time to examine into the details of the fight. We had lost twelve men, the enemy probably twice as many. The action, three years later, would have been considered only a roadside skirmish, but it was then an affair of importance. Every man with General Lyon felt far more elation over the result than has since been felt over battles of much greater moment. We had won a signal victory; the enemy had suffered an equally signal defeat.

During the battle, a chaplain, provided with four men to look after the wounded, came suddenly upon a group of twenty-four Rebels. An imperative demand for their surrender was promptly complied with, and the chaplain, with his force of four, brought twenty-four prisoners into town. He was so delighted at his success that he subsequently took a commission in the line. In time he was honored with the stars of a brigadier-general.

General Lyon was my personal friend, but he very nearly did me great injustice. Seeing myself and a fellow-journalist on a distant part of the field, he mistook us for scouts of the enemy, and ordered his sharp-shooters to pick us off. His chief-of-staff looked in our direction, and fortunately recognized us in time to countermand the order. I was afterward on the point of being shot at by an infantry captain, through a similar mistake. A civilian's dress on the battle-field (a gray coat formed a part of mine) subjects the wearer to many dangers from his friends, as most war correspondents can testify.

While approaching the town, I stopped to slake my thirst at a well. A group of our soldiers joined me while I was drinking. I had drank very freely from the bucket, and transferred it to a soldier, when the resident of a neighboring house appeared, and informed us that the well had been poisoned by the Rebels, and the water was certain to produce death. The soldiers desisted, and looked at me with much pity. For a moment, I confess, the situation did not appear cheerful, but I concluded the injury, if any, was already done, and I must make the best of it. The soldiers watched me as I mounted my horse, evidently expecting me to fall within a hundred yards. When I met one of them the following day, he opened his eyes in astonishment at seeing me alive. From that day, I entertained a great contempt for poisoned wells.

In Booneville the incidents were not of a startling character. I found the strongest secession sympathy was entertained by the wealthier inhabitants, while the poor were generally loyal. Some cases of determined loyalty I found among the wealthy; but they were the exception rather than the rule. Accompanied by a small squad of soldiers, myself and companion visited the house of a gentleman holding office under the United States Government. We obtained from that house several Rebel cockades and small flags, which had been fabricated by the ladies.

With the same squad we visited the principal bank of Booneville, and persuaded the cashier to give us a Rebel flag which had been floating for several days from a staff in front of the building. This flag was ten yards in length, and the materials of which it was made were of the finest quality. The interview between the cashier and ourselves was an amusing one. He protested he knew nothing of the flag or its origin, and at first declared it was not about the building. According to his own representation, he was too good a Union man to harbor any thing of the sort. Just as he was in the midst of a very earnest profession of loyalty the flag was discovered.

"Somebody must have put that there to ruin me," was his exclamation. "Gentlemen, I hope you won't harm me; and, if you want me to do so, I will take the oath of allegiance this minute."

Soon after the occupation of Booneville, General Lyon sent a small expedition to Syracuse, twenty-five miles in the interior. This force returned in a few days, and then preparations were begun for a march to Springfield. Colonel Blair left Booneville for St. Louis and Washington, while General Lyon attended to the preliminaries for his contemplated movement. The First Iowa Infantry joined him, and formed a part of his expeditionary force. The Rebels gathered at Lexington, and thence moved southward to reach the Arkansas line, to form a junction with the then famous Ben McCulloch.

The prospect was good that Central Missouri would soon be clear of Rebels. Our general success in the State depended upon occupying and holding the Southwest. General Lyon was to move thither from Booneville. General Sweeney had already gone there by way of Rolla, while another force, under Major Sturgis, was moving from Leavenworth in a southeasterly direction. All were to unite at Springfield and form an army of occupation.

Preparations went on slowly, as the transportation was to be gathered from the surrounding country. Foreseeing that the expedition would be slow to reach Springfield, I returned to St. Louis. There I made preparations to join the army, when its march should be completed, by a more expeditious route than the one General Lyon would follow.

At Booneville, General Lyon established a temporary blockade of the Missouri River, by stopping all boats moving in either direction. In most cases a single shot across the bow of a boat sufficed to bring it to land. One day the *White Cloud*, on her way from Kansas City to St. Louis, refused to halt until three shots had been fired, the last one grazing the top of the pilot-house. When brought before General Lyon, the captain of the *White Cloud* apologized for neglecting to obey the first signal, and said his neglect was due to his utter ignorance of military usage.

The apology was deemed sufficient. The captain was dismissed, with a gentle admonition not to make a similar mistake in future.

At that time the public was slow to understand the power and extent of military law and military rule. When martial law was declared in St. Louis, in August, 1861, a citizen waited upon the provost-marshal, in order to ascertain the precise state of affairs.

After some desultory conversation, he threw out the question:--

"What does martial law do?"

"Well," said Major McKinstry, the provost-marshal, "I can explain the whole thing in a second. Martial law does pretty much as it d--n pleases."

Before the year was ended the inhabitants of St. Louis learned that the major's assertion was not far from the truth.

CHAPTER V
TO SPRINGFIELD AND BEYOND

The success of the Union arms at Booneville did not silence the Secessionists in St. Louis. They continued to hold meetings, and arrange plans for assisting their friends in the field. At many places, one could hear expressions of indignation at the restrictions which the proper authorities sought to put upon the secession movement. Union flags were torn from the front of private buildings--generally in the night or early morning. Twice, when Union troops were marching along the streets, they were fired upon by citizens. A collision of this kind had occurred at the corner of Fifth and Walnut streets, on the day after the capture of Camp Jackson. The soldiers returned the fire, and killed several persons; but this did not deter the Secessionists from repeating the experiment. In the affairs that took place after the battle of Booneville, the result was the same. Unfortunately, in each collision, a portion of those killed were innocent on-lookers. After a few occurrences of this kind, soldiers were allowed to march through the streets without molestation.

About the first of July, there were rumors that an insurrection would be attempted on the National holiday. Ample provision was made to give the insurgents a warm reception. Consequently, they made no trouble. The printer of the bills of fare at a prominent hotel noticed the Fourth of July by ornamenting his work with a National flag, in colors. This roused the indignation of a half-dozen guests, whose sympathies lay with the Rebellion. They threatened to leave, but were so far in arrears that they could not settle their accounts. The hotel-keeper endeavored to soothe them by promising to give his printing, for the future, to another house. Several loyal guests were roused at this offer, and threatened to secede at once if it were carried out. The affair resulted in nothing but words.

On the morning of the 11th of July I left St. Louis, to join General Lyon in the Southwest. It was a day's ride by rail to Rolla, the terminus of the Southwest Branch of the Pacific road. I well recollect the strange and motley group that filled the cars on that journey. There were a few officers and soldiers *en route* to join their comrades in the field. Nearly all of them were fresh from civil life. They wore their uniforms uneasily, as a farmer's boy wears his Sunday suit. Those who carried sabers experienced much inconvenience when walking, on account of the propensity of those weapons to get between their legs. In citizen's dress, at my side, sat an officer of the old army, who looked upon these newly-made warriors with much contempt, mingled with an admiration of their earnestness. After an outburst of mild invective, he pronounced a well-merited tribute to their patriotism.

"After all," said he, "they are as good as the material the Rebels have for their army. In some respects, they are better. The Northern blood is cold; the Southern is full of life and passion. In the first onset, our enemies will prove more impetuous than we, and will often overpower us. In the beginning of the struggle, they will prove our superiors, and may be able to boast of the first victories. But their physical energy will soon be exhausted, while ours will steadily increase. Patience, coolness, and determination will be sure to bring us the triumph in the end. These raw recruits, that are at present worthless before trained soldiers, distrusting themselves as we distrust them, will yet become veterans, worthy to rank with the best soldiers of the Old World."

The civilian passengers on a railway in Missouri are essentially different from the same class in the East. There are very few women, and the most of these are not as carefully dressed as their Oriental sisters. Their features lack the fineness that one observes in New York and New England. The "hog and hominy," the general diet of the Southwest, is plainly perceptible in the physique of the women. The male travelers, who are not indigenous to the soil, are more roughly clothed and more careless in manner than the same order of passengers between New York and Boston. Of those who enter and leave at way-stations, the men are clad in that yellow, homespun material known as "butternut." The casual observer inclines to the opinion that there are no good bathing-places where these men reside. They are inquisitive, ignorant, unkempt, but generally civil. The women are the reverse of attractive, and are usually uncivil and ignorant. The majority are addicted to smoking, and generally make use of a cob-pipe. Unless objection is made by some passenger, the conductors ordinarily allow the women to indulge in this pastime.

The region traversed by the railway is sparsely settled, the ground being generally unfavorable to agriculture. For some time after this portion of the road was opened, the natives refused to give it patronage, many of them declaring that the old mode of travel, by horseback, was the best of all. During the first week after opening the Southwest Branch, the company ran a daily freight train each way. All the freight offered in that time was a bear and a keg of honey. Both were placed in the same car. The bear ate the honey, and the company was compelled to pay for the damage.

I have heard a story concerning the origin of the name of Rolla, which is interesting, though I cannot vouch for its truth. In selecting a name for the county seat of Phelps County, a North Carolinian residing there, suggested that it should do honor to the capital of his native State. The person who reduced the request to writing, used the best orthography that occurred to him, so that what should have been "Raleigh," became "Rolla." The request thus written was sent to the Legislature, and the name of the town became fixed. The inhabitants generally pronounce it as if the intended spelling had been adopted.

The journey from Rolla to Springfield was accomplished by stage, and required two days of travel. For fifty miles the road led over mountains, to the banks of the Gasconade, one of the prettiest rivers I have ever seen. The mountain streams of Southwest Missouri, having their springs in the limestone rock, possess a peculiarity unknown in the Eastern States. In a depth of two feet or less, the water is apparently as clear as that of the purest mountain brook in New England. But when the depth reaches, or exceeds, three feet, the water assumes a deep-blue tinge, like that of the sky in a clear day. Viewed from an elevation, the picture is one that cannot be speedily forgotten. The blue water makes a marked contrast with surrounding objects, as the streams wind through the forests and fields on their banks. Though meandering through mountains, these rivers have few sharp falls or roaring rapids. Their current is usually gentle, broken here and there into a ripple over a slightly descending shallow, but observing uniformity in all its windings.

My first night from Rolla was passed on the banks of the Gasconade. Another day's ride, extended far into the second night, found me at Springfield. When I reached my room at the hotel, and examined the bed, I found but one sheet where we usually look for two. Expostulations were of no avail. The porter curtly informed me, "People here use only one sheet. Down in St. Louis you folks want two sheets, but in this part of the country we ain't so nice."

I appreciated my fastidiousness when I afterward saw, at a Tennessee hotel, the following notice:--

"Gentlemen who wish towels in their rooms must deposit fifty cents at the office, as security for their return."

Travel in the Border and Southern States will acquaint a Northerner with strange customs. To find an entire household occupying a single large room is not an unfrequent occurrence. The rules of politeness require that, when bedtime has arrived, the men shall go out of doors to contemplate the stars, while the ladies disrobe and retire. The men then return and proceed to bed. Sometimes the ladies amuse themselves by studying the fire while the men find their way to their couches, where they gallantly turn their faces to the wall, and permit the ladies to don their *robes de nuit*.

Notwithstanding the scarcity of accommodations, the traveler seeking a meal or resting-place will rarely meet a refusal. In New York or New England, one can journey many a mile and find a cold denial at every door. In the West and Southwest "the latch-string hangs out," and the stranger is always welcome. Especially is this the case among the poorer classes.

Springfield is the largest town in Southwest Missouri, and has a fine situation. Before the war it was a place of considerable importance, as it controlled the trade of a large region around it. East of it the country is quite broken, but on the south and west there are stretches of rolling prairie, bounded by rough wood-land. Considered in a military light, Springfield was the key to that portion of the State. A large number of public roads center at that point. Their direction is such that the possession of the town by either army would control any near position of an adversary of equal or inferior strength. General Lyon was prompt in seeing its value, and determined to make an early movement for its occupation. When he started from St. Louis for Booneville, he ordered General Sweeney to march from Rolla to Springfield as speedily as possible.

General Sweeney moved with three regiments of infantry and a battery of artillery, and reached Springfield in five days from the time of starting; the distance being a hundred and twenty miles. He then divided his forces, sending Colonel Sigel to Carthage, nearly fifty miles further toward the west, in the hope of cutting off the Rebel retreat in that direction. Major Sturgis was moving from Leavenworth toward Springfield, and expected to arrive there in advance of General Lyon.

Major Sturgis was delayed in crossing a river, so that the Rebels arrived at Carthage before Colonel Sigel had been reinforced. The latter, with about eleven hundred men, encountered the Rebel column, twice as large as his own. The battle raged for several hours, neither side losing very heavily. It resulted in Sigel's retreat to avoid being surrounded by the enemy. Wonderful stories were told at that time of the terrific slaughter in the Rebel ranks, but these stories could never be traced to a reliable source. It is proper to say that the Rebels made equally large estimates of our own loss.

On General Lyon's arrival all the troops were concentrated in the vicinity of Springfield. It was known that the Rebels were encamped near the Arkansas border, awaiting the re-enforcements which had been promised from the older States of the Confederacy. General Fremont had been assigned to the command of the Western Department, and was daily expected at St. Louis to assume the direction of affairs. Our scouts were kept constantly employed in bringing us news from the Rebel camp, and it is quite probable the Rebels were equally well informed of our own condition. We were able to learn that their number was on the increase, and that they would soon be largely re-enforced. After three weeks of occupation our strength promised to be diminished. Half of General Lyon's command consisted of "three-months men," whose period of enlistment was drawing to a close. A portion of these men went to St. Louis, some volunteered to remain as long as the emergency required their presence, and others were kept against their will. Meantime, General Lyon made the most urgent requests for re-enforcements, and declared he would be compelled to abandon the Southwest if not speedily strengthened. General Fremont promised to send troops to his assistance. After he made the promise, Cairo was threatened by General Pillow, and the re-enforcing column turned in that direction. General Lyon was left to take care of himself.

By the latter part of July, our situation had become critical. Price's army had been re-enforced by a column of Arkansas and Louisiana troops, under General McCulloch. This gave the Rebels upward of twelve thousand men, while we could muster less than six thousand. General Price assumed the offensive, moving slowly toward Springfield, as if sure of his ability to overpower the National forces. General Lyon determined to fall upon the enemy before he could reach Springfield, and moved on the 1st of August with that object in view.

On the second day of our march a strong scouting party of Rebels was encountered, and a sharp skirmish ensued, in which they were repulsed. This encounter is known in the Southwest as "the fight at Dug Spring." The next day another skirmish occurred, and, on the third morning, twenty-five miles from Springfield, General Lyon called a council of war. "Councils of war do not fight" has grown into a proverb. The council on this occasion decided that we should return to Springfield without attacking the enemy. The decision was immediately carried out.

The beginning of August, in Southwest Missouri, is in the midst of the warm season. The day of the march to Dug Spring was one I shall never forget. In Kansas, before the war, I once had a walk of several miles under a burning sun, in a region where not a drop of water could be found. When I finally reached it, the only water to be found was in a small, stagnant pool, covered with a green scum nearly an inch in thickness. Warm, brackish, and fever-laden as that water was, I had never before tasted any thing half so sweet. Again, while crossing the Great Plains in 1860, I underwent a severe and prolonged thirst, only quenching it with the bitter alkali-water of the desert. On neither of these occasions were my sufferings half as great as in the advance to Dug Spring.

A long ride in that hot atmosphere gave me a thirst of the most terrible character. Making a detour to the left of the road in a vain search for water, I fell behind the column as it marched slowly along. As I moved again to the front, I passed scores of men who had fallen from utter exhaustion. Many were delirious, and begged piteously for water in ever so small a quantity. Several died from excessive heat, and others were for a long time unfit for duty. Reaching the spring which gave its name to the locality, I was fortunate in finding only the advance of the command. With considerable effort I succeeded in obtaining a pint cupful of water, and thus allayed my immediate thirst.

According to the custom in that region, the spring was covered with a frame building, about eight feet square. There are very few cellars in that part of the country, and the spring-house, as it is called, is used for preserving milk and other articles that require a low temperature. As the main portion of the column came up, the crowd around the spring-house became so dense that those once inside could not get out. The building was lifted and thrown away from the spring, but this only served to increase the confusion. Officers found it impossible to maintain discipline. When the men caught sight of the crowd at the spring, the lines were instantly broken. At the spring, officers and men were mingled without regard to rank, all struggling for the same object. A few of the former, who had been fortunate in commencing the day with full canteens, attempted to bring order out of chaos, but found the effort useless. No command was heeded. The officers of the two regiments of "regulars" had justly boasted of the superior discipline of their men. On this occasion the superiority was not apparent. Volunteers and regulars were equally subject to thirst, and made equal endeavor to quench it.

Twenty yards below the spring was a shallow pool, where cattle and hogs were allowed to run. Directly above it was a trough containing a few gallons of warm water, which had evidently been there several days. This was speedily taken by the men. Then the hot, scum-covered pool was resorted to. In a very few minutes the trampling of the soldiers' feet had stirred this pool till its substance was more like earth than water. Even from this the men would fill their cups and canteens, and drink with the utmost eagerness. I saw a private soldier emerge from the crowd with a canteen full of this worse than ditch-water. An officer tendered a five-dollar gold piece for the contents of the canteen, and found his offer indignantly refused. To such a frenzy were men driven by thirst that they tore up handfuls of moist earth, and swallowed the few drops of water that could be pressed out.

In subsequent campaigns I witnessed many scenes of hunger and thirst, but none to equal those of that day at Dug Spring.

CHAPTER VI
THE BATTLE OF WILSON CREEK

The return of General Lyon from Dug Spring emboldened the enemy to move nearer to Springfield. On the 7th of August the Rebels reached Wilson Creek, ten miles from Springfield, and formed their camp on both sides of that stream. General Ben. McCulloch was their commander-in-chief. On the night of the 8th, General Lyon proposed to move from Springfield for the purpose of attacking their position. The design was not carried out, on account of the impossibility of securing proper disposition of our forces in season to reach the enemy's camp at daylight.

During the 8th and the forenoon of the 9th, preparations were made for resisting an attack in Springfield, in case the enemy should come upon us. In the afternoon of the 9th, General Lyon decided to assault the Rebel camp at daylight of the following morning. A council of war had determined that a defeat would be less injurious than a retreat without a battle, provided the defeat were not too serious. "To abandon the Southwest without a struggle," said General Lyon, "would be a sad blow to our cause, and would greatly encourage the Rebels. We will fight, and hope for the best."

In arranging a plan of battle, Colonel Sigel suggested that the forces should be divided, so that a simultaneous attack would be made upon either extremity of the enemy's camp. The two columns were to move from Springfield at sunset, bivouac within four miles of the proposed battle-field, and begin their march early enough to fall upon the enemy's camp a little past daylight. We left Springfield about sunset on the 9th, General Lyon taking about three thousand men, while Colonel Sigel took less than two thousand. Exceptions have frequently been made to this mode of attack. Had it been successful, I presume no one would have found it faulty. It is an easy matter to criticise the plans of others, after their result is known.

The columns moved by different roads to obtain the desired positions. The march was as silent as possible. The only sounds were the rumbling of wheels and the occasional clank of arms. No one was heavily encumbered, as we expected to return to Springfield before the following night. Midnight found us in a hay-field, four miles from the Rebel camp. There we rested till morning.

On the previous night I had been almost without sleep, and therefore took speedy advantage of the halt. Two journeys over the Plains, a little trip into New Mexico, and some excursions among the Rocky Mountains, had taught me certain rules of campaign life. I rarely moved without my blankets and rubber "poncho," and with a haversack more or less well filled. On this occasion I was prepared for sleeping in the open air.

One bivouac is much like another. When one is weary, a blanket on the ground is just as comfortable as a bed of down under a slated roof. If accustomed to lie under lace curtains, a tree or a bush will make an excellent substitute. "Tired nature's sweet restorer" comes quickly to an exhausted frame. Realities of the past, expectations of the future, hopes, sorrows, wishes, regrets--all are banished as we sink into sweet repose.

At dawn we were in motion. At daylight the smoke hanging over the enemy's camp was fully before us. Sunrise was near at hand when the hostile position was brought to our view. It lay, as we had anticipated, stretched along the banks of Wilson Creek.

Until our advance drove in the pickets, a thousand yards from their camp, the Rebels had no intimation of our approach. Many of them were reluctant to believe we were advancing to attack them, and thought the firing upon the pickets was the work of a scouting party. The opening of our artillery soon undeceived them, a shell being dropped in the middle of their camp.

A Rebel officer afterward told me about our first shell. When the pickets gave the alarm of our approach, the Rebel commander ordered his forces to "turn out." An Arkansas colonel was in bed when the order reached him, and lazily asked, "Is that official?" Before the bearer of the order could answer, our shell tore through the colonel's tent, and exploded a few yards beyond it. The officer waited for no explanation, but ejaculated, "That's official, anyhow," as he sprang out of his blankets, and arrayed himself in fighting costume.

Before the Rebels could respond to our morning salutation, we heard the booming of Sigel's cannon on the left. Colonel Sigel reached the spot assigned him some minutes before we were able to open fire from our position. It had been stipulated that he should wait for the sound of our guns before making his attack. His officers said they waited nearly fifteen minutes for our opening shot. They could look into the Rebel camp in the valley of the stream, a few hundred yards distant. The cooks were beginning their preparations for breakfast, and gave our men a fine opportunity to learn the process of making Confederate corn-bread and coffee. Some of the Rebels saw our men, and supposed they were their own forces, who had taken up a new position. Several walked into our lines, and found themselves prisoners of war.

Previous to that day I had witnessed several skirmishes, but this was my first battle of importance. Distances seemed much greater than they really were. I stood by the side of Captain Totten's battery as it opened the conflict.

"How far are you firing?" I asked.

"About eight hundred yards; not over that," was the captain's response.

I should have called it sixteen hundred, had I been called on for an estimate.

Down the valley rose the smoke of Sigel's guns, about a mile distant, though, apparently, two or three miles away.

Opposite Sigel's position was the camp of the Arkansas Division: though it was fully in my sight, and the tents and wagons were plainly visible, I could not get over the impression that they were far off.

The explosions of our shells, and the flashes of the enemy's guns, a short distance up the slope on the opposite side of the creek, seemed to be at a considerable distance.

To what I shall ascribe these illusions, I do not know. On subsequent battle-fields I have never known their recurrence. Greater battles, larger streams, higher hills, broader fields, wider valleys, more extended camps, have come under my observation, but in none of them has the romance exceeded the reality.

The hours did not crowd into minutes, but the minutes almost extended into hours. I frequently found, on consulting my watch, that occurrences, apparently of an hour's duration, were really less than a half or a quarter of that time.

As the sun rose, it passed into a cloud. When it emerged, I fully expected it would be some distance toward the zenith, and was surprised to find it had advanced only a few degrees.

There was a light shower, that lasted less than ten minutes: I judged it had been twenty.

The evolutions of the troops on the field appeared slow and awkward. They were really effected with great promptness.

General Lyon was killed before nine o'clock, as I very well knew. It was some days before I could rid myself of an impression that his death occurred not far from noon. Th e apparent extension of the hours was the experience of several persons on that field. I think it has been known by many, on the occasion of their first battle. At Pea Ridge, an officer told me, there seemed to be about thirty hours between sunrise and sunset. Another thought it was four P.M. when the sun was at the meridian. It was only at Wilson Creek that I experienced this sensation. On subsequent battle-fields I had no reason to complain of my estimate of time.

The first shell from the enemy's guns passed high over my head. I well remember the screech of that missile as it cut through the air and lost itself in the distance. "Too high, Captain Bledsoe," exclaimed our artillery officer, as he planted a shell among the Rebel gunners. In firing a half-dozen rounds the Rebels obtained our range, and then used their guns with some effect. The noise of each of those shells I can distinctly recall, though I have since listened to hundreds of similar sounds, of which I have no vivid recollection. The sound made by a shell, in its passage through the air, cannot be described, and, when once heard, can never be forgotten.

I was very soon familiar with the whistling of musket-balls. Before the end of the action, I thought I could distinguish the noise of a Minié bullet from that of a common rifle-ball, or a ball from a smooth-bored musket. Once, while conversing with the officer in charge of the skirmish line, I found myself the center of a very hot fire. It seemed, at that instant, as if a swarm of the largest and most spiteful bees had suddenly appeared around me. The bullets flew too rapidly to be counted, but I fancied I could perceive a variation in their sound.

After I found a position beyond the range of musketry, the artillery would insist upon searching me out. While I was seated under a small oak-tree, with my left arm through my horse's bridle, and my pencil busy on my note-book, the tree above my head was cut by a shell. Moving from that spot, I had just resumed my writing, when a shot tore up the ground under my arm, and covered me with dirt. Even a remove to another quarter did not answer my purpose, and I finished my notes after reaching the rear.

It is not my intention to give the details of the battle--the movements of each regiment, battalion, or battery, as it performed its part in the work. The official record will be sought by those who desire the purely military history. It is to be regretted that the official report of the engagement at Wilson Creek displays the great hostility of its author toward a fellow-soldier. In the early campaigns in Missouri, many officers of the regular army vied with the Rebels in their hatred of "the Dutch." This feeling was not confined to Missouri alone, but was apparent in the East as well as in the West. As the war progressed the hostility diminished, but it was never entirely laid aside.

The duration of the battle was about four and a half hours. The whole force under the National flag was five thousand men. The Rebels acknowledged having twelve thousand, of all arms. It is probable that this estimate was a low one. The Rebels were generally armed with shot-guns, common rifles, and muskets of the old pattern. About a thousand had no arms whatever. Their artillery ammunition was of poorer quality than our own. These circumstances served to make the disparity less great than the actual strength of the hostile forces would imply. Even with these considerations, the odds against General Lyon were quite large.

Our loss was a little less than one-fifth our whole strength. Up to that time, a battle in which one-tenth of those engaged was placed *hors de combat*, was considered a very sanguinary affair. During the war there were many engagements where the defeated party suffered a loss of less than one-twentieth. Wilson Creek can take rank as one of the best-fought battles, when the number engaged is brought into consideration.

The First Missouri Infantry went into action with seven hundred and twenty-six men. Its casualty list was as follows:--

Killed	77
Dangerously wounded	93
Otherwise wounded	126
Captured	2
Missing	15

Total	313

The First Kansas Infantry, out of seven hundred and eighty-five men, lost two hundred and ninety-six. The loss in other regiments was quite severe, though not proportionately as heavy as the above. These two regiments did not break during the battle, and when they left the ground they marched off as coolly as from a parade.

At the time our retreat was ordered our ammunition was nearly exhausted and the ranks fearfully thinned. The Rebels had made a furious attack, in which they were repulsed. General Sweeney insisted that it was their last effort, and if we remained on the ground we would not be molested again. Major Sturgis, upon whom the command devolved after General

Lyon's death, reasoned otherwise, and considered it best to fall back to Springfield. The Rebels afterward admitted that General McCulloch had actually given the order for retreat a few moments before they learned of our withdrawal. Of course he countermanded his order at once. There were several battles in the late Rebellion in which the circumstances were similar. In repeated instances the victorious party thought itself defeated, and was much astonished at finding its antagonist had abandoned the struggle.

In our retreat we brought away many of our wounded, but left many others on the field. When the Rebels took possession they cared for their own men as well as the circumstances would permit, but gave no assistance to ours. There were reports, well authenticated, that some who lay helpless were shot or bayoneted. Two days after the battle a surgeon who remained at Springfield was allowed to send out wagons for the wounded. Some were not found until after four days' exposure. They crawled about as best they could, and, by searching the haversacks of dead men, saved themselves from starvation. One party of four built a shelter of branches of trees as a protection against the sun. Another party crawled to the bank of the creek, and lay day and night at the water's edge. Several men sought shelter in the fence corners, or by the side of fallen trees.

Two days before the battle, ten dollars were paid to each man of the First Kansas Infantry. The money was in twenty-dollar pieces, and the payment was made by drawing up the regiment in the customary two ranks, and giving a twenty-dollar piece to each man in the front rank. Three-fourths of those killed or wounded in that regiment were of the front rank. The Rebels learned of this payment, and made rigid search of all whom they found on the field. Nearly a year after the battle a visitor to the ground picked up one of these gold coins.

During the battle several soldiers from St. Louis and its vicinity recognized acquaintances on the opposite side. These recognitions were generally the occasion of many derisive and abusive epithets. In the Border States each party had a feeling of bitter hostility toward the other. Probably the animosity was greater in Missouri than elsewhere.

A lieutenant of the First Missouri Infantry reported that he saw one of the men of his regiment sitting under a tree during the battle, busily engaged in whittling a bullet.

"What are you doing there?" said the officer.

"My ammunition is gone, and I'm cutting down this bullet to fit my gun." (The soldier's musket was a "54-caliber," and the bullet was a "59.")

"Look around among the wounded men," was the order, "and get some 54-cartridges. Don't stop to cut down that bullet."

"I would look around, lieutenant," the soldier responded, "but I can't move. My leg is shot through. I won't be long cutting this down, and then I want a chance to hit some of them."

Captain Gordon Granger was serving on the staff of General Lyon. When not actively engaged in his professional duties, he visited all parts of the field where the fight was hottest. Though himself somewhat excited, he was constantly urging the raw soldiers to keep cool and not throw away a shot. Wherever there was a weak place in our line, he was among the first to discover it and devise a plan for making it good. On one occasion, he found a gap between two regiments, and noticed that the Rebels were preparing to take advantage of it. Without a moment's delay, he transferred three companies of infantry to the spot, managing to keep them concealed behind a small ridge.

"Now, lie still; don't raise your heads out of the grass," said Granger; "I'll tell you when to fire."

The Rebels advanced toward the supposed gap. Granger stood where he could see and not be seen. He was a strange compound of coolness and excitement. While his judgment was of the best, and his resources were ready for all emergencies, a by-stander would have thought him heated almost to frenzy. The warmth of his blood gave him a wonderful energy and rendered him ubiquitous; his skill and decision made his services of the highest importance.

"There they come; steady, now; let them get near enough; fire low; give them h--l."

The Rebels rushed forward, thinking to find an easy passage. When within less than fifty yards, Granger ordered his men to fire. The complete repulse of the Rebels was the result.

"There, boys; you've done well. D--n the scoundrels; they won't come here again." With this, the captain hastened to some other quarter.

The death of General Lyon occurred near the middle of the battle. So many accounts of this occurrence have been given, that I am not fully satisfied which is the correct one. I know at least half a dozen individuals in whose arms General Lyon expired, and think there are as many more who claim that sad honor. There is a similar mystery concerning his last words, a dozen versions having been given by persons who claim to have heard them. It is my belief that General Lyon was killed while reconnoitering the enemy's line and directing the advance of a regiment of infantry. I believe he was on foot at the instant, and was caught, as he fell, in the arms of "Lehman," his orderly. His last utterance was, doubtless, the order for the infantry to advance, and was given a moment before he received the fatal bullet. From the nature of the wound, his death, if not instantaneous, was very speedy. A large musket-ball entered his left side, in the region of the heart, passing nearly through to the right. A reported wound in the breast was made with a bayonet in the hands of a Rebel soldier, several hours afterward. The body was brought to Springfield on the night after the battle.

It was my fortune to be acquainted with General Lyon. During the progress of the war I met no one who impressed me more than he, in his devotion to the interests of the country. If he possessed ambition for personal glory, I was unable to discover it. He declared that reputation was a bubble, which no good soldier should follow. Wealth was a shadow, which no man in the country's service should heed. His pay as an officer was sufficient for all his wants, and he desired nothing more. He gave to the Nation, as the friend he loved the dearest, a fortune which he had inherited. If his death could aid in the success of the cause for which he was fighting, he stood ready to die. The gloom that spread throughout the North when the news of his loss was received, showed a just appreciation of his character.

"How sleep the brave who sink to rest
By all their country's wishes blest!"

At that battle there was the usual complement of officers for five thousand men. Two years later there were seven major-generals and thirteen brigadier-generals who had risen from the Wilson Creek Army. There were colonels, lieutenant-colonels, and majors, by the score, who fought in the line or in the ranks on that memorable 10th of August. In 1863, thirty-two commissioned officers were in the service from one company of the First Iowa Infantry. Out of one company of the First Missouri Infantry, twenty-eight men received commissions. To the majority of the officers from that army promotion was rapid, though a few cases occurred in which the services they rendered were tardily acknowledged.

CHAPTER VII
THE RETREAT FROM SPRINGFIELD

On the night after the battle, the army was quartered at Springfield. The Rebels had returned to the battle-ground, and were holding it in possession. The court-house and a large hotel were taken for hospitals, and received such of our wounded as were brought in. At a council of war, it was decided to fall back to Rolla, a hundred and twenty miles distant, and orders were given to move at daylight.

The journalists held a council of war, and decided to commence their retreat at half-past two o'clock in the morning, in order to be in advance of the army. The probabilities were in favor of the enemy's cavalry being at the junction of certain roads, five miles east of the town. We, therefore, divested ourselves of every thing of a compromising character. In my own saddle-bags I took only such toilet articles as I had long carried, and which were not of a warlike nature. We destroyed papers that might give information to the enemy, and kept only our note-books, from which all reference to the strength of our army was carefully stricken out. We determined, in case of capture, to announce ourselves as journalists, and display our credentials.

One of our party was a telegraph operator as well as a journalist. He did not wish to appear in the former character, as the Missouri Rebels were then declaring they would show no quarter to telegraphers. Accordingly, he took special care to divest himself of all that pertained to the transmission of intelligence over the wires. A pocket "instrument," which he had hitherto carried, he concealed in Springfield, after carefully disabling the office, and leaving the establishment unfit for immediate use.

We passed the dangerous point five miles from town, just as day was breaking. No Rebel cavalry confronted us in the highway, nor shouted an unwelcome "halt!" from a roadside thicket. All was still, though we fancied we could hear a sound of troops in motion far in the distance toward Wilson Creek. The Rebels were doubtless astir, though they did not choose to interfere with the retreat of our army.

As day broke and the sun rose, we found the people of both complexions thronging to the road, and seeking, anxiously, the latest intelligence. At first we bore their questions patiently, and briefly told them what had occurred. Finding that we lost much time, we began, early in the day, to give the shortest answers possible. As fast as we proceeded the people became more earnest, and would insist upon delaying us. Soon after mid-day we commenced denying we had been at the battle, or even in Springfield. This was our only course if we would avoid detention. Several residents of Springfield, and with them a runaway captain from a Kansas regiment, had preceded us a few hours and told much more than the truth. Some of them had advised the people to abandon their homes and go to Rolla or St. Louis, assuring them they would all be murdered if they remained at home.

In pursuance of this advice many were loading a portion of their household goods upon wagons and preparing to precede or follow the army in its retreat. We quieted their alarm as much as possible, advising them to stay at home and trust to fortune. We could not imagine that the Rebels would deal severely with the inhabitants, except in cases where they had been conspicuous in the Union cause. Some of the people took our advice, unloaded their wagons, and waited for further developments. Others persisted in their determination to leave. They knew the Rebels better than we, and hesitated to trust their tender mercies. A year later we learned more of "the barbarism of Slavery."

Southwest Missouri is a region of magnificent distances. A mile in that locality is like two miles in the New England or Middle States. The people have an easy way of computing distance by the survey lines. Thus, if it is the width of a township from one point to another, they call the distance six miles, even though the road may follow the tortuosities of a creek or of the crest of a ridge, and be ten or twelve miles by actual measurement.

From Springfield to Lebanon it is called fifty miles, as indicated by the survey lines. A large part of the way the route is quite direct, but there are places where it winds considerably among the hills, and adds several miles to the length of the road. No account is taken of this, but all is thrown into the general reckoning.

There is a popular saying on the frontier, that they measure the roads with a fox-skin, and make no allowance for the tail. Frequently I have been told it was five miles to a certain point, and, after an hour's riding, on inquiry, found that the place I sought was still five, and sometimes six, miles distant. Once, when I essayed a "short cut" of two miles, that was to save me twice that distance, I rode at a good pace for an hour and a half to accomplish it, and traveled, as I thought, at least eight miles.

On the route from Springfield to Lebanon we were much amused at the estimates of distance. Once I asked a rough-looking farmer, "How far is it to Sand Springs?"

"Five miles, stranger," was the reply. "May be you won't find it so much."

After riding three miles, and again inquiring, I was informed it was "risin' six miles to Sand Springs." Who could believe in the existence of a reliable countryman, after that?

Thirty miles from Springfield, we stopped at a farm-house for dinner. While our meal was being prepared, we lay upon the grass in front of the house, and were at once surrounded by a half-dozen anxious natives. We answered their questions to the best of our abilities, but nearly all of us fell asleep five minutes after lying down. When aroused for dinner, I was told I had paused in the middle of a word of two syllables, leaving my hearers to exercise their imaginations on what I was about to say.

Dinner was the usual "hog and hominy" of the Southwest, varied with the smallest possible loaf of wheaten bread. Outside the house, before dinner, the men were inquisitive. Inside the house, when we were seated for dinner, the women were unceasing in their inquiries. Who can resist the questions of a woman, even though she be an uneducated and unkempt Missourian? The dinner and the questions kept us awake, and we attended faithfully to both.

The people of this household were not enthusiastic friends of the Union. Like many other persons, they were anxious to preserve the good opinion of both sides, by doing nothing in behalf of either. Thus neutral, they feared they would be less kindly treated by the Rebels than by the National forces. Though they had no particular love for our army, I think they were sorry to see it departing. A few of the Secessionists were not slow to express the fear that their own army would not be able to pay in full for all it wanted, as our army had done.

Horses and riders refreshed, our journey was resumed. The scenes of the afternoon were like those of the morning: the same alarm among the people, the same exaggerated reports, and the same advice from ourselves, when we chose to give it. The road stretched out in the same way it had hitherto done, and the information derived from the inhabitants was as unreliable as ever. It was late in the evening, in the midst of a heavy shower, that we reached Lebanon, where we halted for the night.

I have somewhere read of a Persian king who beheaded his subjects for the most trivial or imaginary offenses. The officers of his cabinet, when awaking in the morning, were accustomed to place their hands to their necks, to ascertain if their heads still remained. The individuals comprising our party had every reason to make a similar examination on the morning after our stay in this town, and to express many thanks at the gratifying result.

On reaching the only hotel at Lebanon, long after dark, we found the public room occupied by a miscellaneous assemblage. It was easy to see that they were more happy than otherwise at the defeat which our arms had sustained. While our supper was being prepared we made ready for it, all the time keeping our eyes on the company. We were watched as we went to supper, and, on reaching the table, found two persons sitting so near our allotted places that we could not converse freely.

After supper several individuals wished to talk with us concerning the recent events. We made the battle appear much better than it had really been, and assured them that a company of cavalry was following close behind us, and would speedily arrive. This information was unwelcome, as the countenances of the listeners plainly indicated.

One of our party was called aside by a Union citizen, and informed of a plan to rob, and probably kill, us before morning. This was not pleasing. It did not add to the comfort of the situation to know that a collision between the Home Guards and a company of Secessionists was momentarily expected. At either end of the town the opposing parties were reported preparing for a fight. As the hotel was about half-way between the two points, our position became interesting.

Next came a report from an unreliable contraband that our horses had been stolen. We went to the stable, as a man looks in a wallet he knows to be empty, and happily found our animals still there. We found, however, that the stable had been invaded and robbed of two horses in stalls adjacent to those of our own. The old story of the theft of a saw-mill, followed by that of the dam, was brought to our minds, with the exception, that the return of the thief was not likely to secure his capture. The stable-keeper offered to lock the door and resign the key to our care. His offer was probably well intended, but we could see little advantage in accepting it, as there were several irregular openings in the side of the building, each of them ample for the egress of a horse.

In assigning us quarters for the night, the landlord suggested that two should occupy a room at one end of the house, while the rest were located elsewhere. We objected to this, and sustained our objection. With a little delay, a room sufficient for all of us was obtained. We made arrangements for the best possible defense in case of attack, and then lay down to sleep.

Our Union friend called upon us before we were fairly settled to rest, bringing us intelligence that the room, where the guns of the Home Guard were temporarily stored, had been invaded while the sentinels were at supper. The locks had been removed from some of the muskets, but there were arms enough to make some resistance if necessary. Telling him we would come out when the firing began, and requesting the landlord to send the cavalry commander to our room as soon as he arrived, we fell asleep.

No one of our party carried his fears beyond the waking hours. In five minutes after dismissing our friend, all were enjoying a sleep as refreshing and undisturbed as if we had been in the most secure and luxurious dwelling of New York or Chicago. During several years of travel under circumstances of greater or less danger, I have never found my sleep disturbed, in the slightest degree, by the nature of my surroundings. Apprehensions of danger may be felt while one is awake, but they generally vanish when slumber begins.

In the morning we found ourselves safe, and were gratified to discover that our horses had been let alone. The landlord declared every thing was perfectly quiet, and had been so through the night, with the exception of a little fight at one end of the town. The Home Guards were in possession, and the Secessionists had dispersed. The latter deliberated upon the policy of attacking us, and decided that their town might be destroyed by our retreating army in case we were disturbed. They left us our horses, that we might get away from the place as speedily as possible. So we bade adieu to Lebanon with much delight. That we came unmolested out of that nest of disloyalty, was a matter of much surprise. Subsequent events, there and elsewhere, have greatly increased that surprise.

After a ride of thirteen miles we reached the Gasconade River, which we found considerably swollen by recent rains. The proprietor of the hotel where we breakfasted was a country doctor, who passed in that region as a man of great wisdom. He was intensely disloyal, and did not relish the prospect of having, as he called it, "an Abolition army" moving anywhere in his vicinity. He was preparing to leave for the South, with his entire household, as soon as his affairs could be satisfactorily arranged. He had taken the oath of allegiance, to protect himself from harm at the hands of our soldiers, but his negroes informed us that he belonged to a company of "Independent Guards," which had been organized with the design of joining the Rebel army.

This gentleman was searching for his rights. I passed his place six months afterward. The doctor's negroes had run away to the North, and the doctor had vanished with his family in the opposite direction. His house had been burned, his stables stripped of every thing of value, and the whole surroundings formed a picture of desolation. The doctor had found a reward for his vigilant search. There was no doubt he had obtained his rights.

Having ended our breakfast, we decided to remain at that place until late in the afternoon, for the purpose of writing up our accounts. With a small table, and other accommodations of the worst character, we busied ourselves for several hours. To the persona of the household we were a curiosity. They had never before seen men who could write with a journalist's ordinary rapidity, and were greatly surprised at the large number of pages we succeeded in passing over. We were repeatedly interrupted, until forced to make a request to be let alone. The negroes took every opportunity to look at us, and, when none but ourselves could see them, they favored us with choice bits of local information. When we departed, late in the afternoon, four stout negroes ferried us across the river.

A hotel known as the California House was our stopping-place, ten miles from the Gasconade. As an evidence of our approaching return to civilization, we found each bed at this house supplied with two clean sheets, a luxury that Springfield was unable to furnish. I regretted to find, several months later, that the California House had been burned by the Rebels. At the time of our retreat, the landlord was unable to determine on which side of the question he belonged, and settled the matter, in conversation with me, by saying he was a hotel-keeper, and could not interfere in the great issue of the day. I inclined to the belief that he was a Union man, but feared to declare himself on account of the dubious character of his surroundings.

The rapidity with which the Secessionists carried and received news was a matter of astonishment to our people. While on that ride through the Southwest, I had an opportunity of learning their *modus operandi*. Several times we saw horsemen ride to houses or stables, and, after a few moments' parley, exchange their wearied horses for fresh ones. The parties with whom they effected their exchanges would be found pretty well informed concerning the latest news. By this irregular system of couriers, the Secessionists maintained a complete communication with each other. All along the route, I found they knew pretty well what had transpired, though their news was generally mixed up with much falsehood.

Even in those early days, there was a magnificence in the Rebel capacity for lying. Before the war, the Northern States produced by far the greatest number of inventions, as the records of the Patent Office will show. During the late Rebellion, the brains of the Southern States were wonderfully fertile in the manufacture of falsehood. The inhabitants of Dixie invent neither cotton-gins, caloric engines, nor sewing-machines, but when they apply their faculties to downright lying, the mudsill head is forced to bow in reverence.

In the last day of this ride, we passed over a plateau twelve miles across, also over a mountain of considerable height. Near the summit of this mountain, we struck a small brook, whose growth was an interesting study. At first, barely perceptible as it issued from a spring by the roadside, it grew, mile by mile, until, at the foot of the mountain, it formed a respectable stream. The road crossed it every few hundred yards, and at each crossing we watched its increase. At the base of the mountain it united with another and larger stream, which we followed on our way to Rolla.

Late in the afternoon we reached the end of our journey. Weary, dusty, hungry, and sore, we alighted from our tired horses, and sought the office of the commandant of the post. All were eager to gather the latest intelligence, and we were called upon to answer a thousand questions.

With our story ended, ourselves refreshed from the fatigue of our long ride, a hope for the safety of our gallant but outnumbered army, we bade adieu to Rolla, and were soon whirling over the rail to St. Louis.

CHAPTER VIII
GENERAL FREMONT'S PURSUIT OF PRICE

After the battle of Wilson Creek and the occupation of Springfield, a quarrel arose between the Rebel Generals, Price and McCulloch. It resulted in the latter being ordered to Arkansas, leaving General Price in command of the army in Missouri. The latter had repeatedly promised to deliver Missouri from the hands of the United States forces, and made his preparations for an advance into the interior. His intention, openly declared, was to take possession of Jefferson City, and reinstate Governor Jackson in control of the State. The Rebels wisely considered that a perambulating Governor was not entitled to great respect, and were particularly anxious to see the proclamations of His Excellency issued from the established capital.

Accordingly, General Price, with an army twenty thousand strong, marched from Springfield in the direction of Lexington. This point was garrisoned by Colonel Mulligan with about twenty-five hundred men. After a siege of four days, during the last two of which the garrison was without water, the fort was surrendered. Price's army was sufficiently large to make a complete investment of the fortifications occupied by Colonel Mulligan, and thus cut off all access to the river. The hemp warehouses in Lexington were drawn upon to construct movable breast-works for the besieging force. Rolling the bales of hemp before them, the Rebel sharp-shooters could get very near the fort without placing themselves in great danger.

The defense was gallant, but as no garrisons can exist without water, Colonel Mulligan was forced to capitulate. It afterward became known that Price's army had almost exhausted its stock of percussion-caps--it having less than two thousand when the surrender was made. General Fremont was highly censured by the Press and people for not re-enforcing the garrison, when it was known that Price was moving upon Lexington. One journal in St. Louis, that took occasion to comment adversely upon his conduct, was suddenly suppressed. After a stoppage of a few days, it was allowed to resume publication.

During the siege a small column of infantry approached the north bank of the river, opposite Lexington, with the design of joining Colonel

Mulligan. The attempt was considered too hazardous, and no junction was effected. Mr. Wilkie, of the New York *Times*, accompanied this column, and was much disappointed when the project of reaching Lexington was given up.

Determined to see the battle, he crossed the river and surrendered himself to General Price, with a request to be put on parole until the battle was ended. The Rebel commander gave him quarters in the guardhouse till the surrender took place. Mr. Wilkie was then liberated, and reached St. Louis with an exclusive account of the affair.

While General Price was holding Lexington, General Fremont commenced assembling an army at Jefferson City, with the avowed intention of cutting off the retreat of the Rebels through Southwest Missouri. From Jefferson City our forces moved to Tipton and Syracuse, and there left the line of railway for a march to Springfield. Our movements were not conducted with celerity, and before we left Jefferson City the Rebels had evacuated Lexington and moved toward Springfield.

The delay in our advance was chiefly owing to a lack of transportation and a deficiency of arms for the men. General Fremont's friends charged that he was not properly sustained by the Administration, in his efforts to outfit and organize his army. There was, doubtless, some ground for this charge, as the authorities, at that particular time, were unable to see any danger, except at Washington. They often diverted to that point *matériel* that had been originally designed for St. Louis.

As the army lay at Jefferson City, preparing for the field, some twelve or fifteen journalists, representing the prominent papers of the country, assembled there to chronicle its achievements. They waited nearly two weeks for the movement to begin. Some became sick, others left in disgust, but the most of them remained firm. The devices of the journalists to kill time were of an amusing nature. The town had no attractions whatever, and the gentlemen of the press devoted themselves to fast riding on the best horses they could obtain. Their horseback excursions usually terminated in lively races, in which both riders and steeds were sufferers. The representatives of two widely-circulated dailies narrowly escaped being sent home with broken necks.

Evenings at the hotels were passed in reviving the "sky-larking" of school-boy days. These scenes were amusing to participants and spectators. Sober, dignified men, the majority of them heads of families, occupied themselves in devising plans for the general amusement.

One mode of enjoyment was to assemble in a certain large room, and throw at each other every portable article at hand, until exhaustion ensued.

Every thing that could be thrown or tossed was made use of. Pillows, overcoats, blankets, valises, saddle-bags, bridles, satchels, towels, books, stove-wood, bed-clothing, chairs, window-curtains, and, ultimately, the fragments of the bedsteads, were transformed into missiles. I doubt if that house ever before, or since, knew so much noise in the same time. Everybody enjoyed it except those who occupied adjoining rooms, and possessed a desire for sleep. Some of these persons were inclined to excuse our hilarity, on the ground that the boys ought to enjoy themselves. "The boys!" Most of them were on the shady side of twenty-five, and some had seen forty years.

About nine o'clock in the forenoon of the day following Price's evacuation of Lexington, we obtained news of the movement. The mail at noon, and the telegraph before that time, carried all we had to say of the affair, and in a few hours we ceased to talk of it. On the evening of that day, a good-natured "contractor" visited our room, and, after indulging in our varied amusements until past eleven, bade us good-night and departed.

Many army contractors had grown fat in the country's service, but this man had a large accumulation of adipose matter before the war broke out. A rapid ascent of a long flight of stairs was, therefore, a serious matter with him. Five minutes after leaving us, he dashed rapidly up the stairs and entered our room. As soon as he could speak, he asked, breathing between, the words--

"Have you heard the news?"

"No," we responded; "what is it?"

"Why" (with more efforts to recover his breath), "Price has evacuated Lexington!"

"Is it possible?"

"Yes," he gasped, and then sank exhausted into a large (very large) arm-chair.

We gave him a glass of water and a fan, and urged him to proceed with the story. He told all he had just heard in the bar-room below, and we listened with the greatest apparent interest.

When he had ended, we told him *our* story. The quality and quantity of the wine which he immediately ordered, was only excelled by his hearty appreciation of the joke he had played upon himself.

Every army correspondent has often been furnished with "important intelligence" already in his possession, and sometimes in print before his well-meaning informant obtains it.

A portion of General Fremont's army marched from Jefferson City to Tipton and Syracuse, while the balance, with most of the transportation, was sent by rail. General Sigel was the first to receive orders to march his division from Tipton to Warsaw, and he was very prompt to obey. While other division commanders were waiting for their transportation to arrive from St. Louis, Sigel scoured the country and gathered up every thing with wheels. His train was the most motley collection of vehicles it has ever been my lot to witness. There were old wagons that made the journey from Tennessee to Missouri thirty years before, farm wagons and carts of every description, family carriages, spring wagons, stage-coaches, drays, and hay-carts. In fact, every thing that could carry a load was taken along. Even pack-saddles were not neglected. Horses, mules, jacks, oxen, and sometimes cows, formed the motive power. To stand by the roadside and witness the passage of General Sigel's train, was equal to a visit to Barnum's Museum, and proved an unfailing source of mirth.

Falstaff's train (if he had one) could not have been more picturesque. Even the Missourians, accustomed as they were to sorry sights, laughed heartily at the spectacle presented by Sigel's transportation. The Secessionists made several wrong deductions from the sad appearance of that train. Some of them predicted that the division with *such* a train would prove to be of little value in battle. Never were men more completely deceived. The division marched rapidly, and, on a subsequent campaign, evinced its ability to fight.

One after another, the divisions of Fremont's army moved in chase of the Rebels; a pursuit in which the pursued had a start of seventy-five miles, and a clear road before them. Fremont and his staff left Tipton, when three divisions had gone, and overtook the main column at Warsaw. A few days later, Mr. Richardson, of the *Tribune*, and myself started from Syracuse at one o'clock, one pleasant afternoon, and, with a single halt of an hour's duration, reached Warsaw, forty-seven miles distant, at ten o'clock at night. In the morning we found the general's staff comfortably quartered in the village. On the staff there were several gentlemen from New York and other Eastern cities, who were totally unaccustomed to horseback exercise. One of these recounted the story of their "dreadful" journey of fifty miles from Tipton.

"Only think of it!" said he; "we came through all that distance in less than three days. One day the general made us come *twenty-four* miles."

"That was very severe, indeed. I wonder how you endured it."

"It *was* severe, and nearly broke some of us down. By-the-way, Mr. K----, how did you come over?"

"Oh," said I, carelessly, "Richardson and I left Syracuse at noon yesterday, and arrived here at ten last night."

Before that campaign was ended, General Fremont's staff acquired some knowledge of horsemanship.

At Warsaw the party of journalists passed several waiting days, and domiciled themselves in the house of a widow who had one pretty daughter. Our natural bashfulness was our great hinderance, so that it was a day or two before we made the acquaintance of the younger of the women. One evening she invited a young lady friend to visit her, and obliged us with introductions. The ladies persistently turned the conversation upon the Rebellion, and gave us the benefit of their views. Our young hostess, desiring to say something complimentary, declared she did not dislike the Yankees, but despised the Dutch and the Black Republicans."

"Do you dislike the Black Republicans very much?" said the *Tribune* correspondent.

"Oh! yes; I *hate* them. I wish they were all dead."

"Well," was the quiet response, "we are Black Republicans. I am the blackest of them all."

The fair Secessionist was much confused, and for fully a minute remained silent. Then she said--

"I must confess I did not fully understand what Black Republicans were. I never saw any before."

During the evening she was quite courteous, though persistent in declaring her sentiments. Her companion launched the most bitter invective at every thing identified with the Union cause, and made some horrid wishes about General Fremont and his army. A more vituperative female Rebel I have never seen. She was as pretty as she was disloyal, and was, evidently, fully aware of it.

A few months later, I learned that both these young ladies had become the wives of United States officers, and were complimenting, in high terms, the bravery and patriotism of the soldiers they had so recently despised.

The majority of the inhabitants of Warsaw were disloyal, and had little hesitation in declaring their sentiments. Most of the young men were in the Rebel army or preparing to go there. A careful search of several warehouses revealed extensive stores of powder, salt, shoes, and other military supplies. Some of these articles were found in a cave a few miles from Warsaw, their locality being made known by a negro who was present at their concealment.

Warsaw boasted a newspaper establishment, but the proprietor and editor of the weekly sheet had joined his fortunes to those of General Price. Two years before the time of our visit, this editor was a member of the State Legislature, and made an earnest effort to secure the expulsion of the reporter of *The Missouri Democrat*, on account of the radical tone of that paper. He was unsuccessful, but the aggrieved individual did not forgive him.

When our army entered Warsaw this reporter held a position on the staff of the general commanding. Not finding his old adversary, he contented himself with taking possession of the printing-office, and "confiscating" whatever was needed for the use of head-quarters.

About twenty miles from Warsaw, on the road to Booneville, there was a German settlement, known as Cole Camp. When the troubles commenced in Missouri, a company of Home Guards was formed at Cole Camp. A few days after its formation a company of Secessionists from Warsaw made a night-march and attacked the Home Guards at daylight.

Though inflicting severe injury upon the Home Guards, the Secessionists mourned the loss of the most prominent citizens of Warsaw. They were soon after humiliated by the presence of a Union army.

CHAPTER IX
THE SECOND CAMPAIGN TO SPRINGFIELD

The army was detained at Warsaw, to wait the construction of a bridge over the Osage for the passage of the artillery and heavy transportation. Sigel's Division was given the advance, and crossed before the bridge was finished. The main column moved as soon as the bridge permitted--the rear being brought up by McKinstry's Division. A division from Kansas, under General Lane, was moving at the same time, to form a junction with Fremont near Springfield, and a brigade from Rolla was advancing with the same object in view. General Sturgis was in motion from North Missouri, and there was a prospect that an army nearly forty thousand strong would be assembled at Springfield.

While General Fremont was in St. Louis, before setting out on this expedition, he organized the "Fremont Body-Guard," which afterward became famous. This force consisted of four companies of cavalry, and was intended to form a full regiment. It was composed of the best class of the young men of St. Louis and Cincinnati. From the completeness of its outfit, it was often spoken of as the "Kid-Gloved Regiment." General Fremont designed it as a special body-guard for himself, to move when he moved, and to form a part of his head-quarter establishment. The manner of its organization was looked upon by many as a needless outlay, at a time when the finances of the department were in a disordered condition. The officers and the rank and file of the Body-Guard felt their pride touched by the comments upon them, and determined to take the first opportunity to vindicate their character as soldiers.

When we were within fifty miles of Springfield, it was ascertained that the main force of the Rebels had moved southward, leaving behind them some two or three thousand men. General Fremont ordered a cavalry force, including the Body-Guard, to advance upon the town. On reaching Springfield the cavalry made a gallant charge upon the Rebel camp, which was situated in a large field, bordered by a wood, within sight of the court-house.

In this assault the loss of our forces, in proportion to the number engaged, was quite severe, but the enemy was put to flight, and the town occupied for a few hours. We gained nothing of a material nature, as the Rebels would have quietly evacuated Springfield at the approach of our main army. The courage of the Body-Guard, which no sensible man had doubted, was fully evinced by this gallant but useless charge. When the fight was over, the colonel in command ordered a retreat of twenty miles, to meet the advance of the army.

A corporal with a dozen men became separated from the command while in Springfield, and remained there until the following morning. He received a flag of truce from the Rebels, asking permission to send a party to bury the dead. He told the bearer to wait until he could consult his "general," who was supposed to be lying down in the back office. The "general" replied that his "division" was too much exasperated to render it prudent for a delegation from the enemy to enter town, and therefore declined to grant the request. At the same time he promised to send out strong details to attend to the sad duty. At sunrise he thought it best to follow the movements of his superior officer, lest the Rebels might discover his ruse and effect his capture.

Two days after the charge of the Body-Guard, the advance of the infantry entered Springfield without the slightest opposition. The army gradually came up, and the occupation of the key of Southwest Missouri was completed. The Rebel army fell back toward the Arkansas line, to meet a force supposed to be marching northward from Fayetteville. There was little expectation that the Rebels would seek to engage us. The only possible prospect of their assuming the offensive was in the event of a junction between Price and McCulloch, rendering them numerically superior to ourselves.

During our occupation of Springfield I paid a visit to the Wilson Creek battle-ground. It was eleven weeks from the day I had left it. Approaching the field, I was impressed by its stillness, so different from the tumult on the 10th of the previous August. It was difficult to realize that the spot, now so quiet, had been the scene of a sanguinary contest. The rippling of the creek, and the occasional chirp of a bird, were the only noises that came to our ears. There was no motion of the air, not enough to disturb the leaves freshly fallen from the numerous oak-trees on the battle-field. At each step I could but contrast the cool, calm, Indian-summer day, with the hot, August morning, when the battle took place.

All sounds of battle were gone, but the traces of the encounter had not disappeared. As we followed the route leading to the field, I turned from the beaten track and rode among the trees. Ascending a slight acclivity, I found my horse half-stumbling over some object between his feet. Looking down, I discovered a human skull, partly covered by the luxuriant grass. At a little distance lay the dismembered skeleton to which the skull evidently belonged. It was doubtless that of some soldier who had crawled there while wounded, and sunk exhausted at the foot of a tree. The bits of clothing covering the ground showed that either birds or wild animals had been busy with the remains. Not far off lay another skeleton, disturbed and dismembered like the other.

Other traces of the conflict were visible, as I moved slowly over the field. Here were scattered graves, each for a single person; there a large grave, that had received a dozen bodies of the slain. Here were fragments of clothing and equipments, pieces of broken weapons; the shattered wheel of a caisson, and near it the exploded shell that destroyed it. Skeletons of horses, graves of men, scarred trees, trampled graves, the ruins of the burned wagons of the Rebels, all formed their portion of the picture. It well illustrated the desolation of war.

The spot where General Lyon fell was marked by a rude inscription upon the nearest tree. The skeleton of the general's favorite horse lay near this tree, and had been partially broken up by relic-seekers. The long, glossy mane was cut off by the Rebel soldiers on the day after the battle, and worn by them as a badge of honor. Subsequently the teeth and bones were appropriated by both Rebels and Unionists. Even the tree that designated the locality was partially stripped of its limbs to furnish souvenirs of Wilson Creek.

During the first few days of our stay in Springfield, there were vague rumors that the army was preparing for a long march into the enemy's country. The Rebel army was reported at Cassville, fifty-five miles distant, fortifying in a strong position. General Price and Governor Jackson had convened the remnant of the Missouri Legislature, and caused the State to be voted out of the Union. It was supposed we would advance and expel the Rebels from the State.

While we were making ready to move, it was reported that the Rebel army at Cassville had received large re-enforcements from Arkansas, and was moving in our direction. Of course, all were anxious for a battle, and hailed this intelligence with delight. At the same time there were rumors of trouble from another direction--trouble to the commander-in-chief. The vague reports of his coming decapitation were followed by the arrival, on the 2d of November, of the unconditional order removing General Fremont from command, and appointing General Hunter in his stead.

Just before the reception of this order, "positive" news was received that the enemy was advancing from Cassville toward Springfield, and would either attack us in the town, or meet us on the ground south of it. General Hunter had not arrived, and therefore General Fremont formed his plan of battle, and determined on marching out to meet the enemy.

On the morning of the 3d, the scouts brought intelligence that the entire Rebel army was in camp on the old Wilson Creek battle-ground, and would fight us there. A council of war was called, and it was decided to attack the enemy on the following morning, if General Hunter did not arrive before that time. Some of the officers were suspicious that the Rebels were not in force at Wilson Creek, but when Fremont announced it officially there could be little room for doubt.

Every thing was put in readiness for battle. Generals of division were ordered to be ready to move at a moment's notice. The pickets were doubled, and the grand guards increased to an unusual extent. Four pieces of artillery formed a portion of the picket force on the Fayetteville road, the direct route to Wilson Creek. If an enemy had approached on that night he would have met a warm reception.

About seven o'clock in the evening, a staff officer, who kept the journalists informed of the progress of affairs, visited General Fremont's head-quarters. He soon emerged with important intelligence.

"It is all settled. The army is ready to move at the instant. Orders will be issued at two o'clock, and we will be under way before daylight. Skirmishing will begin at nine, and the full battle will be drawn on at twelve."

"Is the plan arranged?"

"Yes, it is all arranged; but I did not ask how."

"Battle sure to come off--is it?"

"Certainly, unless Hunter comes and countermands the order."

Alas, for human calculations! General Hunter arrived before midnight. Two o'clock came, but no orders to break camp. Daylight, and no orders to march. Breakfast-time, and not a hostile shot had been heard. Nine o'clock, and no skirmish. Twelve o'clock, and no battle.

General Fremont and staff returned to St. Louis. General Hunter made a reconnoissance to Wilson Creek, and ascertained that the only enemy that had been in the vicinity was a scouting party of forty or fifty men. At the time we were to march out, there was not a Rebel on the ground. Their whole army was still at Cassville, fifty-five miles from Springfield.

On the 9th of November the army evacuated Springfield and returned to the line of the Pacific Railway.

General Fremont's scouts had deceived him. Some of these individuals were exceedingly credulous, while others were liars of the highest grade known to civilization. The former obtained their information from the frightened inhabitants; the latter manufactured theirs with the aid of vivid imaginations. I half suspect the fellows were like the showman in the story, and, at length, religiously believed what they first designed as a hoax. Between the two classes of scouts a large army of Rebels was created.

The scouting service often develops characters of a peculiar mould. Nearly every man engaged in it has some particular branch in which he excels. There was one young man accompanying General Fremont's army, whose equal, as a special forager, I have never seen elsewhere. Whenever we entered camp, this individual, whom I will call the captain, would take a half-dozen companions and start on a foraging tour. After an absence of from four to six hours, he would return well-laden with the spoils of war. On one occasion he brought to camp three horses, two cows, a yoke of oxen, and a wagon. In the latter he had a barrel of sorghum molasses, a firkin of butter, two sheep, a pair of fox-hounds, a hoop-skirt, a corn-sheller, a baby's cradle, a lot of crockery, half a dozen padlocks, two hoes, and a rocking-chair. On the next night he returned with a family carriage drawn by a horse and a mule. In the carriage he had, among other things, a parrot-cage which contained a screaming parrot, several pairs of ladies' shoes, a few yards of calico, the stock of an old musket, part of a spinning-wheel, and a box of garden seeds. In what way these things would contribute to the support of the army, it was difficult to understand.

On one occasion the captain found a trunk full of clothing, concealed with a lot of salt in a Rebel warehouse. He brought the trunk to camp, and, as the quartermaster refused to receive it, took it to St. Louis when the expedition returned. At the hotel where he was stopping, some detectives were watching a suspected thief, and, by mistake, searched the captain's room. They found a trunk containing thirteen coats of all sizes, with no pants or vests. Naturally considering this a strange wardrobe for a gentleman, they took the captain into custody. He protested earnestly that he was not, and had never been, a thief, but it was only on the testimony of the quartermaster that he was released. I believe he subsequently acted as a scout under General Halleck, during the siege of Corinth.

After the withdrawal of our army, General Price returned to Springfield and went into winter-quarters. McCulloch's command formed a cantonment at Cross Hollows, Arkansas, about ninety miles southwest of Springfield. There was no prospect of further activity until the ensuing spring. Every thing betokened rest.

From Springfield I returned to St. Louis by way of Rolla, designing to follow the example of the army, and seek a good locality for hibernating. On my way to Rolla I found many houses deserted, or tenanted only by women and children. Frequently the crops were standing, ungathered, in the field. Fences were prostrated, and there was no effort to restore them. The desolation of that region was just beginning.

CHAPTER X
TWO MONTHS OF IDLENESS

Early in the December following the events narrated in the last chapter, General Pope captured a camp in the interior of the State, where recruits were being collected for Price's army. After the return of Fremont's army from Springfield, the Rebels boasted they would eat their Christmas dinner in St. Louis. Many Secessionists were making preparations to receive Price and his army, and some of them prophesied the time of their arrival. It was known that a goodly number of Rebel flags had been made ready to hang out when the conquerors should come. Sympathizers with the Rebellion became bold, and often displayed badges, rosettes, and small flags, indicative of their feelings. Recruiting for the Rebel army went on, very quietly, of course, within a hundred yards of the City Hall. At a fair for the benefit of the Orphan Asylum, the ladies openly displayed Rebel insignia, but carefully excluded the National emblems.

This was the state of affairs when eight hundred Rebels arrived in St. Louis. They redeemed their promise to enjoy a Christmas dinner in St. Louis, though they had counted upon more freedom than they were then able to obtain. In order that they might carry out, in part, their original intention, their kind-hearted jailers permitted the friends of the prisoners to send a dinner to the latter on Christmas Day. The prisoners partook of the repast with much relish.

The capture of those recruits was accompanied by the seizure of a supply train on its way to Springfield. Our success served to diminish the Rebel threats to capture St. Louis, or perform other great and chivalric deeds. The inhabitants of that city continued to prophesy its fall, but they were less defiant than before.

General Fremont commanded the Western Department for just a hundred days. General Hunter, his successor, was dressed in brief authority for fifteen days, and yielded to General Halleck. The latter officer endeavored to make his rule as unlike that of General Fremont as could well be done. He quietly made his head-quarters at the Government Buildings, in the center of St. Louis, instead of occupying a "palatial mansion" on Chouteau

Avenue. The body-guard, or other cumbersome escort, was abolished, and the new general moved unattended about the city. Where General Fremont had scattered the Government funds with a wasteful hand, General Halleck studied economy. Where Fremont had declared freedom to the slaves of traitors, Halleck issued his famous "Order No. 3," forbidding fugitive slaves to enter our lines, and excluding all that were then in the military camps. Where General Fremont had surrounded his head-quarters with so great a retinue of guards that access was almost impossible, General Halleck made it easy for all visitors to see him. He generally gave them such a reception that few gentlemen felt inclined to make a second call.

The policy of scattering the military forces in the department was abandoned, and a system of concentration adopted. The construction of the gun-boat fleet, and accompanying mortar-rafts, was vigorously pushed, and preparations for military work in the ensuing spring went on in all directions. Our armies were really idle, and we were doing very little on the Mississippi; but it was easy to see that we were making ready for the most vigorous activity in the future.

In the latter part of December many refugees from the Southwest began to arrive in St. Louis. In most cases they were of the poorer class of the inhabitants of Missouri and Northern Arkansas, and had been driven from their homes by their wealthier and disloyal neighbors. Their stories varied little from each other. Known or suspected to be loyal, they were summarily expelled, generally with the loss of every thing, save a few articles of necessity. There were many women and children among them, whose protectors had been driven into the Rebel ranks, or murdered in cold blood. Many of them died soon after they reached our lines, and there were large numbers who perished on their way.

Among those who arrived early in January, 1862, was a man from Northern Arkansas. Born in Pennsylvania, he emigrated to the Southwest in 1830, and, after a few years' wandering, settled near Fayetteville. When the war broke out, he had a small farm and a comfortable house, and his two sons were married and living near him.

In the autumn of '61, his elder son was impressed into the Rebel service, where he soon died. The younger was ordered to report at Fayetteville, for duty. Failing to do so on the day specified, he was shot down in his own house on the following night. His body fell upon one of his children standing near him, and his blood saturated its garments.

The day following, the widow, with two small children, was notified to leave the dwelling, as orders had been issued for its destruction. Giving her no time to remove any thing, the Rebel soldiers, claiming to act under military command, fired the house. In this party were two persons who had been well acquainted with the murdered man. The widow sought shelter with her husband's parents.

The widow of the elder son went to the same place of refuge. Thus there were living, under one roof, the old man, his wife, a daughter of seventeen, and the two widows, one with two, and the other with three, children. A week afterward, all were commanded to leave the country. No cause was assigned, beyond the fact that the man was born in the North, and had been harboring the family of his son, who refused to serve in the Rebel ranks. They were told they could have two days for preparation, but within ten hours of the time the notice was served, a gang of Rebels appeared at the door, and ordered an instant departure.

They made a rigid search of the persons of the refugees, to be sure they took away nothing of value. Only a single wagon was allowed, and in this were placed a few articles of necessity. As they moved away, the Rebels applied the torch to the house and its out-buildings. In a few moments all were in flames. The house of the elder son's widow shared the same fete.

They were followed to the Missouri line, and ordered to make no halt under penalty of death. It was more than two hundred miles to our lines, and winter was just beginning. One after another fell ill and died, or was left with Union people along the way. Only four of the party reached our army at Rolla. Two of these died a few days after their arrival, leaving only a young child and its grandfather. At St. Louis the survivors were kindly cared for, but the grief at leaving home, the hardships of the winter journey, and their destitution among strangers, had so worn upon them that they soon followed the other members of their family.

There have been thousands of cases nearly parallel to the above. The Rebels claimed to be fighting for political freedom, and charged the National Government with the most unheard-of "tyranny." We can well be excused for not countenancing a political freedom that kills men at their firesides, and drives women and children to seek protection under another flag. We have heard much, in the past twenty years, of "Southern chivalry." If the deeds of which the Rebels were guilty are characteristic of chivalry, who would wish to be a son of the Cavaliers? The insignia worn in the Middle Ages are set aside, to make room for the torch and the knife. The chivalry that deliberately starves its prisoners, to render them unable to return to the field, and sends blood-hounds on the track of those who attempt an escape from their hands, is the chivalry of modern days. Winder is the Coeur-de-Leon, and Quantrel the Bayard, of the nineteenth century; knights "without fear and without reproach."

Early in January, the Army of the Southwest, under General Curtis, was put in condition for moving. Orders were issued cutting down the allowance of transportation, and throwing away every thing superfluous. Colonel Carr, with a cavalry division, was sent to the line of the Gasconade, to watch the movements of the enemy. It was the preliminary to the march into Arkansas, which resulted in the battle of Pea Ridge and the famous campaign of General Curtis from Springfield to Helena.

As fast as possible, the gun-boat fleet was pushed to completion. One after another, as the iron-clads were ready to move, they made their rendezvous at Cairo. Advertisements of the quartermaster's department, calling for a large number of transports, showed that offensive movements were to take place. In February, Fort Henry fell, after an hour's shelling from Admiral Foote's gun-boats. This opened the way up the Tennessee River to a position on the flank of Columbus, Kentucky, and was followed by the evacuation of that point.

I was in St. Louis on the day the news of the fall of Fort Henry was received. The newspapers issued "extras," with astonishing head-lines. It was the first gratifying intelligence after a long winter of inactivity, following a year which, closed with general reverses to our arms.

In walking the principal streets of St. Louis on that occasion, I could easily distinguish the loyal men of my acquaintance from the disloyal, at half a square's distance. The former were excited with delight; the latter were downcast with sorrow. The Union men walked rapidly, with, faces "wreathed in smiles;" the Secessionists moved with alternate slow and quick steps, while their countenances expressed all the sad emotions.

The newsboys with the tidings of our success were patronized by the one and repelled by the other. I saw one of the venders of intelligence enter the store of a noted Secessionist, where he shouted the nature of the news at the highest note of his voice. A moment later he emerged from the door, bringing the impress of a Secessionist's boot.

The day and the night witnessed much hilarity in loyal circles, and a corresponding gloom in quarters where treason ruled. I fear there were many men in St. Louis whose conduct was no recommendation to the membership of a temperance society.

All felt that a new era had dawned upon us. Soon after came the tidings of a general advance of our armies. We moved in Virginia, and made the beginning of the checkered campaign of '62. Along the Atlantic coast we moved, and Newbern fell into our hands. Further down the Atlantic, and at the mouth of the Mississippi, we kept up the aggression. Grant, at Donelson, "moved immediately upon Buckner's works;" and, in Kentucky, the Army of the Ohio occupied Bowling Green and prepared to move upon Nashville. In Missouri, Curtis had already occupied Lebanon, and was making ready to assault Price at Springfield. Everywhere our flag was going forward.

CHAPTER XI
ANOTHER CAMPAIGN IN MISSOURI

On the 9th of February I left St. Louis to join General Curtis's army. Arriving at Rolla, I found the mud very deep, but was told the roads were in better condition a few miles to the west. With an *attaché* of the Missouri *Democrat*, I started, on the morning of the 10th, to overtake the army, then reported at Lebanon, sixty-five miles distant. All my outfit for a two or three months' campaign, was strapped behind my saddle, or crowded into my saddle-bags. Traveling with a trunk is one of the delights unknown to army correspondents, especially to those in the Southwest. My companion carried an outfit similar to mine, with the exception of the saddle-bags and contents. I returned to Rolla eight weeks afterward, but he did not reach civilization till the following July.

From Rolla to Lebanon the roads were bad--muddy in the valleys of the streams, and on the higher ground frozen into inequalities like a gigantic rasp.

Over this route our army of sixteen thousand men had slowly made its way, accomplishing what was then thought next to impossible. I found the country had changed much in appearance since I passed through on my way to join General Lyon. Many houses had been burned and others deserted. The few people that remained confessed themselves almost destitute of food. Frequently we could not obtain entertainment for ourselves and horses, particularly the latter. The natives were suspicious of our character, as there was nothing in our dress indicating to which side we belonged. At such times the cross-questioning we underwent was exceedingly amusing, though coupled with the knowledge that our lives were not entirely free from danger.

From Lebanon we pushed on to Springfield, through a keen, piercing wind, that swept from the northwest with unremitting steadiness. The night between those points was passed in a log-house with a single room, where ourselves and the family of six persons were lodged. In the bitter cold morning that followed, it was necessary to open the door to give us sufficient light to take breakfast, as the house could not boast of a window.

The owner of the establishment said he had lived there eighteen years, and found it very comfortable. He tilled a small farm, and had earned sufficient money to purchase three slaves, who dwelt in a similar cabin, close beside his own, but not joining it. One of these slaves was cook and housemaid, and another found the care of four children enough for her attention. The third was a man upward of fifty years old, who acted as stable-keeper, and manager of the out-door work of the establishment.

The situation of this landholder struck me as peculiar, though his case was not a solitary one. A house of one room and with no window, a similar house for his human property, and a stable rudely constructed of small poles, with its sides offering as little protection against the wind and storms as an ordinary fence, were the only buildings he possessed. His furniture was in keeping with the buildings. Beds without sheets, a table without a cloth, some of the plates of tin and others of crockery--the former battered and the latter cracked--a less number of knives and forks than there were persons to be supplied, tin cups for drinking coffee, an old fruit-can for a sugar-bowl, and two teaspoons for the use of a large family, formed the most noticeable features. With such surroundings he had invested three thousand dollars in negro property, and considered himself comfortably situated.

Reaching Springfield, I found the army had passed on in pursuit of Price, leaving only one brigade as a garrison. The quartermaster of the Army of the Southwest had his office in one of the principal buildings, and was busily engaged in superintending the forwarding of supplies to the front. Every thing under his charge received his personal attention, and there was no reason to suppose the army would lack for subsistence, so long as he should remain to supply its wants. Presenting him a letter of introduction, I received a most cordial welcome. I found him a modest and agreeable gentleman, whose private excellence was only equaled by his energy in the performance of his official duties.

This quartermaster was Captain Philip H. Sheridan. The double bars that marked his rank at that time, have since been exchanged for other insignia. The reader is doubtless familiar with the important part taken by this gallant officer, in the suppression of the late Rebellion.

General Curtis had attempted to surround and capture Price and his army, before they could escape from Springfield. Captain Sheridan told me that General Curtis surrounded the town on one side, leaving two good roads at the other, by which the Rebels marched out. Our advance from Lebanon was as rapid as the circumstances would permit, but it was impossible to keep the Rebels in ignorance of it, or detain them against their will. One of the many efforts to "bag" Price had resulted like all the others.

We closed with the utmost care every part of the bag except the mouth; out of this he walked by the simple use of his pedals. Operations like those of Island Number Ten, Vicksburg, and Port Hudson, were not then in vogue.

Price was in full retreat toward Arkansas, and our army in hot pursuit. General Sigel, with two full divisions, marched by a road parallel to the line of Price's retreat, and attempted to get in his front at a point forty miles from Springfield. His line of march was ten miles longer than the route followed by the Rebels, and he did not succeed in striking the main road until Price had passed.

I had the pleasure of going through General Price's head-quarters only two days after that officer abandoned them. There was every evidence of a hasty departure. I found, among other documents, the following order for the evacuation of Springfield:--

> HEAD-QUARTERS MISSOURI STATE GUARD,
> SPRINGFIELD, *February* 13, 1862.
>
> The commanders of divisions will instanter, and without the least delay, see that their entire commands are ready for movement at a moment's notice.
>
> By order of Major-General S. Price. H.H. Brand, A.A.G.

There was much of General Price's private correspondence, together with many official documents. Some of these I secured, but destroyed them three weeks later, at a moment when I expected to fall into the hands of the enemy. One letter, which revealed the treatment Union men were receiving in Arkansas, I forwarded to *The Herald*. I reproduce its material portions:--

> DOVER, POPE CO., ARKANSAS, *December* 7, 1861.
>
> MAJOR-GENERAL PRICE:
>
> I wish to obtain a situation as surgeon in your army. Our men over the Boston Mountains are penning and hanging the mountain boys who oppose Southern men. They have in camp thirty, and in the Burrowville jail seventy-two, and have sent twenty-seven to Little Rock. We will kill all we get, certain: every one is so many less. I hope you will soon get help enough to clear out the last one in your State. If you know them, they ought to be killed, as the older they grow the more stubborn they get.
>
> Your most obedient servant,
> JAMES L. ADAMS.

In his departure, General Price had taken most of his personal property of any value. He left a very good array of desks and other appurtenances of his adjutant-general's office, which fell into General Curtis's hands. These articles were at once put into use by our officers, and remained in Springfield as trophies of our success. There was some war *matériel* at the founderies and temporary arsenals which the Rebels had established. One store full of supplies they left undisturbed. It was soon appropriated by Captain Sheridan.

The winter-quarters for the soldiers were sufficiently commodious to contain ten thousand men, and the condition in which we found them showed how hastily they were evacuated. Very little had been removed from the buildings, except those articles needed for the march. We found cooking utensils containing the remains of the last meal, pans with freshly-mixed dough, on which the impression of the maker's hand was visible, and sheep and hogs newly killed and half dressed. In the officers' quarters was a beggarly array of empty bottles, and a few cases that had contained cigars. One of our soldiers was fortunate in finding a gold watch in the straw of a bunk. There were cribs of corn, stacks of forage, and a considerable quantity of army supplies. Every thing evinced a hasty departure.

CHAPTER XII
THE FLIGHT AND THE PURSUIT

When it became certain the army would continue its march into Arkansas, myself and the *Democrat's* correspondent pushed forward to overtake it. Along the road we learned of the rapid retreat of the Rebels, and the equally rapid pursuit by our own forces. About twenty miles south of Springfield one of the natives came to his door to greet us. Learning to which army we belonged, he was very voluble in his efforts to explain the consternation of the Rebels. A half-dozen of his neighbors were by his side, and joined in the hilarity of the occasion. I saw that something more than usual was the cause of their assembling, and inquired what it could be.

"My wife died this morning, and my friends have come here to see me," was the answer I received from the proprietor of the house.

Almost at the instant of completing the sentence, he burst into a laugh, and said,

"It would have done you good to see how your folks captured a big drove of Price's cattle. The Rebs were driving them along all right, and your cavalry just came up and took them. It was rich, I tell you. Ha! ha!"

Not knowing what condolence to offer a man who could be so gay after the death of his wife, I bade him good-morning, and pushed on. He had not, as far as I could perceive, the single excuse of being intoxicated, and his display of vivacity appeared entirely genuine. In all my travels I have never met his equal.

Up to the time of this campaign none of our armies had been into Arkansas. When General Curtis approached the line, the head of the column was halted, the regiments closed up, and the men brought their muskets to the "right shoulder shift," instead of the customary "at will" of the march. Two bands were sent to the front, where a small post marked the boundary, and were stationed by the roadside, one in either State. Close by them the National flag was unfurled. The bands struck up "The Arkansas Traveler," the order to advance was given, and, with many cheers in honor of the event, the column moved onward. For several days "The Arkansas Traveler" was exceedingly popular with the entire command. On the night after crossing the line the news of the fall of Fort Donelson was received.

Soon after entering Arkansas on his retreat, General Price met General McCulloch moving northward to join him. With their forces united, they determined on making a stand against General Curtis, and, accordingly, halted near Sugar Creek. A little skirmish ensued, in which the Rebels gave way, the loss on either side being trifling. They did not stop until they reached Fayetteville. Their halt at that point was very brief.

At Cross Hollows, in Benton County, Arkansas, about two miles from the main road, there is one of the finest springs in the Southwest. It issues from the base of a rocky ledge, where the ravine is about three hundred yards wide, and forms the head of a large brook. Two small flouring mills are run during the entire year by the water from this spring. The water is at all times clear, cold, and pure, and is said never to vary in quantity.

Along the stream fed by this spring, the Rebels had established a cantonment for the Army of Northern Arkansas, and erected houses capable of containing ten or twelve thousand men. The cantonment was laid out with the regularity of a Western city. The houses were constructed of sawed lumber, and provided with substantial brick chimneys.

Of course, this establishment was abandoned when the Rebel army retreated. The buildings were set on fire, and all but a half-dozen of them consumed. When our cavalry reached the place, the rear-guard of the Rebels had been gone less than half an hour. There were about two hundred chickens running loose among the burning buildings. Our soldiers commenced killing them, and had slaughtered two-thirds of the lot when one of the officers discovered that they were game-cocks. This class of chickens not being considered edible, the killing was stopped and the balance of the flock saved. Afterward, while we lay in camp, they were made a source of much amusement. The cock-fights that took place in General Curtis's army would have done honor to Havana or Vera Cruz. Before we captured them the birds were the property of the officers of a Louisiana regiment. We gave them the names of the Rebel leaders. It was an every-day affair for Beauregard, Van Dorn, and Price to be matched against Lee, Johnston, and Polk. I remember losing a small wager on Magruder against Breckinridge. I should have won if Breck had not torn the feathers from Mac's neck, and injured his right wing by a foul blow. I never backed Magruder after that.

From Cross Hollows, General Curtis sent a division in pursuit of Price's army, in its retreat through Fayetteville, twenty-two miles distant. On reaching the town they found the Rebels had left in the direction of Fort Smith. The pursuit terminated at this point. It had been continued for a hundred and ten miles--a large portion of the distance our advance being within a mile or two of the Rebel rear.

In retreating from Fayetteville, the Rebels were obliged to abandon much of the supplies for their army. A serious quarrel is reported to have taken place between Price and McCulloch, concerning the disposition to be made of these supplies. The former was in favor of leaving the large amount of stores, of which, bacon was the chief article, that it might fall into our hands. He argued that we had occupied the country, and would stay there until driven out. Our army would be subsisted at all hazards. If we found this large quantity of bacon, it would obviate the necessity of our foraging upon the country and impoverishing the inhabitants.

General McCulloch opposed this policy, and accused Price of a desire to play into the enemy's hands. The quarrel became warm, and resulted in the discomfiture of the latter. All the Rebel warehouses were set on fire. When our troops entered Fayetteville the conflagration was at its height. It resulted as Price had predicted. The inhabitants were compelled, in great measure, to support our army.

The Rebels retreated across the Boston Mountains to Fort Smith, and commenced a reorganization of their army. Our army remained at Cross Hollows as its central point, but threw out its wings so as to form a front nearly five miles in extent. Small expeditions were sent in various directions to break up Rebel camps and recruiting stations. In this way two weeks passed with little activity beyond a careful observation of the enemy's movements. There were several flouring mills in the vicinity of our camp, which were kept in constant activity for the benefit of the army.

I accompanied an expedition, commanded by Colonel Vandever, of the Ninth Iowa, to the town of Huntsville, thirty-five miles distant. Our march occupied two days, and resulted in the occupation of the town and the dispersal of a small camp of Rebels. We had no fighting, scarcely a shot being fired in anger. The inhabitants did not greet us very cordially, though some of them professed Union sentiments.

In this town of Huntsville, the best friend of the Union was the keeper of a whisky-shop. This man desired to look at some of our money, but declined to take it. An officer procured a canteen of whisky and tendered a Treasury note in payment. The note was refused, with a request for either gold or Rebel paper.

The officer then exhibited a large sheet of "promises to pay," which he had procured in Fayetteville a few days before, and asked how they would answer.

"That is just what I want," said the whisky vender.

The officer called his attention to the fact that the notes had no signatures.

"That don't make any difference," was the reply; "nobody will know whether they are signed or not, and they are just as good, anyhow."

I was a listener to the conversation, and at this juncture proffered a pair of scissors to assist in dividing the notes. It took but a short time to cut off enough "money" to pay for twenty canteens of the worst whisky I ever saw.

At Huntsville we made a few prisoners, who said they were on their way from Price's army to Forsyth, Missouri. They gave us the important information that the Rebel army, thirty thousand strong, was on the Boston Mountains the day previous; and on the very day of our arrival at Huntsville, it was to begin its advance toward our front. These men, and some others, had been sent away because they had no weapons with which to enter the fight.

Immediately on learning this, Colonel Vandever dispatched a courier to General Curtis, and prepared to set out on his return to the main army. We marched six miles before nightfall, and at midnight, while we were endeavoring to sleep, a courier joined us from the commander-in-chief. He brought orders for us to make our way back with all possible speed, as the Rebel army was advancing in full force.

At two o'clock we broke camp, and, with only one halt of an hour, made a forced march of forty-one miles, joining the main column at ten o'clock at night. I doubt if there were many occasions during the war where better marching was done by infantry than on that day. Of course, the soldiers were much fatigued, but were ready, on the following day, to take active part in the battle.

On the 5th of March, as soon as General Curtis learned of the Rebel advance, he ordered General Sigel, who was in camp at Bentonville, to fall back to Pea Ridge, on the north bank of Sugar Creek. At the same time he withdrew Colonel Jeff. C. Davis's Division to the same locality. This placed the army in a strong, defensible position, with the creek in its front. On the ridge above the stream our artillery and infantry were posted.

The Rebel armies under Price and McCulloch had been united and strongly re-enforced, the whole being under the command of General Van Dorn. Their strength was upward of twenty thousand men, and they were confident of their ability to overpower us. Knowing our strong front line, General Van Dorn decided upon a bold movement, and threw himself around our right flank to a position between us and our base at Springfield.

In moving to our right and rear, the Rebels encountered General Sigel's Division before it had left Bentonville, and kept up a running fight during the afternoon of the 6th. Several times the Rebels, in small force, secured positions in Sigel's front, but that officer succeeded in cutting his way through and reaching the main force, with a loss of less than a hundred men.

The position of the enemy at Bentonville showed us his intentions, and we made our best preparations to oppose him. Our first step was to obstruct the road from Bentonville to our rear, so as to retard the enemy's movements. Colonel Dodge, of the Fourth Iowa (afterward a major-general), rose from a sick-bed to perform this work. The impediments which he placed in the way of the Rebels prevented their reaching the road in our rear until nine o'clock on the morning of the 7th.

Our next movement was to reverse our position. We had been facing south--it was now necessary to face to the north. The line that had been our rear became our front. A change of front implied that our artillery train should take the place of the supply train, and *vice versâ*. "Elkhorn Tavern" had been the quartermaster's depot. We made all haste to substitute artillery for baggage-wagons, and boxes of ammunition for boxes of hard bread. This transfer was not accomplished before the battle began, and as our troops were pressed steadily back on our new front, Elkhorn Tavern fell into the hands of the Rebels.

The sugar, salt, and bread which they captured, happily not of large quantity, were very acceptable, and speedily disappeared. Among the quartermaster's stores was a wagon-load of desiccated vegetables, a very valuable article for an army in the field. All expected it would be made into soup and eaten by the Rebels. What was our astonishment to find, two days later, that they had opened and examined a single case, and, after scattering its contents on the ground, left the balance undisturbed!

Elkhorn Tavern was designated by a pair of elk-horns, which occupied a conspicuous position above the door. After the battle these horns were removed by Colonel Carr, and sent to his home in Illinois, as trophies of the victory.

A family occupied the building at the time of the battle, and remained there during the whole contest. When the battle raged most fiercely the cellar proved a place of refuge. Shells tore through the house, sometimes from the National batteries, and sometimes from Rebel guns. One shell exploded in a room where three women were sitting. Though their clothes were torn by the flying fragments, they escaped without personal injury. They announced their determination not to leave home so long as the house remained standing.

Among other things captured at Elkhorn Tavern by the Rebels, was a sutler's wagon, which, had just arrived from St. Louis. In the division of the spoils, a large box, filled with wallets, fell to the lot of McDonald's Battery. For several weeks the officers and privates of this battery could boast of a dozen wallets each, while very few had any money to carry. The Rebel soldiers complained that the visits of the paymaster were like those of angels.

CHAPTER XIII
THE BATTLE OF PEA RIDGE

About nine o'clock on the morning of the 7th, the Rebels made a simultaneous attack on our left and front, formerly our right and rear. General Price commanded the force on our front, and General McCulloch that on our left; the former having the old Army of Missouri, re-enforced by several Arkansas regiments, and the latter having a corps made up of Arkansas, Texas, and Louisiana troops. They brought into the fight upward of twenty thousand men, while we had not over twelve thousand with which to oppose them.

The attack on our left was met by General Sigel and Colonel Davis. That on our front was met by Colonel Carr's Division and the division of General Asboth. On our left it was severe, though not long maintained, the position we held being too strong for the enemy to carry.

It was on this part of the line that the famous Albert Pike, the lawyer-poet of Arkansas, brought his newly-formed brigades of Indians into use. Pike was unfortunate with his Indians. While he was arranging them in line, in a locality where the bushes were about eight feet in height, the Indians made so much noise as to reveal their exact position. One of our batteries was quietly placed within point-blank range of the Indians, and suddenly opened upon them with grape and canister. They gave a single yell, and scattered without waiting for orders.

The Indians were not, as a body, again brought together during the battle. In a charge which our cavalry made upon a Rebel brigade we were repulsed, leaving several killed and wounded upon the ground. Some of Pike's Indians, after their dispersal, came upon these, and scalped the dead and living without distinction. A Rebel officer subsequently informed me that the same Indians scalped several of their own slain, and barbarously murdered some who had been only slightly injured.

On this part of the field we were fortunate, early in the day, in killing General McCulloch and his best lieutenant, General McIntosh. To this misfortune the Rebels have since ascribed their easy defeat. At the time of this reverse to the enemy, General Van Dorn was with. Price in our front.

After their repulse and the death of their leader, the discomfited Rebels joined their comrades in the front, who had been more successful. It was nightfall before the two forces were united.

In our front, Colonel Carr's Division fought steadily and earnestly during the entire day, but was pressed back fully two-thirds of a mile. General Curtis gave it what re-enforcements he could, but there were very few to be spared. When it was fully ascertained that the Rebels on our left had gone to our front, we prepared to unite against them. Our left was drawn in to re-enforce Colonel Carr, but the movement was not completed until long after dark.

Thus night came. The rebels were in full possession of our communications. We had repulsed them on the left, but lost ground, guns, and men on our front. The Rebels were holding Elkhorn Tavern, which we had made great effort to defend. Colonel Carr had repeatedly wished for either night or re-enforcements. He obtained both.

The commanding officers visited General Curtis's head-quarters, and received their orders for the morrow. Our whole force was to be concentrated on our front. If the enemy did not attack us at daylight, we would attack him as soon thereafter as practicable.

Viewed in its best light, the situation was somewhat gloomy. Mr. Fayel, of the *Democrat*, and myself were the only journalists with the army, and the cessation of the day's fighting found us deliberating on our best course in case of a disastrous result. We destroyed all documents that could give information to the enemy, retaining only our note-books, and such papers as pertained to our profession. With patience and resignation we awaited the events of the morrow.

I do not know that any of our officers expected we should be overpowered, but there were many who thought such an occurrence probable. The enemy was nearly twice as strong as we, and lay directly between us and our base. If he could hold out till our ammunition was exhausted, we should be compelled to lay down our arms. There was no retreat for us. We must be victorious or we must surrender.

In camp, on that night, every thing was confusion. The troops that had been on the left during the day were being transferred to the front. The quartermaster was endeavoring to get his train in the least dangerous place. The opposing lines were so near each other that our men could easily hear the conversation of the Rebels. The night was not severely cold; but the men, who were on the front, after a day's fighting, found it quite uncomfortable. Only in the rear was it thought prudent to build fires.

The soldiers of German birth were musical. Throughout the night I repeatedly heard their songs. The soldiers of American parentage were generally profane, and the few words I heard them utter were the reverse of musical. Those of Irish origin combined the peculiarities of both Germans and Americans, with their tendencies in favor of the latter.

I sought a quiet spot within the limits of the camp, but could not find it. Lying down in the best place available, I had just fallen asleep when a mounted orderly rode his horse directly over me. I made a mild remonstrance, but the man was out of hearing before I spoke. Soon after, some one lighted a pipe and threw a coal upon my hand. This drew from me a gentle request for a discontinuance of that experiment. I believe it was not repeated. During the night Mr. Fayel's beard took fire, and I was roused to assist in staying the conflagration.

The vocal music around me was not calculated to encourage drowsiness. Close at hand was the quartermaster's train, with the mules ready harnessed for moving in any direction. These mules had not been fed for two whole days, and it was more than thirty-six hours since they had taken water. These facts were made known in the best language the creatures possessed. The bray of a mule is never melodious, even when the animal's throat is well moistened. When it is parched and dusty the sound becomes unusually hoarse. Each hour added to the noise as the thirst of the musicians increased. Mr. Fayel provoked a discussion concerning the doctrine of the transmigration of souls; and thought, in the event of its truth, that the wretch was to be pitied who should pass into a mule in time of war.

With the dawn of day every one was astir. At sunrise I found our line was not quite ready, though it was nearly so. General Curtis was confident all would result successfully, and completed the few arrangements then requiring attention. We had expected the Rebels would open the attack; but they waited for us to do so. They deserved many thanks for their courtesy. The smoke of the previous day's fight still hung over the camp, and the sun rose through it, as through a cloud. A gentle wind soon dissipated this smoke, and showed us a clear sky overhead. The direction of the wind was in our favor.

The ground selected for deciding the fate of that day was a huge cornfield, somewhat exceeding two miles in length and about half a mile in width. The western extremity of this field rested upon the ridge which gave name to the battle-ground. The great road from Springfield to Fayetteville crossed this field about midway from the eastern to the western end.

It was on this road that the two armies took their positions. The lines were in the edge of the woods on opposite sides of the field--the wings of the armies extending to either end. On the northern side were the Rebels, on the southern was the National army. Thus each army, sheltered by the forest, had a cleared space in its front, affording a full view of the enemy.

By half-past seven o'clock our line was formed and ready for action. A little before eight o'clock the cannonade was opened. Our forces were regularly drawn up in order of battle. Our batteries were placed between the regiments as they stood in line. In the timber, behind these regiments and batteries, were the brigades in reserve, ready to be brought forward in case of need. At the ends of the line were battalions of cavalry, stretching off to cover the wings, and give notice of any attempt by the Rebels to move on our flanks. Every five minutes the bugle of the extreme battalion would sound the signal "All's well." The signal would be taken by the bugler of the next battalion, and in this way carried down the line to the center. If the Rebels had made any attempt to outflank us, we could hardly have failed to discover it at once.

Our batteries opened; the Rebel batteries responded. Our gunners proved the best, and our shot had the greatest effect. We had better ammunition than that of our enemies, and thus reduced the disparity caused by their excess of guns. Our cannonade was slow and careful; theirs was rapid, and was made at random. At the end of two hours of steady, earnest work, we could see that the Rebel line was growing weaker, while our own was still unshaken. The work of the artillery was winning us the victory.

In the center of the Rebel line was a rocky hill, eighty or a hundred feet in height. The side which faced us was almost perpendicular, but the slope to the rear was easy of ascent. On this hill the Rebels had stationed two regiments of infantry and a battery of artillery. The balance of their artillery lay at its base. General Curtis ordered that the fire of all our batteries should be concentrated on this hill at a given signal, and continued there for ten minutes. This was done. At the same time our infantry went forward in a charge on the Rebel infantry and batteries that stood in the edge of the forest. The cleared field afforded fine opportunity for the movement.

The charge was successful. The Rebels fell back in disorder, leaving three guns in our hands, and their dead and wounded scattered on the ground. This was the end of the battle. We had won the victory at Pea Ridge.

I followed our advancing forces, and ascended to the summit of the elevation on which our last fire was concentrated. Wounded men were gathered in little groups, and the dead were lying thick about them. The range of our artillery had been excellent. Rocks, trees, and earth attested the severity of our fire. This cannonade was the decisive work of the day. It was the final effort of our batteries, and was terrible while it lasted.

The shells, bursting among the dry leaves, had set the woods on fire, and the flames were slowly traversing the ground where the battle had raged. We made every effort to remove the wounded to places of safety, before the fire should reach them. At that time we thought we had succeeded. Late in the afternoon I found several wounded men lying in secluded places, where they had been terribly burned, though they were still alive. Very few of them survived.

Our loss in this battle was a tenth of our whole force. The enemy lost more than we in numbers, though less in proportion to his strength. His position, directly in our rear, would have been fatal to a defeated army in many other localities. There were numerous small roads, intersecting the great road at right angles. On these roads the Rebels made their lines of retreat. Had we sent cavalry in pursuit, the Rebels would have lost heavily in artillery and in their supply train. As it was, they escaped without material loss, but they suffered a defeat which ultimately resulted in our possession of all Northern Arkansas.

The Rebels retreated across the Boston Mountains to Van Buren and Fort Smith, and were soon ordered thence to join Beauregard at Corinth. Our army moved to Keytsville, Missouri, several miles north of the battle-ground, where the country was better adapted to foraging, and more favorable to recuperating from the effects of the conflict.

From Keytsville it moved to Forsyth, a small town in Taney County, Missouri, fifty miles from Springfield. Extending over a considerable area, the army consumed whatever could be found in the vicinity. It gave much annoyance to the Rebels by destroying the saltpeter works on the upper portion of White River.

The saltpeter manufactories along the banks of this stream were of great importance to the Rebels in the Southwest, and their destruction seriously reduced the supplies of gunpowder in the armies of Arkansas and Louisiana. Large quantities of the crude material were shipped to Memphis and other points, in the early days of the war. At certain seasons White River is navigable to Forsyth. The Rebels made every possible use of their opportunities, as long as the stream remained in their possession.

Half sick in consequence of the hardships of the campaign, and satisfied there would be no more fighting of importance during the summer, I determined to go back to civilization. I returned to St. Louis by way of Springfield and Rolla. A wounded officer, Lieutenant-Colonel Herron (who afterward wore the stars of a major-general), was my traveling companion. Six days of weary toil over rough and muddy roads brought us to the railway, within twelve hours of St. Louis. It was my last campaign in that region. From that date the war in the Southwest had its chief interest in the country east of the Great River.

CHAPTER XIV
UP THE TENNESSEE AND AT
PITTSBURG LANDING

On reaching St. Louis, three weeks after the battle of Pea Ridge, I found that public attention was centered upon the Tennessee River. Fort Henry, Fort Donelson, Columbus, and Nashville had fallen, and our armies were pushing forward toward the Gulf, by the line of the Tennessee. General Pope was laying siege to Island Number Ten, having already occupied New Madrid, and placed his gun-boats in front of that point. General Grant's army was at Pittsburg Landing, and General Buell's army was moving from Nashville toward Savannah, Tennessee. The two armies were to be united at Pittsburg Landing, for a further advance into the Southern States. General Beauregard was at Corinth, where he had been joined by Price and Van Dorn from Arkansas, and by Albert Sidney Johnston from Kentucky. There was a promise of active hostilities in that quarter. I left St. Louis, after a few days' rest, for the new scene of action.

Cairo lay in my route. I found it greatly changed from the Cairo of the previous autumn. Six months before, it had been the rendezvous of the forces watching the Lower Mississippi. The basin in which the town stood, was a vast military encampment. Officers of all rank thronged the hotels, and made themselves as comfortable as men could be in Cairo. All the leading journals of the country were represented, and the dispatches from Cairo were everywhere perused with interest, though they were not always entirety accurate.

March and April witnessed a material change. Where there had been twenty thousand soldiers in December, there were less than one thousand in April. Where a fleet of gun-boats, mortar-rafts, and transports had been tied to the levees during the winter months, the opening spring showed but a half-dozen steamers of all classes. The transports and the soldiers were up the Tennessee, the mortars were bombarding Island Number Ten, and the gun-boats were on duty where their services were most needed. The journalists had become war correspondents in earnest, and were scattered to the points of greatest interest.

Cairo had become a vast depot of supplies for the armies operating on the Mississippi and its tributaries. The commander of the post was more a forwarding agent than a military officer. The only steamers at the levee were loading for the armies. Cairo was a map of busy, muddy life.

The opening year found Cairo exulting in its deep and all-pervading mud. There was mud everywhere.

Levee, sidewalks, floors, windows, tables, bed-clothing, all were covered with it. On the levee it varied from six to thirty inches in depth. The luckless individual whose duties obliged him to make frequent journeys from the steamboat landing to the principal hotel, became intimately acquainted with its character.

Sad, unfortunate, derided Cairo! Your visitors depart with unpleasant memories. Only your inhabitants, who hold titles to corner lots, speak loudly in your praise. When it rains, and sometimes when it does not, your levee is unpleasant to walk upon. Your sidewalks are dangerous, and your streets are unclean. John Phenix declared you destitute of honesty. Dickens asserted that your physical and moral foundations were insecurely laid. Russell did not praise you, and Trollope uttered much to your discredit. Your musquitos are large, numerous, and hungry. Your atmosphere does not resemble the spicy breezes that blow soft o'er Ceylon's isle. Your energy and enterprise are commendable, and your geographical location is excellent, but you can never become a rival to Saratoga or Newport.

Cairo is built in a basin formed by constructing a levee to inclose the peninsula at the junction of the Ohio and Mississippi Rivers. Before the erection of the levee, this peninsula was overflowed by the rise of either river. Sometimes, in unusual floods, the waters reach the top of the embankment, and manage to fill the basin. At the time of my visit, the Ohio was rising rapidly. The inhabitants were alarmed, as the water was gradually gaining upon them. After a time it took possession of the basin, enabling people to navigate the streets and front yards in skiffs, and exchange salutations from house-tops or upper windows. Many were driven from their houses by the flood, and forced to seek shelter elsewhere. In due time the waters receded and the city remained unharmed. It is not true that a steamer was lost in consequence of running against a chimney of the St. Charles Hotel.

Cairo has prospered during the war, and is now making an effort to fill her streets above the high-water level, and insure a dry foundation at all seasons of the year. This once accomplished, Cairo will become a city of no little importance.

Proceeding up the Tennessee, I reached Pittsburg Landing three days after the great battle which has made that locality famous.

The history of that battle has been many times written. Official reports have given the dry details,--the movements of division, brigade, regiment, and battery, all being fully portrayed. A few journalists who witnessed it gave the accounts which were circulated everywhere by the Press. The earliest of these was published by *The Herald.* The most complete and graphic was that of Mr. Reid, of *The Cincinnati Gazette.* Officers, soldiers, civilians, all with greater or less experience, wrote what they had heard and seen. So diverse have been the statements, that a general officer who was prominent in the battle, says he sometimes doubts if he was present.

In the official accounts there have been inharmonious deductions, and many statements of a contradictory character. Some of the participants have criticised unfavorably the conduct of others, and a bitterness continuing through and after the war has been the result.

In February of 1862, the Rebels commenced assembling an army at Corinth. General Beauregard was placed in command. Early in March, Price and Van Dorn were ordered to take their commands to Corinth, as their defeat at Pea Ridge had placed them on the defensive against General Curtis. General A. S. Johnston had moved thither, after the evacuation of Bowling Green, Kentucky, and from all quarters the Rebels were assembling a vast army. General Johnston became commander-in-chief on his arrival.

General Halleck, who then commanded the Western Department, ordered General Grant, after the capture of Forts Henry and Donelson, to move to Pittsburg Landing, and seize that point as a base against Corinth. General Buell, with the Army of the Ohio, was ordered to join him from Nashville, and with other re-enforcements we would be ready to take the offensive.

Owing to the condition of the roads, General Buell moved very slowly, so that General Grant was in position at Pittsburg Landing several days before the former came up. This was the situation at the beginning of April; Grant encamped on the bank of the Tennessee nearest the enemy, and Buell slowly approaching the opposite bank. It was evidently the enemy's opportunity to strike his blow before our two armies should be united.

On the 4th of April, the Rebels prepared to move from Corinth to attack General Grant's camp, but, on account of rain, they delayed their advance till the morning of the 6th. At daylight of the 6th our pickets were driven in, and were followed by the advance of the Rebel army.

The division whose camp was nearest to Corinth, and therefore the first to receive the onset of the enemy, was composed of the newest troops in the army. Some of the regiments had received their arms less than two weeks before. The outposts were not sufficiently far from camp to allow much time for getting under arms after the first encounter. A portion of this division was attacked before it could form, but its commander, General Prentiss, promptly rallied his men, and made a vigorous fight. He succeeded, for a time, in staying the progress of the enemy, but the odds against him were too great. When his division was surrounded and fighting was no longer of use, he surrendered his command. At the time of surrender he had little more than a thousand men remaining out of a division six thousand strong. Five thousand were killed, wounded, or had fled to the rear.

General Grant had taken no precautions against attack. The vedettes were but a few hundred yards from our front, and we had no breast-works of any kind behind which to fight. The newest and least reliable soldiers were at the point where the enemy would make his first appearance. The positions of the various brigades and divisions were taken, more with reference to securing a good camping-ground, than for purposes of strategy. General Grant showed himself a soldier in the management of the army after the battle began, and he has since achieved a reputation as the greatest warrior of the age. Like the oculist who spoiled a hatful of eyes in learning to operate for the cataract, he improved his military knowledge by his experience at Shiloh. Never afterward did he place an army in the enemy's country without making careful provision against assault.

One division, under General Wallace, was at Crump's Landing, six miles below the battle-ground, and did not take part in the action till the following day. The other divisions were in line to meet the enemy soon after the fighting commenced on General Prentiss's front, and made a stubborn resistance to the Rebel advance.

The Rebels well knew they would have no child's play in that battle. They came prepared for hot, terrible work, in which thousands of men were to fall. The field attests our determined resistance; it attests their daring advance. A day's fighting pushed us slowly, but steadily, toward the Tennessee. Our last line was formed less than a half mile from its bank. Sixty pieces of artillery composed a grand battery, against which the enemy rushed. General Grant's officers claim that the enemy received a final check when he attacked that line. The Rebels claim that another hour of daylight, had we received no re-enforcements, would have seen our utter defeat. Darkness and a fresh division came to our aid.

General Buell was to arrive at Savannah, ten miles below Pittsburg, and on the opposite bank of the river, on the morning of the 6th. On the evening of the 5th, General Grant proceeded to Savannah to meet him, and was there when the battle began on the following morning. His boat was immediately headed for Pittsburg, and by nine o'clock the General was on the battle-field. From that time, the engagement received his personal attention. When he started from Savannah, some of General Buell's forces were within two miles of the town. They were hurried forward as rapidly as possible, and arrived at Pittsburg, some by land and others by water, in season to take position on our left, just as the day was closing. Others came up in the night, and formed a part of the line on the morning of the 7th.

General Nelson's Division was the first to cross the river and form on the left of Grant's shattered army. As he landed, Nelson rode among the stragglers by the bank and endeavored to rally them. Hailing a captain of infantry, he told him to get his men together and fall into line. The captain's face displayed the utmost terror. "My regiment is cut to pieces," was the rejoinder; "every man of my company is killed."

"Then why ain't you killed, too, you d----d coward?" thundered Nelson. "Gather some of these stragglers and go back into the battle."

The man obeyed the order.

General Nelson reported to General Grant with his division, received his orders, and then dashed about the field, wherever his presence was needed. The division was only slightly engaged before night came on and suspended the battle.

At dawn on the second day the enemy lay in the position it held When darkness ended the fight. The gun-boats had shelled the woods during the night, and prevented the Rebels from reaching the river on our left. A creek and ravine prevented their reaching it on the right. None of the Rebels stood on the bank of the Tennessee River on that occasion, except as prisoners of war.

As they had commenced the attack on the 6th, it was our turn to begin it on the 7th. A little past daylight we opened fire, and the fresh troops on the left, under General Buell, were put in motion. The Rebels had driven us on the 6th, so we drove them on the 7th. By noon of that day we held the ground lost on the day previous.

The camps which the enemy occupied during the night were comparatively uninjured, so confident were the Rebels that our defeat was assured.

It was the arrival of General Buell's army that saved us. The history of that battle, as the Rebels have given it, shows that they expected to overpower General Grant before General Buell could come up. They would then cross the Tennessee, meet and defeat Buell, and recapture Nashville. The defeat of these two armies would have placed the Valley of the Ohio at the command of the Rebels. Louisville was to have been the next point of attack.

The dispute between the officers of the Army of the Tennessee and those of the Army of the Ohio is not likely to be terminated until this generation has passed away. The former contend that the Rebels were repulsed on the evening of the 6th of April, before the Army of the Ohio took part in the battle. The latter are equally earnest in declaring that the Army of the Tennessee would have been defeated had not the other army arrived. Both parties sustain their arguments by statements in proof, and by positive assertions. I believe it is the general opinion of impartial observers, that the salvation of General Grant's army is due to the arrival of the army of General Buell. With the last attack on the evening of the 6th, in which our batteries repulsed the Rebels, the enemy did not retreat. Night came as the fighting ceased. Beauregard's army slept where it had fought, and gave all possible indication of a readiness to renew the battle on the following day. So near was it to the river that our gun-boats threw shells during the night to prevent our left wing being flanked.

Beauregard is said to have sworn to water his horse in the Tennessee, or in Hell, on that night. It is certain that the animal did not quench his thirst in the terrestrial stream. If he drank from springs beyond the Styx, I am not informed.

CHAPTER XV
SHILOH AND THE SIEGE OF CORINTH

The fatal error of the Rebels, was their neglect to attack on the 4th, as originally intended. They were informed by their scouts that Buell could not reach Savannah before the 9th or 10th; and therefore a delay of two days would not change the situation. Buell was nearer than they supposed.

The surgeon of the Sixth Iowa Infantry fell into the enemy's hands early on the morning of the first day of the battle, and established a hospital in our abandoned camp. His position was at a small log-house close by the principal road. Soon after he took possession, the enemy's columns began to file past him, as they pressed our army. The surgeon says he noticed a Louisiana regiment that moved into battle eight hundred strong, its banners flying and the men elated at the prospect of success. About five o'clock in the afternoon this regiment was withdrawn, and went into bivouac a short distance from the surgeon's hospital. It was then less than four hundred strong, but the spirit of the men was still the same. On the morning of the 7th, it once more went into battle. About noon it came out, less than a hundred strong, pressing in retreat toward Corinth. The men still clung to their flag, and declared their determination to be avenged.

The story of this regiment was the story of many others. Shattered and disorganized, their retreat to Corinth had but little order. Only the splendid rear-guard, commanded by General Bragg, saved them from utter confusion. The Rebels admitted that many of their regiments were unable to produce a fifth of their original numbers, until a week or more after the battle. The stragglers came in slowly from the surrounding country, and at length enabled the Rebels to estimate their loss. There were many who never returned to answer at roll-call.

In our army, the disorder was far from small. Large numbers of soldiers wandered for days about the camps, before they could ascertain their proper locations. It was fully a week, before all were correctly assigned. We refused to allow burying parties from the Rebels to come within our lines, preferring that they should not see the condition of our camp. Time was required to enable us to recuperate. I presume the enemy was as much in need of time as ourselves.

A volume could be filled with the stories of personal valor during that battle. General Lew Wallace says his division was, at a certain time, forming on one side of a field, while the Rebels were on the opposite side. The color-bearer of a Rebel regiment stepped in front of his own line, and waved his flag as a challenge to the color-bearer that faced him. Several of our soldiers wished to meet the challenge, but their officers forbade it. Again the Rebel stepped forward, and planted his flag-staff in the ground. There was no response, and again and again he advanced, until he had passed more than half the distance between the opposing lines. Our fire was reserved in admiration of the man's daring, as he stood full in view, defiantly waving his banner. At last, when the struggle between the divisions commenced, it was impossible to save him, and he fell dead by the side of his colors.

On the morning of the second day's fighting, the officers of one of our gun-boats saw a soldier on the river-bank on our extreme left, assisting another soldier who was severely wounded. A yawl was sent to bring away the wounded man and his companion. As it touched the side of the gun-boat on its return, the uninjured soldier asked to be sent back to land, that he might have further part in the battle. "I have," said he, "been taking care of this man, who is my neighbor at home. He was wounded yesterday morning, and I have been by his side ever since. Neither of us has eaten any thing for thirty hours, but, if you will take good care of him, I will not stop now for myself. I want to get into the battle again at once." The man's request was complied with. I regret my inability to give his name.

A drummer-boy of the Fifteenth Iowa Infantry was wounded five times during the first day's battle, but insisted upon going out on the second day. He had hardly started before he fainted from loss of blood, and was left to recover and crawl back to the camp.

Colonel Sweeney, of the Fifty-second Illinois Infantry, who lost an arm in Mexico and was wounded in the leg at Wilson Creek, received a wound in his arm on the first day of the battle. He kept his saddle, though he was unable to use his arm, and went to the hospital after the battle was over. When I saw him he was venting his indignation at the Rebels, because they had not wounded him in the stump of his amputated arm, instead of the locality which gave him so much inconvenience. It was this officer's fortune to be wounded on nearly every occasion when he went into battle.

During the battle, Dr. Cornyn, surgeon of Major Cavender's battalion of Missouri Artillery, saw a section of a battery whose commander had been killed. The doctor at once removed the surgeon's badge from his hat and the sash from his waist, and took command of the guns. He placed them in position, and for several hours managed them with good effect. He was twice wounded, though not severely. "I was determined they should not kill or capture me as a surgeon when I had charge of that artillery," said the doctor afterward, "and so removed every thing that marked my rank."

The Rebels made some very desperate charges against our artillery, and lost heavily in each attack. Once they actually laid their hands on the muzzles of two guns in Captain Stone's battery, but were unable to capture them.

General Hurlbut stated that his division fought all day on Sunday with heavy loss, but only one regiment broke. When he entered the battle on Monday morning, the Third Iowa Infantry was commanded by a first-lieutenant, all the field officers and captains having been disabled or captured. Several regiments were commanded by captains.

Colonel McHenry, of the Seventeenth Kentucky, said his regiment fought a Kentucky regiment which was raised in the county where his own was organized. The fight was very fierce. The men frequently called out from one to another, using taunting epithets. Two brothers recognized each other at the same moment, and came to a tree midway between the lines, where they conversed for several minutes.

The color-bearer of the Fifty-second Illinois was wounded early in the battle. A man who was under arrest for misdemeanor asked the privilege of carrying the colors. It was granted, and he behaved so admirably that he was released from arrest as soon as the battle was ended.

General Halleck arrived a week after the battle, and commenced a reorganization of the army. He found much confusion consequent upon the battle. In a short time the army was ready to take the offensive. We then commenced the advance upon Corinth, in which we were six weeks moving twenty-five miles. When our army first took position at Pittsburg Landing, and before the Rebels had effected their concentration, General Grant asked permission to capture Corinth. He felt confident of success, but was ordered not to bring on an engagement under any circumstances. Had the desired permission been given, there is little doubt he would have succeeded, and thus avoided the necessity of the battle of Shiloh.

The day following my arrival at Pittsburg Landing I rode over the battle-field. The ground was mostly wooded, the forest being one in which artillery could be well employed, but where cavalry was comparatively useless. The ascent from the river was up a steep bluff that led to a broken table-ground, in which there were many ravines, generally at right angles to the river. On this table-ground our camps were located, and it was there the battle took place.

Everywhere the trees were scarred and shattered, telling, as plainly as by words, of the shower of shot, shell, and bullets, that had fallen upon them. Within rifle range of the river, stood a tree marked by a cannon-shot, showing how much we were pressed back on the afternoon of the 6th. From the moment the crest of the bluff was gained, the traces of battle were apparent.

In front of the line where General Prentiss's Division fought, there was a spot of level ground covered with a dense growth of small trees. The tops of these trees were from twelve to fifteen feet high, and had been almost mowed off by the shower of bullets which passed through them. I saw no place where there was greater evidence of severe work. There was everywhere full proof that the battle was a determined one. Assailant and defendant had done their best.

It was a ride of five miles among scarred trees, over ground cut by the wheels of guns and caissons, among shattered muskets, disabled cannon, broken wagons, and all the heavier débris of battle. Everywhere could be seen torn garments, haversacks, and other personal equipments of soldiers. There were tents where the wounded had been gathered, and where those who could not easily bear movement to the transports were still remaining. In every direction I moved, there were the graves of the slain, the National and the Rebel soldiers being buried side by side. Few of the graves were marked, as the hurry of interment had been great. I fear that many of those graves, undesignated and unfenced, have long since been leveled. A single year, with its rain and its rank vegetation, would leave but a small trace of those mounds.

All through that forest the camps of our army were scattered. During the first few days after the battle they showed much irregularity, but gradually took a more systematic shape. When the wounded had been sent to the transports, the regiments compacted, the camps cleared of superfluous baggage and *matériel*, and the weather became more propitious, the army assumed an attractive appearance.

When the news of the battle reached the principal cities of the West, the Sanitary Commission prepared to send relief. Within twenty-four hours, boats were dispatched from St. Louis and Cincinnati, and hurried to Pittsburg Landing with the utmost rapidity. The battle had not been altogether unexpected, but it found us without the proper preparation. Whatever we had was pushed forward without delay, and the sufferings of the wounded were alleviated as much as possible.

As fast as the boats arrived they were loaded with wounded, and sent to St. Louis and other points along the Mississippi, or to Cincinnati and places in its vicinity. Chicago, St. Louis, and Cincinnati were the principal points represented in this work of humanity. Many prominent ladies of those cities passed week after week in the hospitals or on the transports, doing every thing in their power, and giving their attention to friend and foe alike.

In all cases the Rebels were treated with the same kindness that our own men received. Not only on the boats, but in the hospitals where the wounded were distributed, and until they were fully recovered, our suffering prisoners were faithfully nursed. The Rebel papers afterward admitted this kind treatment, but declared it was a Yankee trick to win the sympathies of our prisoners, and cause them to abandon the insurgent cause. The men who systematically starved their prisoners, and deprived them of shelter and clothing, could readily suspect the humanity of others. They were careful never to attempt to kill by kindness, those who were so unfortunate as to fall into their hands.

It was three weeks after the battle before all the wounded were sent away, and the army was ready for offensive work. When we were once more in fighting trim, our lines were slowly pushed forward. General Pope had been called from the vicinity of Fort Pillow, after his capture of Island Number Ten, and his army was placed in position on the left of the line already formed. When our advance began, we mustered a hundred and ten thousand men. Exclusive of those who do not take part in a battle, we could have easily brought eighty thousand men into action. We began the siege of Corinth with every confidence in our ability to succeed.

In this advance, we first learned how an army should intrench itself. Every time we took a new position, we proceeded to throw up earth-works. Before the siege was ended, our men had perfected themselves in the art of intrenching. The defenses we erected will long remain as monuments of the war in Western Tennessee. Since General Halleck, no other commander has shown such ability to fortify in an open field against an enemy that was acting on the defensive.

It was generally proclaimed that we were to capture Corinth with all its garrison of sixty or seventy thousand men. The civilian observers could not understand how this was to be accomplished, as the Rebels had two lines of railway open for a safe retreat. It was like the old story of "bagging Price" in Missouri. Every part of the bag, except the top and one side, was carefully closed and closely watched. Unmilitary men were skeptical, but the military heads assured them it was a piece of grand strategy, which the public must not be allowed to understand.

During the siege, there was very little for a journalist to record. One day was much like another. Occasionally there would be a collision with the enemy's pickets, or a short struggle for a certain position, usually ending in our possession of the disputed point. The battle of Farmington, on the left of our line, was the only engagement worthy the name, and this was of comparatively short duration. Twenty-four hours after it transpired we ceased to talk about it, and made only occasional reference to the event. There were four weeks of monotony. An advance of a half mile daily was not calculated to excite the nerves.

The chaplains and the surgeons busied themselves in looking after the general health of the army. One day, a chaplain, noted for his advocacy of total abstinence, passed the camp of the First Michigan Battery. This company was raised in Coldwater, Michigan, and the camp-chests, caissons, and other property were marked "Loomis's Coldwater Battery." The chaplain at once sought Captain Loomis, and paid a high compliment to his moral courage in taking a firm and noble stand in favor of temperance. After the termination of the interview, the captain and several friends drank to the long life of the chaplain and the success of the "Coldwater Battery."

Toward the end of the siege, General Halleck gave the journalists a sensation, by expelling them from his lines. The representatives of the Press held a meeting, and waited upon that officer, after the appearance of the order requiring their departure. They offered a protest, which was insolently rejected. We could not ascertain General Halleck's purpose in excluding us just as the campaign was closing, but concluded he desired we should not witness the end of the siege in which so much had been promised and so little accomplished. A week after our departure, General Beauregard evacuated Corinth, and our army took possession. The fruits of the victory were an empty village, a few hundred stragglers, and a small quantity of war *matériel*.

From Corinth the Rebels retreated to Tupelo, Mississippi, where they threw up defensive works. The Rebel Government censured General Beauregard for abandoning Corinth. The evacuation of that point uncovered Memphis, and allowed it to fall into our hands.

Beauregard was removed from command. General Joseph E. Johnston was assigned to duty in his stead. This officer proceeded to reorganize his army, with a view to offensive operations against our lines. He made no demonstrations of importance until the summer months had passed away.

The capture of Corinth terminated the offensive portion of the campaign. Our army occupied the line of the Memphis and Charleston Railway from Corinth to Memphis, and made a visit to Holly Springs without encountering the enemy. A few cavalry expeditions were made into Mississippi, but they accomplished nothing of importance. The Army of the Tennessee went into summer-quarters. The Army of the Ohio, under General Buell, returned to its proper department, to confront the Rebel armies then assembling in Eastern Tennessee. General Halleck was summoned to Washington as commander-in-chief of the armies of the United States.

CHAPTER XVI
CAPTURE OF FORT PILLOW AND BATTLE OF MEMPHIS

While I was tarrying at Cairo, after the exodus of the journalists from the army before Corinth, the situation on the Mississippi became interesting. After the capture of Island Number Ten, General Pope was ordered to Pittsburg Landing with his command. When called away, he was preparing to lay siege to Fort Pillow, in order to open the river to Memphis. His success at Island Number Ten had won him much credit, and he was anxious to gain more of the same article. Had he taken Fort Pillow, he would have held the honor of being the captor of Memphis, as that city must have fallen with the strong fortifications which served as its protection.

The capture of Island Number Ten was marked by the only instance of a successful canal from one bend of the Mississippi to another. As soon as the channel was completed, General Pope took his transports below the island, ready for moving his men. Admiral Foote tried the first experiment of running his gun-boats past the Rebel batteries, and was completely successful. The Rebel transports could not escape, neither could transports or gun-boats come up from Memphis to remove the Rebel army. There was a lake in the rear of the Rebels which prevented their retreat. The whole force, some twenty-eight hundred, was surrendered, with all its arms and munitions of war. General Pope reported his captures somewhat larger than they really were, and received much applause for his success.

The reputation of this officer, on the score of veracity, has not been of the highest character. After he assumed command in Virginia, his "Order Number Five" drew upon him much ridicule. Probably the story of the capture of ten thousand prisoners, after the occupation of Corinth, has injured him more than all other exaggerations combined. The paternity of that choice bit of romance belongs to General Halleck, instead of General Pope. Colonel Elliott, who commanded the cavalry expedition, which General Pope sent out when Corinth was occupied, forwarded a dispatch to Pope, something like the following:--

"I am still pursuing the enemy. The woods are full of stragglers. Some of my officers estimate their number as high as ten thousand. Many have already come into my lines."

Pope sent this dispatch, without alteration, to General Halleck. From the latter it went to the country that "General Pope reported ten thousand prisoners captured below Corinth." It served to cover up the barrenness of the Corinth occupation, and put the public in good-humor. General Halleck received credit for the success of his plans. When it came out that no prisoners of consequence had been taken, the real author of the story escaped unharmed.

At the time of his departure to re-enforce the army before Corinth, General Pope left but a single brigade of infantry, to act in conjunction with our naval forces in the siege of Fort Pillow. This brigade was encamped on the Arkansas shore opposite Fort Pillow, and did some very effective fighting against the musquitos, which that country produces in the greatest profusion. An attack on the fort, with such a small force, was out of the question, and the principal aggressive work was done by the navy at long range.

On the 10th of May, the Rebel fleet made an attack upon our navy, in which they sunk two of our gun-boats, the *Mound City* and the *Cincinnati*, and returned to the protection of Fort Pillow with one of their own boats disabled, and two others somewhat damaged. Our sunken gun-boats were fortunately in shoal water, where they were speedily raised and repaired. Neither fleet had much to boast of as the result of that engagement.

The journalists who were watching Fort Pillow, had their head-quarters on board the steamer *John H. Dickey*, which was anchored in midstream. At the time of the approach of the Rebel gun-boats, the *Dickey* was lying without sufficient steam to move her wheels, and the prospect was good that she might be captured or destroyed. Her commander, Captain Mussleman, declared he was *not* in that place to stop cannon-shot, and made every exertion to get his boat in condition to move. His efforts were fully appreciated by the journalists, particularly as they were successful. The *Dickey*, under the same captain, afterward ran a battery near Randolph, Tennessee, and though pierced in every part by cannon-shot and musket-balls, she escaped without any loss of life.

As soon as the news of the evacuation of Corinth was received at Cairo, we looked for the speedy capture of Fort Pillow. Accordingly, on the 4th of June, I proceeded down the river, arriving off Fort Pillow on the morning of the 5th. The Rebels had left, as we expected, after spiking their guns and destroying most of their ammunition. The first boat to reach the abandoned fort was the *Hetty Gilmore*, one of the smallest transports in the fleet. She landed a little party, which took possession, hoisted the flag, and declared the fort, and all it contained, the property of the United States. The Rebels were, by this time, several miles distant, in full retreat to a safer location.

It was at this same fort, two years later, that the Rebel General Forrest ordered the massacre of a garrison that had surrendered after a prolonged defense. His only plea for this cold-blooded slaughter, was that some of his men had been fired upon after the white flag was raised. The testimony in proof of this barbarity was fully conclusive, and gave General Forrest and his men a reputation that no honorable soldier could desire.

In walking through the fort after its capture, I was struck by its strength and extent. It occupied the base of a bluff near the water's edge. On the summit of the bluff there were breast-works running in a zigzag course for five or six miles, and inclosing a large area. The works along the river were very strong, and could easily hold a powerful fleet at bay.

From Fort Pillow to Randolph, ten miles lower down, was less than an hour's steaming. Randolph was a small, worthless village, partly at the base of a bluff, and partly on its summit. Here the Rebels had erected a powerful fort, which they abandoned when they abandoned Fort Pillow. The inhabitants expressed much agreeable astonishment on finding that we did not verify all the statements of the Rebels, concerning the barbarity of the Yankees wherever they set foot on Southern soil. The town was most bitterly disloyal. It was afterward burned, in punishment for decoying a steamboat to the landing, and then attempting her capture and destruction. A series of blackened chimneys now marks the site of Randolph.

Our capture of these points occurred a short time after the Rebels issued the famous "cotton-burning order," commanding all planters to burn their cotton, rather than allow it to fall into our hands. The people showed no particular desire to comply with the order, except in a few instances. Detachments of Rebel cavalry were sent to enforce obedience. They enforced it by setting fire to the cotton in presence of its owners. On both banks of the river, as we moved from Randolph to Memphis, we could see the smoke arising from plantations, or from secluded spots in the forest where cotton had been concealed. In many cases the bales were broken open and rolled into the river, dotting the stream with floating cotton. Had it then possessed the value that attached to it two years later, I fear there would have been many attempts to save it for transfer to a Northern market.

On the day before the evacuation of Fort Pillow, Memphis determined she would never surrender. In conjunction with other cities, she fitted up several gun-boats, that were expected to annihilate the Yankee fleet. In the event of the failure of this means of defense, the inhabitants were pledged to do many dreadful things before submitting to the invaders. Had we placed any confidence in the resolutions passed by the Memphians, we should have expected all the denizens of the Bluff City to commit *hari-kari*, after first setting fire to their dwellings.

On the morning of the 6th of June, the Rebel gun-boats, eight in number, took their position just above Memphis, and prepared for the advance of our fleet. The Rebel boats were the *Van Dorn* (flag-ship), *General Price*, *General Bragg*, *General Lovell*, *Little Rebel*, *Jeff. Thompson*, *Sumter*, and *General Beauregard*. The *General Bragg* was the New Orleans and Galveston steamer *Mexico* in former days, and had been strengthened, plated, and, in other ways made as effective as possible for warlike purposes. The balance of the fleet consisted of tow-boats from the Lower Mississippi, fitted up as rams and gun-boats. They were supplied with very powerful engines, and were able to choose their positions in the battle. The Rebel fleet was commanded by Commodore Montgomery, who was well known to many persons on our own boats.

The National boats were the iron-clads *Benton*, *Carondelet*, *St. Louis*, *Louisville*, and *Cairo*. There was also the ram fleet, commanded by Colonel Ellet. It comprised the *Monarch*, *Queen of the West*, *Lioness*, *Switzerland*, *Mingo*, *Lancaster No. 3*, *Fulton*, *Horner*, and *Samson*. The *Monarch* and *Queen of the West* were the only boats of the ram fleet that took part in the action. Our forces were commanded by Flag-officer Charles H. Davis, who succeeded Admiral Foote at the time of the illness of the latter.

The land forces, acting in conjunction with our fleet, consisted of a single brigade of infantry, that was still at Fort Pillow. It did not arrive in the vicinity of Memphis until after the battle was over.

Early in the morning the battle began. It was opened by the gun-boats on the Rebel side, and for some minutes consisted of a cannonade at long range, in which very little was effected. Gradually the boats drew nearer to each other, and made better use of their guns.

Before they arrived at close quarters the rams *Monarch* and *Queen of the West* steamed forward and engaged in the fight. Their participation was most effective. The *Queen of the West* struck and disabled one of the Rebel gun-boats, and was herself disabled by the force of the blow. The *Monarch* steered straight for the *General Lovell*, and dealt her a tremendous blow, fairly in the side, just aft the wheel. The sides of the *Lovell* were crushed as if they had been made of paper, and the boat sank in less than three minutes, in a spot where the plummet shows a depth of ninety feet.

Grappling with the *Beauregard*, the *Monarch* opened upon her with a stream of hot water and a shower of rifle-balls, which effectually prevented the latter from using a gun. In a few moments she cast off and drifted a short distance down the river. Coming up on the other side, the *Monarch* dealt her antagonist a blow that left her in a sinking condition. Herself comparatively uninjured, she paused to allow the gun-boats to take a part. Those insignificant and unwieldy rams had placed three of the enemy's gun-boats *hors de combat* in less than a quarter of an hour's time.

Our gun-boats ceased firing as the rams entered the fight; but they now reopened. With shot and shell the guns were rapidly served. The effect was soon apparent. One Rebel boat was disabled and abandoned, after grounding opposite Memphis. A second was grounded and blown up, and two others were disabled, abandoned, and captured.

It was a good morning's work. The first gun was fired at forty minutes past five o'clock, and the last at forty-three minutes past six. The Rebels boasted they would whip us before breakfast. We had taken no breakfast when the fight began. After the battle was over we enjoyed our morning meal with a relish that does not usually accompany defeat.

The following shows the condition of the two fleets after the battle:--

General Beauregard,	sunk.
General Lovell,	sunk.
General Price,	injured and captured.
Little Rebel,	" " "
Sumter,	" " "
General Bragg,	" " "
Jeff. Thompson,	burned.
General Van Dorn,	escaped.

THE NATIONAL FLEET.

Benton,	unhurt.
Carondelet,	"
St. Louis,	"
Louisville,	"
Cairo,	"
Monarch (ram),	unhurt.
Queen of the West (ram),	disabled.

The captured vessels were refitted, and, without alteration of names, attached to the National fleet. The *Sumter* was lost a few months later, in consequence of running aground near the Rebel batteries in the vicinity of Bayou Sara. The *Bragg* was one of the best boats in the service in point of speed, and proved of much value as a dispatch-steamer on the lower portion of the river.

The people of Memphis rose at an early hour to witness the naval combat. It had been generally known during the previous night that the battle would begin about sunrise. The first gun brought a large crowd to the bluff overlooking the river, whence a full view of the fight was obtained. Some of the spectators were loyal, and wished success to the National fleet, but the great majority were animated by a strong hope and expectation of our defeat.

A gentleman, who was of the lookers-on, subsequently told me of the conduct of the populace. As a matter of course, the disloyalists had all the conversation their own way. While they expressed their wishes in the loudest tones, no one uttered a word in opposition. Many offered wagers on the success of their fleet, and expressed a readiness to give large odds. No one dared accept these offers, as their acceptance would have been an evidence of sympathy for the Yankees. Americans generally, but particularly in the South, make their wagers as they hope or wish. In the present instance no man was allowed to "copper" on the Rebel flotilla.

CHAPTER XVII
IN MEMPHIS AND UNDER THE FLAG

The somewhat widely (though not favorably) known Rebel chieftain, Jeff. Thompson, was in Memphis on the day of the battle, and boasted of the easy victory the Rebels would have over the National fleet.

"We will chaw them up in just an hour," said Jeff., as the battle began.

"Are you sure of that?" asked a friend.

"Certainly I am; there is no doubt of it." Turning to a servant, he sent for his horse, in order, as he said, to be able to move about rapidly to the best points for witnessing the engagement.

In an hour and three minutes the battle was over. Jeff, turned in his saddle, and bade his friend farewell, saying he had a note falling due that day at Holly Springs, and was going out to pay it. The "chawing up" of our fleet was not referred to again.

As the *Monarch* struck the *Lovell*, sinking the latter in deep water, the crowd stood breathless. As the crew of the sunken boat were floating helplessly in the strong current, and our own skiffs were putting off to aid them, there was hardly a word uttered through all that multitude. As the Rebel boats, one after another, were sunk or captured, the sympathies of the spectators found vent in words. When, at length, the last of the Rebel fleet disappeared, and the Union flotilla spread its flags in triumph, there went up an almost universal yell of indignation from that vast crowd. Women tore their bonnets from their heads, and trampled them on the ground; men stamped and swore as only infuriated Rebels can, and called for all known misfortunes to settle upon the heads of their invaders. The profanity was not entirely monopolized by the men.

This scene of confusion lasted for some time, and ended in anxiety to know what we would do next. Some of the spectators turned away, and went, in sullen silence, to their homes. Others remained, out of curiosity, to witness the end of the day's work. A few were secretly rejoicing at the result, but the time had not come when they could display their sympathies.

The crowd eagerly watched our fleet, and noted every motion of the various boats.

The press correspondents occupied various positions during the engagement. Mr. Coffin, of the Boston *Journal*, was on the tug belonging to the flag-ship, and had a fine view of the whole affair. One of *The Herald* correspondents was in the pilot-house of the gun-boat *Cairo*, while Mr. Colburn, of *The World*, was on the captured steamer *Sovereign*. "Junius," of *The Tribune*, and Mr. Vizitelly, of the London *Illustrated News*, with several others, were on the transport *Dickey*, the general rendezvous of the journalists. The representative of the St. Louis *Republican* and myself were on the *Platte Valley*, in rear of the line of battle. The *Platte Valley* was the first private boat that touched the Memphis landing after the capture of the city.

The battle being over, we were anxious to get on shore and look at the people and city of Memphis. Shortly after the fighting ceased, Colonel Ellet sent the ram *Lioness*, under a flag-of-truce, to demand the surrender of the city. To this demand no response was given. A little later, Flag-Officer Davis sent the following note to the Mayor, at the hands of one of the officers of the gun-boat *Benton*:--

> UNITED STATES FLAG-STEAMER BENTON,
> OFF MEMPHIS, *June* 6, 1862.
>
> SIR:--I have respectfully to request that you will surrender the city of Memphis to the authority of the United States, which I have the honor to represent. I am, Mr. Mayor, with high respect, your most obedient servant, C. H. DAVIS, *Flag-Officer Commanding*.
>
> To his Honor, the Mayor of Memphis.

To this note the following reply was received:--

> MAYOR'S OFFICE, MEMPHIS, *June* 6, 1862.
>
> C. H. Davis, *Flag-Officer Commanding*:
>
> SIR:--Your note of this date is received and contents noted. In reply I have only to say that, as the civil authorities have no means of defense, by the force of circumstances the city is in your hands. Respectfully, John Park, *Mayor of Memphis*.

At the meeting, four days before, the citizens of Memphis had solemnly pledged themselves never to surrender. There was a vague understanding that somebody was to do a large amount of fighting, whenever Memphis was attacked. If this fighting proved useless, the city was to be fired in every house, and only abandoned after its complete destruction. It will be seen that the note of the mayor, in response to a demand for surrender, vindicates the honor of Memphis. It merely informs the United States officer that the city has fallen "by the force of circumstances." Since that day I have frequently heard its citizens boast that the place was not surrendered. "You came in," say they, "and took possession, but we did not give up to you. We declared we would never surrender, and we kept our word."

About eleven o'clock in the forenoon, the transports arrived with our infantry, and attempted to make a landing. As their mooring-lines were thrown on shore they were seized by dozens of persons in the crowd, and the crews were saved the trouble of making fast. This was an evidence that the laboring class, the men with blue shirts and shabby hats, were not disloyal. We had abundant evidence of this when our occupation became a fixed fact. It was generally the wealthy who adhered to the Rebel cause.

As a file of soldiers moved into the city, the people stood at a respectful distance, occasionally giving forth wordy expression of their anger. When I reached the office of *The Avalanche*, one of the leading journals of Memphis, and, of course, strongly disloyal, I found the soldiers removing a Rebel flag from the roof of the building. The owner of the banner made a very vehement objection to the proceeding. His indignation was so great that his friends were obliged to hold him, to prevent his throwing himself on the bayonet of the nearest soldier. I saw him several days later, when his anger had somewhat cooled. He found relief from his troubles, before the end of June, by joining the Rebel army at Holly Springs.

On the bluff above the levee was a tall flag-staff. The Rebels had endeavored to make sure of their courage by nailing a flag to the top of this staff. A sailor from one of the gun-boats volunteered to ascend the staff and bring down the banner. When he had ascended about twenty feet, he saw two rifles bearing upon him from the window of a neighboring building. The sailor concluded it was best to go no further, and descended at once. The staff was cut down and the obnoxious flag secured.

With the city in our possession, we had leisure to look about us. Memphis had been in the West what Charleston was in the East: an active worker in the secession cause. Her newspapers had teemed with abuse of every thing which opposed their heresy, and advocated the most summary measures. Lynching had been frequent and never rebuked, impressments were of daily and nightly occurrence, every foundery and manufactory had been constantly employed by the Rebel authorities, and every citizen had, in some manner, contributed to the insurrection. It was gratifying in the extreme to see the Memphis, of which we at Cairo and St. Louis had heard so much, brought under our control. The picture of five United States gun-boats lying in line before the city, their ports open and their guns shotted, was pleasing in the eyes of loyal men.

Outside of the poorer classes there were some loyal persons, but their number was not large. There were many professing loyalty, who possessed very little of the article, and whose record had been exceedingly doubtful. Prominent among these were the politicians, than whom none had been more self-sacrificing, if their own words could be believed.

There were many men of this class ready, no doubt, to swear allegiance to the victorious side, who joined our standard because they considered the Rebel cause a losing one. They may have become loyal since that time, but it has been only through the force of circumstances. In many cases our Government accepted their words as proof of loyalty, and granted these persons many exclusive privileges. It was a matter of comment that a newly converted loyalist could obtain favors at the hands of Government officials, that would be refused to men from the North. The acceptance of office under the Rebels, and the earnest advocacy he had shown for secession, were generally alleged to have taken place under compulsion, or in the interest of the really loyal men.

A Memphis gentleman gave me an amusing account of the reception of the news of the fall of Fort Donelson. Many boasts had been made of the terrible punishment that was in store for our army, if it ventured an attack upon Fort Donelson. No one would be allowed to escape to tell the tale. All were to be slaughtered, or lodged in Rebel prisons. Memphis was consequently waiting for the best tidings from the Cumberland, and did not think it possible a reverse could come to the Rebel cause.

One Sunday morning, the telegraph, without any previous announcement, flashed the intelligence that Fort Donelson, with twelve thousand men, had surrendered, and a portion of General Grant's army was moving on Nashville, with every prospect of capturing that city. Memphis was in consternation. No one could tell how long the Yankee army would stop at Nashville before moving elsewhere, and it was certain that Memphis was uncovered by the fall of Fort Donelson.

My informant first learned the important tidings in the rotunda of the Gayoso House. Seeing a group of his acquaintances with faces depicting the utmost gloom, he asked what was the matter.

"Bad enough," said one. "Fort Donelson has surrendered with nearly all its garrison."

"That is terrible," said my friend, assuming a look of agony, though he was inwardly elated.

"Yes, and the enemy are moving on Nashville."

"Horrible news," was the response; "but let us not be too despondent. Our men are good for them, one against three, and they will never get out of Nashville alive, if they should happen to take it."

With another expression of deep sorrow at the misfortune which had befallen the Rebel army, this gentleman hastened to convey the glad news to his friends. "I reached home," said he, "locked my front door, called my wife and sister into the parlor, and instantly jumped over the center-table. They both cried for joy when I told them the old flag floated over Donelson."

The Secessionists in Memphis, like their brethren elsewhere, insisted that all the points we had captured were given up because they had no further use for them. The evacuation of Columbus, Fort Pillow, Fort Henry, and Bowling Green, with the surrender of Donelson, were parts of the grand strategy of the Rebel leaders, and served to lure us on to our destruction. They would never admit a defeat, but contended we had invariably suffered.

An uneducated farmer, on the route followed by one of our armies in Tennessee, told our officers that a Rebel general and his staff had taken dinner with him during the retreat from Nashville. The farmer was anxious to learn something about the military situation, and asked a Rebel major how the Confederate cause was progressing.

"Splendidly," answered the major. "We have whipped the Yankees in every battle, and our independence will soon be recognized."

The farmer was thoughtful for a minute or two, and then deliberately said:

"I don't know much about war, but if we are always whipping the Yankees, how is it they keep coming down into our country after every battle?"

The major grew red in the face, and told the farmer that any man who asked such an absurd question was an Abolitionist, and deserved hanging to the nearest tree. The farmer was silenced, but not satisfied.

I had a fine illustration of the infatuation of the Rebel sympathizers, a few days after Memphis was captured. One evening, while making a visit at the house of an acquaintance, the hostess introduced me to a young lady of the strongest secession proclivities. Of course, I endeavored to avoid the topics on which we were certain to differ, but my new acquaintance was determined to provoke a discussion. With a few preliminaries, she throw out the question:

"Now, don't you think the Southern soldiers have shown themselves the bravest people that ever lived, while the Yankees have proved the greatest cowards?"

"I can hardly agree with you," I replied. "Your people have certainly established a reputation on the score of bravery, but we can claim quite as much."

"But we have whipped you in every battle. We whipped you at Manassas and Ball's Bluff, and we whipped General Grant at Belmont."

"That is very true; but how was it at Shiloh?"

"At Shiloh we whipped you; we drove you to your gun-boats, which was all we wanted to do."

"Ah, I beg your pardon; but what is your impression of Fort Donelson?"

"Fort Donelson!"--and my lady's cheek flushed with either pride or indignation--"Fort Donelson was an unquestioned victory for the South. We stopped your army--all we wanted to; and then General Forrest, General Floyd, and all the troops we wished to bring off, came away. We only left General Buckner and three thousand men for you to capture."

"It seems, then, we labored under a delusion at the North. We thought we had something to rejoice over when Fort Donelson fell. But, pray, what do you consider the capture of Island Number Ten and the naval battle here?"

"At Island Ten we defeated you" (how this was done she did not say), "and we were victorious here. You wanted to capture all our boats; but you only got four of them, and those were damaged."

"In your view of the case," I replied, "I admit the South to have been always victorious. Without wishing to be considered disloyal to the Nation, I can heartily wish you many similar victories."

In the tour which Dickens records, Mark Tapley did not visit the Southern country, but the salient points of his character are possessed by the sons of the cavaliers. "Jolly" under the greatest misfortunes, and extracting comfort and happiness from all calamities, your true Rebel could never know adversity. The fire which consumes his dwelling is a personal boon, as he can readily explain. So is a devastating flood, or a widespread pestilence. The events which narrow-minded mudsills are apt to look upon as calamitous, are only "blessings in disguise" to every supporter and friend of the late "Confederacy."

CHAPTER XVIII
SUPERVISING A REBEL JOURNAL

On the morning of the 6th of June, the newspaper publishers, like most other gentlemen of Memphis, were greatly alarmed. *The Avalanche* and *The Argus* announced that it was impossible for the Yankee fleet to cope successfully with the Rebels, and that victory was certain to perch upon the banners of the latter. The sheets were not dry before the Rebel fleet was a thing of the past. *The Appeal* had not been as hopeful as its contemporaries, and thought it the wisest course to abandon the city. It moved to Grenada, Mississippi, a hundred miles distant, and resumed publication. It became a migratory sheet, and was at last captured by General Wilson at Columbus, Georgia. In ability it ranked among the best of the Rebel journals.

The Avalanche and *The Argus* continued publication, with a strong leaning to the Rebel side. The former was interfered with by our authorities; and, under the name of *The Bulletin*, with new editorial management, was allowed to reappear. *The Argus* maintained its Rebel ground, though with moderation, until the military hand fell upon it. Memphis, in the early days of our occupation, changed its commander nearly every week. One of these changes brought Major-General Wallace into the city. This officer thought it proper to issue the following order:--

> HEAD-QUARTERS THIRD DIVISION, RESERVED CORPS, ARMY OF TENNESSEE, MEMPHIS, *June* 17,1862.
>
> EDITORS DAILY ARGUS:--As the closing of your office might be injurious to you pecuniarily, I send two gentlemen--Messrs. A.D. Richardson and Thos. W. Knox, both of ample experience--to take charge of the editorial department of your paper. The business management of your office will be left to you.
>
> Very respectfully,
> LEWIS WALLACE,
> *General Third Division, Reserved Corps.*

The publishers of *The Argus* printed this order at the head of their columns. Below it they announced that they were not responsible for any thing which should appear editorially, as long as the order was in force. The business management and the general miscellaneous and news matter were not interfered with.

Mr. Richardson and myself entered upon our new duties immediately. We had crossed the Plains together, had published a paper in the Rocky Mountains, had been through many adventures and perils side by side; but we had never before managed a newspaper in an insurrectionary district. The publishers of *The Argus* greeted us cordially, and our whole intercourse with them was harmonious. They did not relish the intrusion of Northern men into their office, to compel the insertion of Union editorials, but they bore the inconvenience with an excellent grace. The foreman of the establishment displayed more mortification at the change, than any other person whom we met.

The editorials we published were of a positive character. We plainly announced the determination of the Government to assert itself and put down and punish treason. We told the Memphis people that the scheme of partisan warfare, which was then in its inception, would work more harm than good to the districts where guerrilla companies were organized. We insisted that the Union armies had entered Memphis and other parts of the South, to stay there, and that resistance to their power was useless. We credited the Rebels with much bravery and devotion to their cause, but asserted always that we had the right and the strong arm in our favor.

It is possible we did not make many conversions among the disloyal readers of *The Argus*, but we had the satisfaction of saying what we thought it necessary they should hear. The publishers said their subscribers were rapidly falling off, on account of the change of editorial tone. Like newspaper readers everywhere, they disliked to peruse what their consciences did not approve. We received letters, generally from women, denying our right to control the columns of the paper for our "base purposes." Some of these letters were not written after the style of Chesterfield, but the majority of them were courteous.

There were many jests in Memphis, and throughout the country generally, concerning the appointment of representatives of *The Herald* and *The Tribune* to a position where they must work together. *The Herald* and *The Tribune* have not been famous, in the past twenty years, for an excess of good-nature toward each other. Mr. Bennett and Mr. Greeley are not supposed to partake habitually of the same dinners and wine, or to join in frequent games of billiards and poker. The compliments which the two great dailies occasionally exchange, are not calculated to promote an intimate friendship between the venerable gentlemen whose names are so well known to the public. No one expects these veteran editors to emulate the example of Damon and Pythias.

At the time Mr. Richardson and myself took charge of *The Argus, The Tribune* and *The Herald* were indulging in one of their well-known disputes. It was much like the Hibernian's debate, "with sticks," and attracted some attention, though it was generally voted a nuisance. Many, who did not know us, imagined that the new editors of *The Argus* would follow the tendencies of the offices from which they bore credentials. Several Northern journals came to hand, in which this belief was expressed. A Chicago paper published two articles supposed to be in the same issue of *The Argus*, differing totally in every line of argument or statement of fact. One editor argued that the harmonious occupancy of contiguous desks by the representatives of *The Herald* and *The Tribune*, betokened the approach of the millennium.

When he issued the order placing us in charge of *The Argus*, General Wallace assured its proprietors that he should remove the editorial supervision as soon as a Union paper was established in Memphis. This event occurred in a short time, and *The Argus* was restored to its original management, according to promise.

As soon as the capture of Memphis was known at the North, there was an eager scramble to secure the trade of the long-blockaded port. Several boat-loads of goods were shipped from St. Louis and Cincinnati, and Memphis was so rapidly filled that the supply was far greater than the demand.

Army and Treasury regulations were soon established, and many restrictions placed upon traffic. The restrictions did not materially diminish the quantity of goods, but they served to throw the trade into a few hands, and thus open the way for much favoritism. Those who obtained permits, thought the system an excellent one. Those who were kept "out in the cold," viewed the matter in a different light. A thousand stories of dishonesty, official and unofficial, were in constant circulation, and I fear that many of them came very near the truth.

In our occupation of cities along the Mississippi, the Rebels found a ready supply from our markets. This was especially the case at Memphis. Boots and shoes passed through the lines in great numbers, either by stealth or by open permit, and were taken at once to the Rebel army. Cloth, clothing, percussion-caps, and similar articles went in the same direction. General Grant and other prominent officers made a strong opposition to our policy, and advised the suppression of the Rebellion prior to the opening of trade, but their protestations were of no avail. We chastised the Rebels with one hand, while we fed and clothed them with the other.

After the capture of Memphis, Colonel Charles R. Ellet, with two boats of the ram fleet, proceeded to explore the river between Memphis and Vicksburg. It was not known what defenses the Rebels might have constructed along this distance of four hundred miles. Colonel Ellet found no hinderance to his progress, except a small field battery near Napoleon, Arkansas. When a few miles above Vicksburg, he ascertained that a portion of Admiral Farragut's fleet was below that point, preparing to attack the city. He at once determined to open communication with the lower fleet.

Opposite Vicksburg there is a long and narrow peninsula, around which the Mississippi makes a bend. It is a mile and a quarter across the neck of this peninsula, while it is sixteen miles around by the course of the river. It was impossible to pass around by the Mississippi, on account of the batteries at Vicksburg. The Rebels were holding the peninsula with a small force of infantry and cavalry, to prevent our effecting a landing. By careful management it was possible to elude the sentinels, and cross from one side of the peninsula to the other.

Colonel Ellet armed himself to make the attempt. He took only a few documents to prove his identity as soon as he reached Admiral Farragut. A little before daylight, one morning, he started on his perilous journey. He waded through swamps, toiled among the thick undergrowth in a portion of the forest, was fired upon by a Rebel picket, and narrowly escaped drowning in crossing a bayou. He was compelled to make a wide detour, to avoid capture, and thus extended his journey to nearly a half-dozen miles.

On reaching the bank opposite one of our gun-boats, he found a yawl near the shore, by which he was promptly taken on board. The officers of this gun-boat suspected him of being a spy, and placed him under guard. It was not until the arrival of Admiral Farragut that his true character became known.

After a long interview with that officer he prepared to return. He concealed dispatches for the Navy Department and for Flag-Officer Davis in the lining of his boots and in the wristbands of his shirt. A file of marines escorted him as far as they could safely venture, and then bade him farewell. Near the place where he had left his own boat, Colonel Ellet found a small party of Rebels, carefully watching from a spot where they could not be easily discovered. It was a matter of some difficulty to elude these men, but he did it successfully, and reached his boat in safety. He proceeded at once to Memphis with his dispatches. Flag-Officer Davis immediately decided to co-operate with Admiral Farragut, in the attempt to capture Vicksburg.

Shortly after the capture of New Orleans, Admiral Farragut ascended the Mississippi as far as Vicksburg. At that time the defensive force was very small, and there were but few batteries erected. The Admiral felt confident of his ability to silence the Rebel guns, but he was unaccompanied by a land force to occupy the city after its capture. He was reluctantly compelled to return to New Orleans, and wait until troops could be spared from General Butler's command. The Rebels improved their opportunities, and concentrated a large force to put Vicksburg in condition for defense. Heavy guns were brought from various points, earth-works were thrown up on all sides, and the town became a vast fortification. When the fleet returned at the end of June, the Rebels were ready to receive it. Their strongest works were on the banks of the Mississippi. They had no dread of an attack from the direction of Jackson, until long afterward.

Vicksburg was the key to the possession of the Mississippi. The Rebel authorities at Richmond ordered it defended as long as defense was possible.

CHAPTER XIX
THE FIRST SIEGE OF VICKSBURG

On the 1st of July, I left Memphis with the Mississippi flotilla, and arrived above Vicksburg late on the following day. Admiral Farragut's fleet attempted the passage of the batteries on the 28th of June. A portion of the fleet succeeded in the attempt, under a heavy fire, and gained a position above the peninsula. Among the first to effect a passage was the flag-ship *Hartford*, with the "gallant old salamander" on board. The *Richmond*, *Iroquois*, and *Oneida* were the sloops-of-war that accompanied the *Hartford*. The *Brooklyn* and other heavy vessels remained below.

The history of that first siege of Vicksburg can be briefly told. Twenty-five hundred infantry, under General Williams, accompanied the fleet from New Orleans, with the design of occupying Vicksburg after the batteries had been silenced by our artillery. Most of the Rebel guns were located at such a height that it was found impossible to elevate our own guns so as to reach them. Thus the occupation by infantry was found impracticable. The passage of the batteries was followed by the bombardment, from the mortar-schooners of Admiral Farragut's fleet and the mortar-rafts which Flag-Officer Davis had brought down. This continued steadily for several days, but Vicksburg did not fall.

A canal across the peninsula was proposed and commenced. The water fell as fast as the digging progressed, and the plan of leaving Vicksburg inland was abandoned for that time. Even had there been a flood in the river, the entrance to the canal was so located that success was impossible. The old steamboat-men laughed at the efforts of the Massachusetts engineer, to create a current in his canal by commencing it in an eddy.

Just as the canal project was agreed upon, I was present at a conversation between General Williams and several residents of the vicinity. The latter, fearing the channel of the river would be changed, visited the general to protest against the carrying out of his plan.

The citizens were six in number. They had selected no one to act as their leader. Each joined in the conversation as he saw fit. After a little preliminary talk, one of them said:

"Are you aware, general, there is no law of the State allowing you to make a cut-off, here?"

"I am sorry to say," replied General Williams, "I am not familiar with the laws of Louisiana. Even if I were, I should not heed them. I believe Louisiana passed an act of secession. According to your own showing you have no claims on the Government now."

This disposed of that objection. There was some hesitation, evidently embarrassing to the delegation, but not to General Williams. Citizen number one was silenced. Number two advanced an idea.

"You may remember, General, that you will subject the parish of Madison to an expenditure of ninety thousand dollars for new levees."

This argument disturbed General Williams no more than the first one. He promptly replied:

"The parish of Madison gave a large majority in favor of secession; did it not?"

"I believe it did," was the faltering response.

"Then you can learn that treason costs something. It will cost you far more before the war is over."

Citizen number two said nothing more. It was the opportunity for number three to speak.

"If this cut-off is made, it will ruin the trade of Vicksburg. It has been a fine city for business, but this will spoil it. Boats will not be able to reach the town, but will find all the current through the short route."

"That is just what we want," said the General. "We are digging the canal for the very purpose of navigating the river without passing near Vicksburg."

Number three went to the rear. Number four came forward.

"If you make this cut-off, all these plantations will be carried away. You will ruin the property of many loyal men."

He was answered that loyal men would be paid for all property taken or destroyed, as soon as their loyalty was proved.

The fifth and last point in the protest was next advanced. It came from an individual who professed to practice law in De Soto township, and was as follows:

"The charter of the Vicksburg and Shreveport Railroad is perpetual, and so declared by act of the Louisiana Legislature. No one has any right to cut through the embankment."

"That is true," was the quiet answer. "The Constitution of the United States is also a perpetual charter, which it was treason to violate. When you and your leaders have no hesitation at breaking national faith, it is absurd to claim rights under the laws of a State which you deny to be in the Union."

This was the end of the delegation. Its members retired without having gained a single point in their case. They were, doubtless, easier in mind when they ascertained, two weeks later, that the canal enterprise was a failure.

The last argument put forth on that occasion, to prevent the carrying out of our plans, is one of the curiosities of legislation. For a long time there were many parties in Louisiana who wished the channel of the Mississippi turned across the neck of the peninsula opposite Vicksburg, thus shortening the river fifteen miles, at least, and rendering the plantations above, less liable to overflow. As Vicksburg lay in another State, her interests were not regarded. She spent much money in the corrupt Legislature of Louisiana to defeat the scheme. As a last resort, it was proposed to build a railway, with a perpetual charter, from the end of the peninsula opposite Vicksburg, to some point in the interior. Much money was required. The capitalists of Vicksburg contributed the funds for lobbying the bill and commencing the road. Up to the time when the Rebellion began, it was rendered certain that no hand of man could legally turn the Mississippi across that peninsula.

The first siege of Vicksburg lasted but twenty days. Our fleet was unable to silence the batteries, and our land force was not sufficient for the work. During the progress of the siege, Colonel Ellet, with his ram fleet, ascended the Yazoo River, and compelled the Rebels to destroy three of their gun-boats, the *Livingston, Polk,* and *Van Dorn,* to prevent their falling into our hands. The *Van Dorn* was the only boat that escaped, out of the fleet of eight Rebel gun-boats which met ours at Memphis on the 6th of June.

At the time of making this expedition, Colonel Ellet learned that the famous ram gun-boat *Arkansas* was completed, and nearly ready to descend the river. He notified Admiral Farragut and Flag-Officer Davis, but they paid little attention to his warnings.

This Rebel gun-boat, which was expected to do so much toward the destruction of our naval forces on the Mississippi, was constructed at Memphis, and hurried from there in a partially finished condition, just before the capture of the city. She was towed to Yazoo City and there completed. The *Arkansas* was a powerful iron-clad steamer, mounting ten guns, and carrying an iron beak, designed for penetrating the hulls of our gun-boats. Her engines were powerful, though they could not be worked with facility at the time of her appearance. Her model, construction, armament, and propelling force, made her equal to any boat of our upper flotilla, and her officers claimed to have full confidence in her abilities.

On the morning of the 15th of July, the *Arkansas* emerged from the Yazoo River, fifteen miles above Vicksburg. A short distance up that stream she encountered two of our gun-boats, the *Carondelet* and *Tyler*, and fought them until she reached our fleet at anchor above Vicksburg. The *Carondelet* was one of our mail-clad gun-boats, built at St. Louis in 1861. The *Tyler* was a wooden gun-boat, altered from an old transport, and was totally unfit for entering into battle. Both were perforated by the Rebel shell, the *Tyler* receiving the larger number. The gallantry displayed by Captain Gwin, her commander, was worthy of special praise.

Our fleet was at anchor four or five miles above Vicksburg--some of the vessels lying in midstream, while others were fastened to the banks. The *Arkansas* fired to the right and left as she passed through the fleet. Her shot disabled two of our boats, and slightly injured two or three others. She did not herself escape without damage. Many of our projectiles struck her sides, but glanced into the river. Two shells perforated her plating, and another entered a port, exploding over one of the guns. Ten men were killed and as many wounded.

The *Arkansas* was not actually disabled, but her commander declined to enter into another action until she had undergone repairs. She reached a safe anchorage under protection of the Vicksburg batteries.

A few days later, a plan was arranged for her destruction. Colonel Ellet, with the ram *Queen of the West*, was to run down and strike the *Arkansas* at her moorings. The gun-boat *Essex* was to join in this effort, while the upper flotilla, assisted by the vessels of Admiral Farragut's fleet, would shell the Rebel batteries.

The *Essex* started first, but ran directly past the *Arkansas*, instead of stopping to engage her, as was expected. The *Essex* fired three guns at the *Arkansas* while in range, from one of which a shell crashed through the armor of the Rebel boat, disabling an entire gun-crew.

The *Queen of the West* attempted to perform her part of the work, but the current was so strong where the *Arkansas* lay that it was impossible to deal an effective blow. The upper flotilla did not open fire to engage the attention of the enemy, and thus the unfortunate *Queen of the West* was obliged to receive all the fire from the Rebel batteries. She was repeatedly perforated, but fortunately escaped without damage to her machinery. The *Arkansas* was not seriously injured in the encounter, though the completion of her repairs was somewhat delayed.

On the 25th of July the first siege of Vicksburg was raised. The upper flotilla of gun-boats, mortar-rafts, and transports, returned to Memphis and Helena. Admiral Farragut took his fleet to New Orleans. General Williams went, with his land forces, to Baton Rouge. That city was soon after attacked by General Breckinridge, with six thousand men. The Rebels were repulsed with heavy loss. In our own ranks the killed and wounded were not less than those of the enemy. General Williams was among the slain, and at one period our chances, of making a successful defense were very doubtful.

The *Arkansas* had been ordered to proceed from Vicksburg to take part in this attack, the Rebels being confident she could overpower our three gun-boats at Baton Rouge. On the way down the river her machinery became deranged, and she was tied up to the bank for repairs. Seeing our gun-boats approaching, and knowing he was helpless against them; her commander ordered the *Arkansas* to be abandoned and blown up. The order was obeyed, and this much-praised and really formidable gun-boat closed her brief but brilliant career.

The Rebels were greatly chagrined at her loss, as they had expected she would accomplish much toward driving the National fleet from the Mississippi. The joy with which they hailed her appearance was far less than the sorrow her destruction evoked.

CHAPTER XX
THE MARCH THROUGH ARKANSAS.-
-THE SIEGE OF CINCINNATI

About the middle of July, General Curtis's army arrived at Helena, Arkansas, ninety miles below Memphis. After the battle of Pea Ridge, this army commenced its wanderings, moving first to Batesville, on the White River, where it lay for several weeks. Then it went to Jacksonport, further down that stream, and remained a short time. The guerrillas were in such strong force on General Curtis's line of communications that they greatly restricted the receipt of supplies, and placed the army on very short rations. For nearly a month the public had no positive information concerning Curtis's whereabouts. The Rebels were continually circulating stories that he had surrendered, or was terribly defeated.

The only reasons for doubting the truth of these stories were, first, that the Rebels had no force of any importance in Arkansas; and second, that our army, to use the expression of one of its officers, "wasn't going round surrendering." We expected it would turn up in some locality where the Rebels did not desire it, and had no fears of its surrender.

General Curtis constructed several boats at Batesville, which were usually spoken of as "the Arkansas navy." These boats carried some six or eight hundred men, and were used to patrol the White River, as the army moved down its banks. In this way the column advanced from Batesville to Jacksonport, and afterward to St. Charles.

Supplies had been sent up the White River to meet the army. The transports and their convoy remained several days at St. Charles, but could get no tidings of General Curtis. The river was falling, and they finally returned. Twelve hours after their departure, the advance of the lost army arrived at St. Charles.

From St. Charles to Helena was a march of sixty miles, across a country destitute of every thing but water, and not even possessing a good supply of that article. The army reached Helena, weary and hungry, but it was speedily supplied with every thing needed, and put in condition to take the offensive. It was soon named in general orders "the Army of Arkansas," and ultimately accomplished the occupation of the entire State.

During July and August there was little activity around Memphis. In the latter month, I found the climate exceedingly uncomfortable. Day after day the atmosphere was hot, still, stifling, and impregnated with the dust that rose in clouds from the parched earth. The inhabitants endured it easily, and made continual prophesy that the *hot* weather "would come in September." Those of us who were strangers wondered what the temperature must be, to constitute "hot" weather in the estimation of a native. The thermometer then stood at eighty-five degrees at midnight, and ninety-eight or one hundred at noon. Few people walked the streets in the day, and those who were obliged to do so generally moved at a snail's pace. Cases of *coup-de-soleil* were frequent. The temperature affected me personally, by changing my complexion to a deep yellow, and reducing my strength about sixty per cent.

I decided upon "A Journey due North." Forty-eight hours after sweltering in Memphis, I was shivering on the shores of Lake Michigan. I exchanged the hot, fever-laden atmosphere of that city, for the cool and healthful air of Chicago. The activity, energy, and enterprise of Chicago, made a pleasing contrast to the idleness and gloom that pervaded Memphis. This was no place for me to exist in as an invalid. I found the saffron tint of my complexion rapidly disappearing, and my strength restored, under the influence of pure breezes and busy life. Ten days in that city prepared me for new scenes of war.

At that time the Rebel army, under General Bragg, was making its advance into Kentucky. General Buell was moving at the same time toward the Ohio River. The two armies were marching in nearly parallel lines, so that it became a race between them for Nashville and Louisville. Bragg divided his forces, threatening Louisville and Cincinnati at the same time. Defenses were thrown up around the former city, to assist in holding it in case of attack, but they were never brought into use. By rapid marching, General Buell reached Louisville in advance of Bragg, and rendered it useless for the latter to fling his army against the city.

Meantime, General Kirby Smith moved, under Bragg's orders, to the siege of Cincinnati. His advance was slow, and gave some opportunity for preparation. The chief reliance for defense was upon the raw militia and such irregular forces as could be gathered for the occasion. The hills of Covington and Newport, opposite Cincinnati, were crowned with fortifications and seamed with rifle-pits, which were filled with these raw soldiers. The valor of these men was beyond question, but they were almost entirely without discipline. In front of the veteran regiments of the Rebel army our forces would have been at great disadvantage.

When I reached Cincinnati the Rebel army was within a few miles of the defenses. On the train which took me to the city, there were many of the country people going to offer their services to aid in repelling the enemy. They entered the cars at the various stations, bringing their rifles, which they well knew how to use. They were the famous "squirrel-hunters" of Ohio, who were afterward the subject of some derision on the part of the Rebels. Nearly twenty thousand of them volunteered for the occasion, and would have handled their rifles to advantage had the Rebels given them the opportunity.

At the time of my arrival at Cincinnati, Major-General Wallace was in command. The Queen City of the West was obliged to undergo some of the inconveniences of martial law. Business of nearly every kind was suspended. A provost-marshal's pass was necessary to enable one to walk the streets in security. The same document was required of any person who wished to hire a carriage, or take a pleasant drive to the Kentucky side of the Ohio. Most of the able-bodied citizens voluntarily offered their services, and took their places in the rifle-pits, but there were some who refused to go. These were hunted out and taken to the front, much against their will. Some were found in or under beds; others were clad in women's garments, and working at wash-tubs. Some tied up their hands as if disabled, and others plead baldness or indigestion to excuse a lack of patriotism. All was of no avail. The provost-marshal had no charity for human weakness.

This severity was not pleasant to the citizens, but it served an admirable purpose. When Kirby Smith arrived in front of the defenses, he found forty thousand men confronting him. Of these, not over six or eight thousand had borne arms more than a week or ten days. The volunteer militia of Cincinnati, and the squirrel-hunters from the interior of Ohio and Indiana, formed the balance of our forces. Our line of defenses encircled the cities of Covington and Newport, touching the Ohio above and below their extreme limits. Nearly every hill was crowned with a fortification. These fortifications were connected by rifle-pits, which were kept constantly filled with men. On the river we had a fleet of gun-boats, improvised from ordinary steamers by surrounding their vulnerable parts with bales of hay. The river was low, so that it was necessary to watch several places where fording was possible. A pontoon bridge was thrown across the Ohio, and continued there until the siege was ended.

It had been a matter of jest among the journalists at Memphis and other points in the Southwest, that the vicissitudes of war might some day enable us to witness military operations from the principal hotels in the Northern cities. "When we can write war letters from the Burnet or the Sherman House," was the occasional remark, "there will be some personal comfort in being an army correspondent." What we had said in jest was now proving true. We could take a carriage at the Burnet House, and in half an hour stand on our front lines and witness the operations of the skirmishers. Later in the war I was enabled to write letters upon interesting topics from Detroit and St. Paul.

The way in which our large defensive force was fed, was nearly as great a novelty as the celerity of its organization. It was very difficult to sever the red tape of the army regulations, and enable the commissary department to issue rations to men that belonged to no regiments or companies. The people of Cincinnati were very prompt to send contributions of cooked food to the Fifth Street Market-House, which was made a temporary restaurant for the defenders of the city. Wagons were sent daily through nearly all the streets to gather these contributed supplies, and the street-cars were free to all women and children going to or from the Market-House. Hundreds walked to the front, to carry the provisions they had prepared with their own hands. All the ordinary edibles of civilized life were brought forward in abundance. Had our men fought at all, they would have fought on full stomachs.

The arrival of General Buell's army at Louisville rendered it impossible for Bragg to take that city. The defenders of Cincinnati were re-enforced by a division from General Grant's army, which was then in West Tennessee. This arrival was followed by that of other trained regiments and brigades from various localities, so that we began to contemplate taking the offensive. The Rebels disappeared from our front, and a reconnoissance showed that they were falling back toward Lexington. They burned the turnpike and railway bridges as they retreated, showing conclusively that they had abandoned the siege.

As soon as the retirement of the Rebels was positively ascertained, a portion of our forces was ordered from Cincinnati to Louisville. General Buell's army took the offensive, and pursued Bragg as he retreated toward the Tennessee River. General Wallace was relieved, and his command transferred to General Wright.

A change in the whole military situation soon transpired. From holding the defensive, our armies became the pursuers of the Rebels, the latter showing little inclination to risk an encounter. The battle of Perryville was the great battle of this Kentucky campaign. Its result gave neither army much opportunity for exultation.

In their retreat through Kentucky and Tennessee, the Rebels gathered all the supplies they could find, and carried them to their commissary depot at Knoxville. It was said that their trains included more than thirty thousand wagons, all of them heavily laden. Large droves of cattle and horses became the property of the Confederacy.

CHAPTER XXI
THE BATTLE OF CORINTH

The Bragg campaign into Kentucky being barren of important results, the Rebel authorities ordered that an attempt should be made to drive us from West Tennessee. The Rebel army in Northern Mississippi commenced the aggressive late in September, while the retreat of Bragg was still in progress. The battle of Iuka resulted favorably to the Rebels, giving them possession of that point, and allowing a large quantity of supplies to fall into their hands. On the 4th of October was the famous battle of Corinth, the Rebels under General Van Dorn attacking General Rosecrans, who was commanding at Corinth.

The Rebels advanced from Holly Springs, striking Corinth on the western side of our lines. The movement was well executed, and challenged our admiration for its audacity and the valor the Rebel soldiery displayed. It was highly important for the success of the Rebel plans in the Southwest that we should be expelled from Corinth. Accordingly, they made a most determined effort, but met a signal defeat.

Some of the best fighting of the war occurred at this battle of Corinth. The Rebel line of battle was on the western and northern side of the town, cutting off our communications with General Grant at Jackson. The Rebels penetrated our line, and actually obtained possession of a portion of Corinth, but were driven out by hard, earnest work. It was a struggle for a great prize, in which neither party was inclined to yield as long as it had any strength remaining to strike a blow.

The key to our position was on the western side, where two earthworks had been thrown up to command the approaches in that direction. These works were known as "Battery Williams" and "Battery Robbinette," so named in honor of the officers who superintended their erection and commanded their garrisons at the time of the assault. These works were on the summits of two small hills, where the ascent from the main road that skirted their base was very gentle. The timber on these slopes had been cut away to afford full sweep to our guns. An advancing force would be completely under our fire during the whole time of its ascent. Whether succeeding or failing, it must lose heavily.

General Van Dorn gave Price's Division the honor of assaulting these works. The division was composed of Missouri, Arkansas, and Texas regiments, and estimated at eight thousand strong. Price directed the movement in person, and briefly told his men that the position must be taken at all hazards. The line was formed on the wooded ground at the base of the hills on which our batteries stood. The advance was commenced simultaneously along the line.

As the Rebels emerged from the forest, our guns were opened. Officers who were in Battery Williams at the time of the assault, say the Rebels moved in splendid order. Grape and shell made frequent and wide gaps through their ranks, but the line did not break nor waver. The men moved directly forward, over the fallen timber that covered the ground, and at length came within range of our infantry, which had been placed in the forts to support the gunners. Our artillery had made fearful havoc among the Rebels from the moment they left the protection of the forest. Our infantry was waiting with impatience to play its part.

When the Rebels were fairly within range of our small-arms, the order was given for a simultaneous volley along our whole line. As the shower of bullets struck the Rebel front, hundreds of men went down. Many flags fell as the color-bearers were killed, but they were instantly seized and defiantly waved. With a wild cheer the Rebels dashed forward up to the very front of the forts, receiving without recoil a most deadly fire. They leaped the ditch and gained the parapet. They entered a bastion of Battery Williams, and for a minute held possession of one of our guns.

Of the dozen or more that gained the interior of the bastion, very few escaped. Nearly all were shot down while fighting for possession of the gun, or surrendered when the parapet was cleared of those ascending it. The retreat of the Rebels was hasty, but it was orderly. Even in a repulse their coolness did not forsake them. They left their dead scattered thickly in our front. In one group of seventeen, they lay so closely together that their bodies touched each other. An officer told me he could have walked along the entire front of Battery Williams, touching a dead or wounded Rebel at nearly every step. Two Rebel colonels were killed side by side, one of them falling with his hand over the edge of the ditch. They were buried where they died. In the attack in which the Rebels entered the edge of the town, the struggle was nearly as great. It required desperate fighting for them to gain possession of the spot, and equally desperate fighting on our part to retake it. All our officers who participated in this battle spoke in admiration of the courage displayed by the Rebels. Praise from an enemy is the greatest praise. The Rebels were not defeated on account of any lack of bravery or of recklessness. They were fully justified in retreating after the efforts they made. Our army was just as determined to hold Corinth as the Rebels were to capture it. Advantages of position turned the scale in our favor, and enabled us to repulse a force superior to our own.

Just before the battle, General Grant sent a division under General McPherson to re-enforce Corinth. The Rebels had cut the railway between the two points, so that the re-enforcement did not reach Corinth until the battle was over.

On the morning following the battle, our forces moved out in pursuit of the retreating Rebels. At the same time a column marched from Bolivar, so as to fall in their front. The Rebels were taken between the two columns, and brought to an engagement with each of them; but, by finding roads to the south, managed to escape without disorganization. Our forces returned to Corinth and Bolivar, thinking it useless to make further pursuit.

Thus terminated the campaign of the enemy against Corinth. There was no expectation that the Rebels would trouble us any more in that quarter for the present, unless we sought them out. Their defeat was sufficiently serious to compel them to relinquish all hope of expelling us from Corinth.

During the time of his occupation of West Tennessee, General Grant was much annoyed by the wandering sons of Israel, who thronged his lines in great numbers. They were engaged in all kinds of speculation in which money could be made. Many of them passed the lines into the enemy's country, and purchased cotton, which they managed to bring to Memphis and other points on the river. Many were engaged in smuggling supplies to the Rebel armies, and several were caught while acting as spies.

On our side of the lines the Jews were Union men, and generally announced their desire for a prompt suppression of the Rebellion. When under the folds of the Rebel flag they were the most ardent Secessionists, and breathed undying hostility to the Yankees. Very few of them had any real sympathy with either side, and were ready, like Mr. Pickwick, to shout with the largest mob on all occasions, provided there was money to be made by the operation. Their number was very great. In the latter half of '62, a traveler would have thought the lost tribes of Israel were holding a reunion at Memphis.

General Grant became indignant, and issued an order banishing the Jews from his lines. The order created much excitement among the Americans of Hebraic descent. The matter was placed before the President, and the obnoxious restriction promptly revoked. During the time it was in force a large number of the proscribed individuals were obliged to go North.

Sometimes the Rebels did not treat the Jews with the utmost courtesy. On one occasion a scouting party captured two Jews who were buying cotton. The Israelites were robbed of ten thousand dollars in gold and United States currency, and then forced to enter the ranks of the Rebel army. They did not escape until six months later.

In Chicago, in the first year of the war, a company of Jews was armed and equipped at the expense of their wealthier brethren. The men composing the company served their full time, and were highly praised for their gallantry.

The above case deserves mention, as it is an exception to the general conduct of the Jews.

CHAPTER XXII
THE CAMPAIGN FROM CORINTH

Two weeks after the battle of Corinth, General Rosecrans was summoned to the Army of the Cumberland, to assume command in place of General Buell. General Grant was placed at the head of the Thirteenth Army Corps, including all the forces in West Tennessee. Preparations for an aggressive movement into the enemy's country had been in progress for some time. Corinth, Bolivar, and Jackson were strongly fortified, so that a small force could defend them. The base of supply was at Columbus, Kentucky, eighty-five miles due north of Jackson, thus giving us a long line of railway to protect.

On the first of November the movement began, by the advance of a column from Corinth and another from Bolivar. These columns met at Grand Junction, twenty-five miles north of Holly Springs, and, after lying there for two weeks, advanced to the occupation of the latter point. The Rebels evacuated the place on our approach, and after a day or two at Holly Springs we went forward toward the south. Abbeville and Oxford were taken, and the Rebels established themselves at Grenada, a hundred miles south of Memphis.

From Corinth I accompanied the division commanded by General Stanley. I had known this officer in Missouri, in the first year of the war, when he claimed to be very "conservative" in his views. During the campaign with General Lyon he expressed himself opposed to a warfare that should produce a change in the social status at the South. When I met him at Corinth he was very "radical" in sentiment, and in favor of a thorough destruction of the "peculiar institution." He declared that he had liberated his own slaves, and was determined to set free all the slaves of any other person that might come in his way. He rejoiced that the war had not ended during the six months following the fall of Fort Sumter, as we should then have allowed slavery to exist, which would have rendered us liable to another rebellion whenever the Southern leaders chose to make it. We could only be taught by the logic of events, and it would take two or three years of war to educate the country to a proper understanding of our position.

It required a war of greater magnitude than was generally expected at the outset. In 1861 there were few people who would have consented to interfere with "slavery in the States." The number of these persons was greater in 1862, but it was not until 1864 that the anti-slavery sentiment took firm hold of the public mind. In 1861 the voice of Missouri would have favored the retention of the old system. In 1864 that State became almost as radical as Massachusetts. The change in public sentiment elsewhere was nearly as great.

During the march from Corinth to Grand Junction, I had frequent opportunity for conversing with the people along the route. There were few able-bodied men at home. It was the invariable answer, when we asked the whereabouts of any citizen, "He's away." Inquiry would bring a reluctant confession that he had gone to the Rebel army. Occasionally a woman would boast that she had sent her husband to fight for his rights and the rights of his State. The violation of State rights and the infringement upon personal prerogative were charged upon the National Government as the causes of the war. Some of the women displayed considerable skill in arguing the question of secession, but their arguments were generally mingled with invective. The majority were unable to make any discussion whatever.

"What's you-uns come down here to fight we-uns for?" said one of the women whose husband was in the Rebel army. "We-uns never did you-uns no hurt." (This addition of a syllable to the personal pronouns of the second and third persons is common in some parts of the South, while in others it will not be heard.)

"Well," said General Stanley, "we came down here because we were obliged to come. Your people commenced a war, and we are trying to help you end it."

"We-uns didn't want to fight, no-how. You-uns went and made the war so as to steal our niggers."

The woman acknowledged that neither her husband nor herself ever owned negroes, or ever expected to do so. She knew nothing about Fort Sumter, and only knew that the North elected one President and the South another, on the same occasion. The South only wanted its president to rule its own region, but the North wanted to extend its control over the whole country, so as to steal the negroes. Hence arose the war.

Some of the poorer whites manifested a loyal feeling, which sprang from a belief that the establishment of the Confederacy would not better their condition. This number was not large, but it has doubtless increased with the termination of the war. The wealthier portion of the people were invariably in sympathy with the Rebel cause.

After we reached Grand Junction, and made our camp a short distance south of that point, we were joined by the column from Bolivar. In the two columns General Grant had more than forty thousand men, exclusive of a force under General Sherman, about to move from Memphis. The Rebel army was at Holly Springs and Abbeville, and was estimated at fifty thousand strong. Every day found a few deserters coming in from the Rebels, but their number was not large. The few that came represented their army to be well supplied with shoes, clothing, and ammunition, and also well fed. They were nearly recovered from the effects of their repulse at Corinth, a month before.

Our soldiers foraged at will on the plantations near our camp. The quantities of supplies that were brought in did not argue that the country had been previously visited by an army. Mules, horses, cattle, hogs, sheep, chickens, and other things used by an army, were found in abundance.

The soldiers did not always confine their foraging to articles of necessity. A clergyman's library was invaded and plundered. I saw one soldier bending under the (avoirdupois) weight of three heavy volumes on theology, printed in the German language. Another soldier, a mere boy, was carrying away in triumph a copy of Scott's Greek Lexicon. In every instance when it came to their knowledge, the officers compelled the soldiers to return the books they had stolen. German theology and Greek Lexicons were not thought advantageous to an army in the field.

One wing of our army was encamped at Lagrange, Tennessee, and honored with the presence of General Grant. Lagrange presented a fair example of the effects of secession upon the interior villages of the South. Before the war it was the center of a flourishing business. Its private residences were constructed with considerable magnificence, and evinced the wealth of their owners. There was a male and a female college; there was a bank, and there were several stores and commission houses.

When the war broke out, the young men at the male college enlisted in the Rebel army. The young women in the female college went to their homes. The bank was closed for want of funds, the hotels had no guests, the stores had few customers, and these had no money, the commission houses could find no cotton to sell and no goods to buy. Every thing was completely stagnated. All the men who could carry muskets went to the field. When we occupied the town, there were not three men remaining who were of the arms-bearing age.

I found in Lagrange a man who *could* keep a hotel. He was ignorant, lazy, and his establishment only resembled the Fifth Avenue or the Continental in the prices charged to the guests. I staid several days with this Boniface, and enjoyed the usual fare of the interior South. Calling for my bill at my departure, I found the charges were only three dollars and fifty cents per day.

My horse had been kept in a vacant and dilapidated stable belonging to the hotel, but the landlord refused to take any responsibility for the animal. He had no corn or hay, and his hostler had "gone to the Yankees!" During my stay I employed a man to purchase corn and give the desired attention to the horse. The landlord made a charge of one dollar per day for "hoss-keeping," and was indignant when I entered a protest. Outside of Newport and Saratoga, I think there are very few hotel-keepers in the North who would make out and present a bill on so small a basis as this.

This taverner's wife and daughter professed an utter contempt for all white persons who degraded themselves to any kind of toil. Of course, their hostility to the North was very great. Beyond a slight supervision, they left every thing to the care of the negroes. A gentleman who was with me sought to make himself acquainted with the family, and succeeded admirably until, on one evening, he constructed a small toy to amuse the children. This was too much. He was skillful with his hands, and must therefore be a "mudsill." His acquaintance with the ladies of that household came to an end. His manual dexterity was his ruin.

There was another hotel in Lagrange, a rival establishment, that bore the reputation of being much the worse in point of comfort. It was owned by a widow, and this widow had a son--a lank, overgrown youth of eighteen. His poverty, on one point, was the greatest I ever knew. He could have been appropriately selected as the hero of a certain popular novel by Wilkie Collins. No name had ever been given him by his parents. In his infancy they spoke of him as "the boy." When he grew large enough to appear on the street with other boys, some one gave him the *sobriquet* of "Rough and Ready." From that time forward, his only praenomen was "Rough." I made several inquiries among his neighbors, but could not ascertain that he bore any other Christian appellative.

The first comprehensive order providing for the care of the negroes in the Southwest, was issued by General Grant while his army lay at Lagrange and Grand Junction. Previous to that time, the negroes had been disposed of as each division and post commander thought best, under his general instructions not to treat them unkindly. Four months earlier, our authorities at Memphis had enrolled several hundred able-bodied negroes into an organization for service in the Quartermaster's Department, in accordance with the provisions of an order from District Head-Quarters. They threw up fortifications, loaded and unloaded steamboats, and performed such other labor as was required. In General Grant's army there was a pioneer corps of three hundred negroes, under the immediate charge of an overseer, controlled by an officer of engineers. No steps were then taken to use them as soldiers.

The number of negroes at our posts and in our camps was rapidly increasing. Under the previous orders, they were registered and employed only on Government work. None but the able-bodied males were thus available. The new arrangements contemplated the employment of all who were capable of performing any kind of field labor. It was expected to bring some revenue to the Government, that would partially cover the expense of providing for the negroes.

The following is the order which General Grant issued:--

HEAD-QUARTERS THIRTEENTH ARMY CORPS,
DEPARTMENT OF THE TENNESSEE,
LAGRANGE, TENNESSEE, *November* 14, 1862.

SPECIAL FIELD ORDER, NO. 4.

I. Chaplain J. Eaton, Jr., of the Twenty-seventh Ohio Volunteers, is hereby appointed to take charge of all fugitive slaves that are now, or may from time to time come, within the military lines of the advancing army in this vicinity, not employed and registered in accordance with General Orders, No. 72, from head-quarters District of West Tennessee, and will open a camp for them at Grand Junction, where they will be suitably cared for, and organized into companies, and set to work, picking, ginning, and baling all cotton now outstanding in fields.

II. Commanding officers of all troops will send all fugitives that come within the lines, together with such teams, cooking utensils, and other baggage as they may bring with them, to Chaplain J. Eaton, Jr., at Grand Junction.

III. One regiment of infantry from Brigadier-General McArthur's Division will be temporarily detailed as guard in charge of such contrabands, and the surgeon of said regiment will be charged with the care of the sick.

IV. Commissaries of subsistence will issue, on the requisitions of Chaplain Eaton, omitting the coffee ration, and substituting rye. By order of Major-General U.S. Grant. JNO. A. RAWLINS, A.A.G.

Chaplain Eaton entered immediately upon the discharge of his duties. Many division and brigade commanders threw obstacles in his way, and were very slow to comply with General Grant's order. Some of the officers of the Commissary Department made every possible delay in filling Chaplain Eaton's requisitions. The people of the vicinity laughed at the experiment, and prophesied speedy and complete failure. They endeavored to insure a failure by stealing the horses and mules, and disabling the machinery which Chaplain Eaton was using. Failing in this, they organized guerrilla parties, and attempted to frighten the negroes from working in the field. They only desisted from this enterprise when some of their number were killed.

All the negroes that came into the army lines were gathered at Grand Junction and organized, in compliance with the order. There were many fields of cotton fully ripened, that required immediate attention. Cotton-picking commenced, and was extensively prosecuted.

The experiment proved a success. The cotton, in the immediate vicinity of Grand Junction and Lagrange was gathered, baled, and made ready for market. For once, the labors of the negro in the Southwest were bringing an actual return to the Government.

The following year saw the system enlarged, as our armies took possession of new districts. In 1863, large quantities of cotton were gathered from fields in the vicinity of Lake Providence and Milliken's Bend, and the cultivation of plantations was commenced. In 1864, this last enterprise was still further prosecuted. Chaplain Eaton became Colonel Eaton, and the humble beginning at Grand Junction grew into a great scheme for demonstrating the practicability of free labor, and benefiting the negroes who-had been left without support by reason of the flight of their owners.

As the army lay in camp near Lagrange for nearly four weeks, and the enemy was twenty-five miles distant, there was very little war correspondence to be written. There was an occasional skirmish near the front, but no important movement whatever. The monotony of this kind of life, and the tables of the Lagrange hotels, were not calculated to awaken much enthusiasm. Learning from a staff officer the probable date when the army would advance, I essayed a visit to St. Louis, and returned in season to take part in the movement into Mississippi.

At the time General Grant advanced from Lagrange, he ordered General Sherman to move from Memphis, so that the two columns would unite in the vicinity of Oxford, Mississippi. General Sherman pushed his column as rapidly as possible, and, by the combined movement, the Rebels were forced out of their defenses beyond Oxford, and compelled to select a new line in the direction of Grenada. Our flag was steadily advancing toward the Gulf.

Satisfied there would be no battle until our army had passed Oxford, I tarried several days at Holly Springs, waiting for the railway to be opened. I found the town a very pleasant one, finely situated, and bearing evidence of the wealth and taste of its inhabitants. When the war broke out, there were only two places in the State that could boast a larger population than Holly Springs.

At the time of my arrival, the hotels of Holly Springs were not open, and I was obliged to take a room at a private house with one of the inhabitants. My host was an earnest advocate of the Rebel cause, and had the fullest confidence in the ultimate independence of the South.

"We intend," said he, "to establish a strong Government, in which there will be no danger of interference by any abolitionists. If you had allowed us to have our own way, there would never have been any trouble. We didn't want you to have slavery in the North, but we wanted to go into the Territories, where we had a perfect right, and do as we pleased about taking our slaves there. The control of the Government belongs to us. The most of the Presidents have been from the South, as they ought to be. It was only when you elected a sectional President, who was sworn to break up slavery, that we objected. You began the war when you refused us the privilege of having a national President."

This gentleman argued, further, that the half of all public property belonged to the South, and it was only just that the State authorities should take possession of forts and arsenals, as they did at the inception of the war. It was the especial right of the South to control the nation. Slavery was instituted from Heaven, for the especial good of both white and black. Whoever displayed any sympathy for the negro, and wished to make him free, was doing a great injustice to the slave and his master, particularly to the latter.

Once he said the destruction of slavery would be unworthy a people who possessed any gallantry. "You will," he declared, "do a cruel wrong to many fine ladies. They know nothing about working with their hands, and consider such knowledge disgraceful. If their slaves are taken from them, these ladies will be helpless."

This gentleman was the possessor of several negroes, though he lived in a house that he did not own. Of course, it was a great injustice to deprive him of his only property, especially as the laws of his State sanctioned such ownership. He declared he would not submit to any theft of that character. I do not think I ever saw a person manifest more passion than was exhibited by this individual on hearings one afternoon, that one of his slaves had taken refuge in our camp, with the avowed intention of going North.

"I don't care for the loss," said he, "but what I do care for is, to be robbed by a nigger. I can endure an injury from a white man; to have a nigger defy me is too much."

Unfortunate and unhappy man! I presume he is not entirely satisfied with the present status of the "Peculiar Institution."

The cotton speculators at Holly Springs were guilty of some sharp transactions. One day a gentleman residing in the vicinity came to town in order to effect a sale of fifty bales. The cotton was in a warehouse a half-dozen miles away.

Remaining over night in Holly Springs, and walking to the railway station in the morning, he found his cotton piled by the track and ready for shipment. Two men were engaged effacing the marks upon the bales. By some means they had obtained a sufficient number of Government wagons to remove the entire lot during the night. It was a case of downright theft. The offenders were banished beyond the lines of the army.

In a public office at Holly Springs our soldiers found a great number of bills on the Northern Bank of Mississippi. They were in sheets, just as they had come from the press. None of them bore dates or signatures.

The soldiers supplied all needed chirography, and the bills obtained a wide circulation. Chickens, pigs, and other small articles were purchased of the whites and negroes, and paid for with the most astonishing liberality.

Counterfeits of the Rebel currency were freely distributed, and could only be distinguished from the genuine by their superior execution.

Among the women in Holly Springs and its vicinity snuff was in great demand. The article is used by them in much the same way that men chew tobacco. The practice is known as "dipping," and is disgusting in the extreme. A stick the size of a common pencil is chewed or beaten at one end until the fibers are separated. In this condition it forms a brush.

This brush is moistened with saliva, and plunged into the snuff. The fine powder which adheres is then rubbed on the gums and among the teeth. A species of partial intoxication is the result.

The effect of continued "dipping" becomes apparent. The gums are inflamed, the teeth are discolored, the lips are shriveled, and the complexion is sallow. The throat is dry and irritated, and there is a constant desire to expectorate.

I trust the habit will never become a Northern one.

CHAPTER XXIII
GRANT'S OCCUPATION OF MISSISSIPPI

The people of Holly Springs were much excited over the slavery question. It was then early in December. The President's proclamation was to have its effect on all States, or portions of States, not represented in Congress on the first of January following. The slaveholders desired to have the northern district of Mississippi represented in Congress before the first of January.

Three or four days after my arrival at Holly Springs I was with a small party of citizens to whom I had received introduction. The great question was being discussed. All were agreed that Northern Mississippi should be represented in Congress at whatever cost.

"Grant has now been in Mississippi nearly two weeks," said the principal speaker; "we are clearly entitled to representation."

"Certainly we are," responded another; "but who will represent us?"

"Hold an election to-morrow, and choose our man."

"Who will we send? None of us would be received. There isn't a man in the district who could swear he has taken no part in the Rebellion."

"I have it," said the individual who first proposed an election. Turning to me, he made a somewhat novel proposition:

"You can represent us in Congress. We've all been so d----d disloyal that we can't go; but that is no reason why we should not send a loyal men. Say yes, and we'll meet to-morrow, a dozen of us, and elect you."

Here was an opportunity for glory. Only four days in a State from which I could go to Congress! I was offered all necessary credentials to insure my reception. My loyalty could be clearly and easily proved. My only duties would be to assist in fastening slavery upon my congressional district. Much as I felt honored at the offer of distinction, I was obliged to decline it. A similar proposition was made to another journalist. He, like myself, was governed by modesty, and begged to be excused from serving.

The desire of this people to be represented in Congress, was a partial proof that they expected the national authority restored throughout the country. They professed to believe that our occupation would be temporary, but their actions did not agree with their words.

They were greatly mortified at the inability of their army to oppose our advance, and frequently abused the Rebel Government without stint. They had anticipated an easy victory from the outset, and were greatly disappointed at the result, up to that time.

"Just see how it is," said a Mississippian one day; "we expected to whip you without the slightest trouble. We threw the war into the Border States to keep it off our soil. Mississippi was very earnest for the Rebellion when Kentucky was the battle-ground. We no more expected you would come here, than that we should get to the moon. It is the fortune of war that you have driven us back, but it is very severe upon the cotton States."

I ventured to ask about the possibilities of repudiation of the Rebel debt, in case the Confederacy was fairly established.

"Of course we shall repudiate," was the response. "It would be far better for the Confederacy to do so than to attempt to pay the debt, or even its interest. Suppose we have a debt of a thousand millions, at eight per cent. This debt is due to our own people, and they have to pay the interest upon it. In twelve years and a half they would have paid another thousand millions, and still be as deeply in debt as ever. Now, if they repudiate the whole, the country will be a thousand millions richer at the end of twelve years and a half, than it otherwise would."

In Mississippi, as well as in other Southern States, I frequently heard this argument. It is not surprising that the confidence of the people in their currency was shaken at a very early period.

In its days of prosperity, Holly Springs boasted of two rival papers, each of them published weekly. One of these died just as the war broke out. The proprietor of the other, who was at the same time its editor, went, with his two sons, into the Rebel army, leaving the paper in charge of his wife. The lady wielded the pen for nearly a year, but the scarcity of printing-paper compelled her to close her office, a few months before our arrival.

One afternoon, I accompanied Mr. Colburn, of *The World*, on a visit to the ex-editress. The lady received our cards and greeted us very cordially. She spoke, with evident pride, of her struggles to sustain her paper in war-time and under war prices, and hoped she could soon resume its publication. She referred to the absence of her husband and sons in the Rebel service, and was gratified that they had always borne a good record. She believed in the

South and in the justness of its cause, but was prompt to declare that all the wrong was not on one side. She neither gave the South extravagant praise, nor visited the North with denunciation.

She regretted the existence of the war, and charged its beginning upon the extremists of both sides. Slavery was clearly its cause, and she should look for its complete destruction in the event of the restoration of national authority. Through justice to itself, the North could demand nothing less, and the South must be willing to abide by the fortune of war.

This woman respected and admired the North, because it was a region where labor was not degrading.

She had always opposed the Southern sentiment concerning labor, and educated her children after her own belief. While other boys were idling in the streets, she had taught her sons all the mysteries of the printing-office, and made them able to care for themselves. She was confident they would vindicate the correctness of her theory, by winning good positions in life. She believed slavery had assisted the development of the South, but was equally positive that its effect upon the white race was ruinous in the extreme.

She had no word of abuse for the Union, but spoke of it in terms of praise. At the same time she expressed an earnest hope for the success of the Rebellion. She saw the evil of slavery, but wished the Confederacy established. How she could reconcile all her views I was unable to ascertain. I do not believe she will take seriously to heart the defeat of the scheme to found a slaveholders' government. In the suppression of the Rebellion she will doubtless discover a brilliant future for "the land of the cypress and myrtle," and bless the day that witnessed the destruction of slavery.

At Oxford, our forces found the residence of the ex-Hon. Jacob Thompson, who has since figured prominently as the Rebel agent in Canada. In his office a letter-book and much correspondence were secured--the letters showing that the design of a rebellion dated much further back than the first election of Mr. Lincoln. Some of this correspondence was given to the public at the time, and proved quite interesting. The balance was sent to the War Department, where it was expected to be of service. The books in Mr. Thompson's library found their way to various parts of the Union, and became scattered where it will be difficult for their owner to gather them, should he desire to restore his collection. If "misery loves company," it was doubtless gratifying to Mr. Thompson to know of the capture of the library and correspondence of Jefferson Davis, several months later.

Our advance into Mississippi was being successfully pushed, early in December, 1862. There was a prospect that it would not accomplish the desired object, the capture of Vicksburg, without some counter-movement. A force was sent from Helena, Arkansas, to cut the railway in rear of the Rebel army. Though accomplishing its immediate object, it did not make a material change in the military situation. The Rebels continued to hold Grenada, which they had strongly fortified. They could only be forced from this position by a movement that should render Grenada of no practical value.

General Grant detached the right wing of his army, with orders to make a rapid march to Memphis, and thence to descend the Mississippi by steamboats to Vicksburg. This expedition was commanded by General Sherman. While the movement was in progress, General Grant was to push forward, on the line he had been following, and attempt to join General Sherman at the nearest practicable point on the Yazoo River above Vicksburg. The fall of Vicksburg was thus thought to be assured, especially as General Sherman's attack was to be made upon the defenses in its rear.

General Sherman moved, to Memphis with due celerity. The garrison of that city was reduced as much as possible to re-enforce his column. The Army of Arkansas, then at Helena, was temporarily added to his command. This gave a force exceeding twenty-eight thousand strong to move upon Vicksburg. It was considered sufficiently large to accomplish the desired object--the garrison of Vicksburg having been weakened to strengthen the army in General Grant's front.

I was in Holly Springs when General Sherman began to move toward Memphis. Thinking there would be active work at Vicksburg, I prepared to go to Columbus by rail, and take a steamboat thence to Memphis. By this route it was nearly four hundred miles; but it was safer and more expeditious to travel in that way than to attempt the "overland" journey of fifty miles in a direct line.

There were rumors that the Rebels contemplated a raid upon Holly Springs, for the purpose of cutting General Grant's communications and destroying the supplies known to be accumulated there. From the most vague and obscurely-worded hints, given by a Secessionist, I inferred that such a movement was expected. The Rebels were arranging a cavalry force to strike a blow somewhere upon our line of railway, and there was no point more attractive than Holly Springs. I attached no importance to the story, as I had invariably known the friends of the Rebels to predict wonderful movements that never occurred.

Meeting the post-commandant shortly afterward, I told him what I had heard. He assured me there was nothing to fear, and that every thing was arranged to insure a successful defense. On this point I did not agree with him. I knew very well that the garrison was not properly distributed to oppose a dash of the enemy. There were but few men on picket, and no precautions had been taken against surprise. Our accumulation of stores was sufficiently large to be worth a strong effort to destroy them. As I was about ready to leave, I concluded to take the first train to Columbus.

Less than forty-eight hours after my departure, General Van Dorn, at the head of five thousand men, entered Holly Springs with very slight opposition. He found every thing nearly as he could have arranged it had he planned the defense himself. The commandant, Colonel Murphy, was afterward dismissed the service for his negligence in preparing to defend the place after being notified by General Grant that the enemy was moving to attack him.

The accumulation of supplies at the railway depot, and all the railway buildings, with their surroundings, were burned. Two trains of cars were standing ready to move, and these shared a similar fate. In the center of the town, a building we were using as a magazine was blown up. The most of the business portion of Holly Springs was destroyed by fire, communicated from this magazine.

During the first year of the war, Holly Springs was selected as the site of a "Confederate States Arsenal," and a series of extensive buildings erected at great expense.

We had converted these buildings into hospitals, and were fitting them up with suitable accommodations for a large number of sick and wounded.

After ordering our surgeons to remove their patients, the Rebels set fire to the hospitals while the yellow flag was floating over them. General Grant subsequently denounced this act as contrary to the usages of war.

The Rebels remained in Holly Springs until five o'clock in the afternoon of the day of their arrival. At their departure they moved in a northerly direction, evidently designing to visit Grand Junction. At Davis's Mill, about half-way between Holly Springs and Grand Junction, they found a small stockade, garrisoned by two companies of infantry, protecting the railway bridge. They sent forward a flag-of-truce, and demanded the instant surrender of the stockade.

Their demand was not complied with. That garrison, of less than two hundred men, fought Van Dorn's entire command four hours, repulsed three successive charges, and finally compelled the Rebels to retreat. Van Dorn's northward movement was checked, and our stores at Grand Junction and Lagrange were saved, by the gallantry of this little force. General Grant subsequently gave special compliment to the bravery of these soldiers and their officers, in an order which was read to every regiment in the Army of the Tennessee.

Our plans were completely deranged by this movement of the enemy. The supplies and ammunition we had relied upon were destroyed, and our communications severed. It was impossible to push further into Mississippi, and preparations were made for immediate retreat. The railway was repaired and the heavy baggage sent to the rear as speedily as possible. When this was accomplished the army began to fall back. Oxford, Abbeville, and Holly Springs were abandoned, and returned to the protection of the Rebel flag. Northern Mississippi again became the field for guerrilla warfare, and a source of supply to the Rebels in the field. The campaign for the capture of Vicksburg took a new shape from the day our lines were severed.

A few days before the surrender of Vicksburg, General Grant, in conversation with some friends, referred to his position in Mississippi, six months before. Had he pressed forward beyond Grenada, he would have been caught in midwinter in a sea of mud, where the safety of his army might have been endangered. Van Dorn's raid compelled him to retreat, saved him from a possible heavier reverse, and prepared the way for the campaign in which Vicksburg finally capitulated. A present disaster, it proved the beginning of ultimate success.

CHAPTER XXIV
THE BATTLE OF CHICKASAW BAYOU

On arriving at Memphis, I found General Sherman's expedition was ready to move toward Vicksburg. A few of the soldiers who escaped from the raid on Holly Springs had reached Memphis with intelligence of that disaster. The news caused much excitement, as the strength of the Rebels was greatly exaggerated. A few of these soldiers thought Van Dorn's entire division of fifteen or twenty thousand men had been mounted and was present at the raid. There were rumors of a contemplated attack upon Memphis, after General Sherman's departure.

Unmilitary men thought the event might delay the movement upon Vicksburg, but it did not have that effect. General Sherman said he had no official knowledge that Holly Springs had been captured, and could do no less than carry out his orders. The expedition sailed, its various divisions making a rendezvous at Friar's Point, twelve miles below Helena, on the night of the 22d of December. From this place to the mouth of the Yazoo, we moved leisurely down the Mississippi, halting a day near Milliken's Bend, almost in sight of Vicksburg. We passed a portion of Christmas-Day near the mouth of the Yazoo.

On the morning of the 26th of December, the fleet of sixty transports, convoyed by several gun-boats, commenced the ascent of the Yazoo. This stream debouches into the Mississippi, fifteen miles above Vicksburg, by the course of the current, though the distance in an airline is not more than six miles. Ten or twelve miles above its mouth, the Yazoo sweeps the base of the range of hills on which Vicksburg stands, at a point nearly behind the city. It was therefore considered a feasible route to the rear of Vicksburg.

In a letter which I wrote on that occasion, I gave the following description of the country adjoining the river, and the incidents of a night bivouac before the battle:--"The bottom-land of the Yazoo is covered with a heavy growth of tall cypress-trees, whose limbs are everywhere interlaced. In many places the forest has a dense undergrowth, and in others it is quite clear, and affords easy passage to mounted men. These huge trees are heavily draped in the 'hanging moss,' so common in the Southern States, which gives them a most gloomy appearance. The moss, everywhere pendent from the limbs of the trees, covers them like a shroud, and in some localities shuts out the sunlight. In these forests there are numerous bayous that form a net-work converting the land into a series of islands. When separated from your companions, you can easily imagine yourself in a wilderness. In the wild woods of the Oregon there is no greater solitude."

"On the afternoon of the 27th, I started from the transports, and accompanied our left wing, which was advancing on the east side of Chickasaw Bayou. The road lay along the crest of the levee which had been thrown up on the bank of the bayou, to protect the fields on that side against inundation. This road was only wide enough for the passage of a single wagon. Our progress was very slow, on account of the necessity for removing heavy logs across the levee. When night overtook us, we made our bivouac in the forest, about three miles from the river.

"I had taken with me but a single blanket, and a haversack containing my note-book and a few crackers. That night in bivouac acquainted me with some of the discomforts of war-making on the Yazoo. The ground was moist from recent rains, so that dry places were difficult to find. A fellow-journalist proposed that we unite our blankets, and form a double bed for mutual advantage. To this I assented. When my friend came forward, to rest in our combined couch, I found his 'blanket' was purely imaginary, having been left on the steamer at his departure. For a while we 'doubled,' but I was soon deserted, on account of the barrenness of my accommodations.

"No fires were allowed, as they might reveal our position to the watchful enemy. The night was cold. Ice formed at the edge of the bayou, and there was a thick frost on the little patches of open ground. A negro who had lived in that region said the swamp usually abounded in moccasins, copperheads, and cane-snakes, in large numbers. An occasional rustling of the leaves at my side led me to imagine these snakes were endeavoring to make my acquaintance.

"Laying aside my snake fancies, it was too cold to sleep. As fast as I would fall into a doze, the chill of the atmosphere would steal through my blanket, and remind me of my location. Half-sleeping and half-waking, I dreamed of every thing disagreeable. I had visions of Greenland's icy mountains, of rambles in Siberia, of my long-past midwinter nights in the snow-drifted gorges of Colorado, of shipwreck, and of burning dwellings, and of all moving accidents by flood and field! These dreams followed each other with a rapidity that far outstripped the workings of the electric telegraph.

"Cold and dampness and snakes and fitful dreams were not the only bodily discomforts. A dozen horses were loose in camp, and trotting gayly about. Several times they passed at a careless pace within a yard of my head. Once the foremost of the *caballada* jumped directly over me, and was followed by the rest. My comments on these eccentricities of that noble animal, the horse, provoked the derision rather than the sympathy of those who heard them.

"A teamster, who mistook me for a log, led his mules over me. A negro, under the same delusion, attempted to convert me into a chair, and another wanted to break me up for fuel, to be used in making a fire after daylight. Each of these little blunders evoked a gentle remonstrance, that effectually prevented a repetition by the same individual.

"A little past daylight a shell from the Rebel batteries exploded within twenty yards of my position, and warned me that it was time to rise. To make my toilet, I pulled the sticks and leaves from my hair and beard, and brushed my overcoat with a handful of moss. I breakfasted on a cracker and a spoonful of whisky. I gave my horse a handful of corn and a large quantity of leaves. The former he ate, but the latter he refused to touch. The column began to move, and I was ready to attend upon its fortunes."

General Sherman's plan was to effect a landing on the Yazoo, and, by taking possession of the bluffs, sever the communication between Vicksburg and the interior. It was thought the garrison of Vicksburg had been greatly weakened to re-enforce the army in General Grant's front, so that our success would be certain when we once gained the bluffs.

A portion of our forces effected a landing on the 26th, but the whole command was not on shore till the 27th. Fighting commenced on the 27th, and became more earnest on the 28th, as we crowded toward the bluffs.

In moving from the steamboat landing to the base of the bluffs on the 28th, our army encountered the enemy at several points, but forced him back without serious loss on either side. It appeared to be the Rebel design not to make any resistance of magnitude until we had crossed the lower ground and were near the base of the line of hills protecting Vicksburg.

Not far from the foot of the bluffs there was a bayou, which formed an excellent front for the first line of the Rebel defenses. On our right we attempted to cross this bayou with a portion of Morgan L. Smith's Division, but the Rebel fire was so severe that we were repulsed. On our extreme right a similar attempt obtained the same result.

On our left the bayou was crossed by General Morgan's and General Steele's Divisions at two or three points, and our forces gained a position close up to the edge of the bluff.

At eleven A. M. on the 29th, an assault was made by three brigades of infantry upon the works of the enemy on this portion of the line. General Blair and General Thayer from Steele's Division, pushed forward through an abatis which skirted the edge of the bayou, and captured the first line of Rebel rifle-pits. From this line the brigades pressed two hundred yards farther up the hillside, and temporarily occupied a portion of the second line. Fifty yards beyond was a small clump of trees, which was gained by one regiment, the Thirteenth Illinois, of General Blair's Brigade.

The Rebels massed heavily against these two brigades. Our assaulting force had not been followed by a supporting column, and was unable to hold the works it captured. It fell back to the bayou and re-formed its line. One of General Morgan's brigades occupied a portion of the rifle-pits at the time the hill was assaulted by the brigades from General Steele's Division.

During the afternoon of the 29th, preparations were made for another assault, but the plan was not carried out. It was found the Rebels had been re-enforced at that point, so that we had great odds against us. The two contending armies rested within view of each other, throwing a few shells each hour, to give notice of their presence.

After the assault, the ground between the contending lines was covered with dead and wounded men of our army. A flag-of-truce was sent out on the afternoon of the 29th, to arrange for burying the dead and bringing away the wounded, but the Rebels would not receive it. Sunrise on the 30th, noon, sunset, and sunrise again, and they lay there still. On the 31st, a truce of five hours was arranged, and the work of humanity accomplished. A heavy rain had fallen, rendering the ground unfit for the rapid moving of infantry and artillery, in front of the Rebel position.

On the evening of the 31st, orders were issued for a new plan of attack at another part of the enemy's lines. A division was to be embarked on the transports, and landed as near as possible to the Rebel fortifications on Haines's Bluff, several miles up the Yazoo. The gun-boats were to take the advance, engage the attention of the forts, and cover the landing. Admiral Porter ordered Colonel Ellet to go in advance, with a boat of his ram fleet, to remove the obstructions the Rebels had placed in the river, under the guns of the fort. A raft was attached to the bow of the ram, and on the end of the raft was a torpedo containing a half ton of powder.

Admiral Porter contended that the explosion of the torpedo would remove the obstructions, so that the fleet could proceed. Colonel Ellet expressed his readiness to obey orders, but gave his opinion that the explosion, while effecting its object, would destroy his boat and all on board. Some officers and civilians, who knew the admiral's antipathy to Colonel Ellet, suggested that the former was of the same opinion, and therefore desirous that the experiment should be made.

Every thing was in readiness on the morning of the 1st of January, but a dense fog prevented the execution of our new plan. On the following day we withdrew from the Yazoo, and ended the second attack upon Vicksburg. Our loss was not far from two thousand men, in all casualties.

General Sherman claimed to have carried out with exactness, the instructions from his superior officers respecting the time and manner of the attack. Van Dorn's raid upon General Grant's lines, previous to Sherman's departure from Memphis, had radically changed the military situation. Grant's advance being stopped, his co-operation by way of Yazoo City could not be given. At the same time, the Rebels were enabled to strengthen their forces at Vicksburg. The assault was a part of the great plan for the conquest of the Mississippi, and was made in obedience to positive orders. Before the orders were carried out, a single circumstance had deranged the whole plan. After the fighting was ended and the army had re-embarked, preparatory to leaving the Yazoo, General Sherman was relieved from command by General McClernand. The latter officer carried out the order for withdrawal. The fleet steamed up the Mississippi to Milliken's Bend, where it remained for a day or two. General McClernand directed that an expedition be made against Arkansas Post, a Rebel fortification on the Arkansas River, fifty miles above its mouth.

After the first attack upon Vicksburg, in June, 1862, the Rebels strengthened the approaches in the rear of the city. They threw up defensive works on the line of bluffs facing the Yazoo, and erected a strong fortification to prevent our boats ascending that stream. Just before General Sherman commenced his assault, the gun-boat *Benton*, aided by another iron-clad, attempted to silence the batteries at Haines's Bluff, but was unsuccessful. Her sides were perforated by the Rebel projectiles, and she withdrew from the attack in a disabled condition. Captain Gwin, her commander, was mortally wounded early in the fight.

Captain Gwin was married but a few weeks before this occurrence. His young wife was on her way from the East to visit him, and was met at Cairo with the news of his death.

About two months before the time of our attack, an expedition descended the Mississippi from Helena, and suddenly appeared near the mouth of the Yazoo. It reached Milliken's Bend at night, surprising and capturing the steamer *Fairplay*, which was loaded with arms and ammunition for the Rebels in Arkansas. So quietly was the capture made, that the officers of the *Fairplay* were not aware of the change in their situation until awakened by their captors.

CHAPTER XXV
BEFORE VICKSBURG

The army moved against Arkansas Post, which was captured, with its entire garrison of five thousand men. The fort was dismantled and the earth-works leveled to the ground. After this was accomplished, the army returned to Milliken's Bend. General Grant arrived a few days later, and commenced the operations which culminated in the fall of Vicksburg.

Before leaving Memphis on the Yazoo expedition, General Sherman issued an order excluding all civilians, except such as were connected with the transports, and threatening to treat as a spy any person who should write accounts for publication which might give information to the enemy. No journalists were to be allowed to take part in the affair. One who applied for permission to go in his professional capacity received a very positive refusal. General Sherman had a strong antipathy to journalists, amounting almost to a mania, and he was determined to discourage their presence in his movements against Vicksburg.

Five or six correspondents accompanied the expedition, some of them on passes from General Grant, which were believed superior to General Sherman's order, and others with passes or invitations from officers in the expedition. I carried a pass from General Grant, and had a personal invitation from an officer who held a prominent command in the Army of Arkansas. I had passed Memphis, almost without stopping, and was not aware of the existence of the prohibitory order until I reached the Yazoo.

I wrote for *The Herald* an account of the battle, which I directed to a friend at Cairo, and placed in the mail on board the head-quarters' boat. The day after mailing my letter, I learned it was being read at General Sherman's head-quarters. The General afterward told me that his mail-agent, Colonel Markland, took my letter, among others, from the mail, with his full assent, though without his order.

I proceeded to rewrite my account, determined not to trust again to the head-quarters' mail. When I was about ready to depart, I received the letter which had been stolen, bearing evident marks of repeated perusal.

Two maps which it originally contained were not returned. I proceeded to Cairo as the bearer of my own dispatches.

On my return to Milliken's Bend, two weeks later, I experienced a new sensation. After two interviews with the indignant general, I received a tender of hospitalities from the provost-marshal of the Army of the Tennessee. The tender was made in such form as left no opportunity for declining it. A few days after my arrest, I was honored by a trial before a military court, consisting of a brigadier-general, four colonels, and two majors. General Sherman had made the following charges against me:--

First.--"*Giving information to the enemy.*"

Second.--"*Being a spy.*"

Third.--"*Disobedience of orders.*"

The first and second charges were based on my published letter. The third declared that I accompanied the expedition without proper authority, and published a letter without official sanction. These were my alleged offenses.

My court had a protracted session. It decided there was nothing in my letter which violated the provisions of the order regulating war correspondence for the Press. It declared me innocent of the first and second charges. It could see nothing criminal in the manner of my accompanying the expedition.

But I was guilty of something. There was a "General Order, Number 67," issued in 1861, of whose existence neither myself nor, as far as I could ascertain, any other journalist, was aware. It provided that no person should write, print, or cause to be printed "any information respecting military movements, without the authority and sanction of the general in command."

Here was the rock on which I split. I had written a letter respecting military movements, and caused it to be printed, "without the sanction of the general in command." Correspondents everywhere had done the same thing, and continued to do it till the end of the war. "Order Number 67" was as obsolete as the laws of the Medes and Persians, save on that single occasion. Dispatches by telegraph passed under the eye of a Government censor, but I never heard of an instance wherein a letter transmitted by mail received any official sanction.

My court was composed of officers from General Sherman's command, and was carefully watched by that distinguished military chieftain, throughout its whole sitting. It wavered in deciding upon the proper "punishment" for my offense. Should it banish me from that spot, or should I receive an official censure? It concluded to send me outside the limits of the Army of the Tennessee.

During the days I passed in the care of the provost-marshal, I perused all the novels that the region afforded. When these were ended, I studied a copy of a well-known work on theology, and turned, for light reading, to the "Pirate's Own Book." A sympathizing friend sent me a bundle of tracts and a copy of the "Adventures of John A. Murrell." A volume of lectures upon temperance and a dozen bottles of Allsop's pale ale, were among the most welcome contributions that I received. The ale disappeared before the lectures had been thoroughly digested.

The chambermaid of the steamboat displayed the greatest sympathy in my behalf. She declined to receive payment of a washing-bill, and burst into tears when I assured her the money was of no use to me.

Her fears for my welfare were caused by a frightful story that had been told her by a cabin-boy. He maliciously represented that I was to be executed for attempting to purchase cotton from a Rebel quartermaster. The verdant woman believed the story for several days.

It may interest some readers to know that the proceedings of a court-martial are made in writing. The judge-advocate (who holds the same position as the prosecuting attorney in a civil case) writes his questions, and then reads them aloud. The answers, as they are given, are reduced to writing. The questions or objections of the prisoner's counsel must be made in writing and given to the judge-advocate, to be read to the court. In trials where a large number of witnesses must be examined, it is now the custom to make use of "short-hand" writers. In this way the length of a trial is greatly reduced.

The members of a court-martial sit in full uniform, including sash and sword, and preserve a most severe and becoming dignity. Whenever the court wishes to deliberate upon any point of law or evidence, the room is cleared, neither the prisoner nor his counsel being allowed to remain. It frequently occurs that the court is thus closed during the greater part of its sessions. With the necessity for recording all its proceedings, and frequent stoppages for deliberation, a trial by a military court is ordinarily very slow.

In obedience to the order of the court, I left the vicinity of the Army of the Tennessee, and proceeded North.

In departing from Young's Point, I could not obey a certain Scriptural injunction, as the mud of Louisiana adheres like glue, and defies all efforts to shake it off. Mr. Albert D. Richardson, of The Tribune, on behalf of many of my professional friends, called the attention of President Lincoln to the little affair between General Sherman and myself.

In his recently published book of experiences during the war, Mr. Richardson has given a full and graphic account of his interview with the President. Mr. Lincoln unbent himself from his official cares, told two of his best stories, conversed for an hour or more upon the military situation, gave his reasons for the removal of General McClellan, and expressed his hope in our ultimate success. Declaring it his inflexible determination not to interfere with the conduct of any military department, he wrote the following document:--

EXECUTIVE MANSION,
WASHINGTON, *March* 20, 1863.

WHOM IT MAY CONCERN:

Whereas it appears to my satisfaction that Thomas W. Knox, a correspondent of *The New York Herald*, has been, by the sentence of a court-martial, excluded from the Military Department under command of Major-General Grant, and also that General Thayer, president of the court-martial, which rendered the sentence, and Major-General McClernand, in command of a corps of that department, and many other respectable persons, are of opinion that Mr. Knox's offense was technical, rather than willfully wrong, and that the sentence should be revoked: Now, therefore, said sentence is hereby so far revoked as to allow Mr. Knox to return to General Grant's head-quarters, to remain if General Grant shall give his express assent; and to again leave the department, if General Grant shall refuse such assent.

A. LINCOLN

With this letter I returned to the army. General Grant referred the question to General Sherman. In consideration of our quarrel, and knowing the unamiable character of the latter officer, I should have been greatly surprised had he given any thing else than a refusal. I had fully expected to return immediately when I left St. Louis, but, like most persons in a controversy, wished to carry my point.

General Sherman long since retrieved his failure at Chickasaw Bayou. Throughout the war he was honored with the confidence and friendship of General Grant. The career of these officers was not marked by the jealousies that are too frequent in military life. The hero of the campaign from Chattanooga to Raleigh is destined to be known in history. In those successful marches, and in the victories won by his tireless and never vanquished army, he has gained a reputation that may well be enduring.

Soon after my return from Young's Point, General Grant crossed the Mississippi at Grand Gulf, and made his daring and successful movement to attain the rear of Vicksburg. Starting with a force less than the one his opponent could bring against him, he cut loose from his communications and succeeded in severing the enemy's line of supplies. From Grand Gulf to Jackson, and from Jackson to the rear of Vicksburg, was a series of brilliant marches and brilliant victories. Once seated where he had his antagonist's army inclosed, General Grant opened his lines to the Yazoo, supplied himself with every thing desired, and pressed the siege at his leisure. With the fall of Vicksburg, and the fall, a few days later, of Port Hudson, "the Father of Waters went unvexed to the Sea."

While the army was crossing the Mississippi at Grand Gulf, three well-known journalists, Albert D. Richardson and Junius H. Browne, of *The Tribune*, and Richard T. Colburn, of *The World*, attempted to run past the Rebel batteries at Vicksburg, on board a tug at midnight. The tug was blown up and destroyed; the journalists were captured and taken to the Rebel prison at Vicksburg. Thence they were removed to Richmond, occupying, while *en route*, the prisons of a half-dozen Rebel cities. Mr. Colburn was soon released, but the companions of his adventure were destined to pass nearly two years in the prisons of the Confederacy. By a fortunate escape and a midwinter march of nearly four hundred miles, they reached our lines in safety. In books and in lecture-rooms, they have since told the story of their captivity and flight.

I have sometimes thought my little quarrel with General Sherman proved "a blessing in disguise," in saving me from a similar experience of twenty months in Rebel prisons.

CHAPTER XXVI
KANSAS IN WAR-TIME

In May, 1863, I made a hasty visit to Western Missouri and Kansas, to observe the effect of the war in that quarter. Seven years earlier the border warfare attracted much attention. The great Rebellion caused Kansas and its troubles to sink into insignificance. Since the first election of Mr. Lincoln to the Presidency, Kansas has been rarely mentioned.

I passed through this young State in the summer of 1860. I was repeatedly told: "We have old grudges that we wish to settle; if the troubles ever break out again in any part of the United States, we hope to cross out our account." When the war opened, the people of Kansas saw their opportunity for "making square work," as they expressed it, with Missouri and the other slave States. They placed two regiments of volunteers in the field with as much celerity as was displayed in many of the older and more populous States. These regiments were followed by others until fully half the able-bodied population of Kansas was in the service. In some localities the proportion was even greater than this.

The dash and daring of these Kansas soldiers became proverbial. At Wilson Creek, two regiments from Kansas had their first experience of battle, and bore themselves most nobly. The conduct of other Kansas soldiers, on other battle-fields, was equally commendable. Their bravery and endurance was only equaled by their ability in foraging.

Horses, mules, cattle, and provisions have, in all times, been considered the legitimate spoils of war. The Kansas soldiers did not confine themselves to the above, but appropriated every thing portable and valuable, whether useful or useless. Their example was contagious, and the entire army soon learned to follow it.

During General Grant's campaign in Mississippi in '62, the Seventh Kansas Cavalry obtained a reputation for ubiquity and lawlessness. Every man who engaged in plundering on his own account, no matter to what regiment he belonged, invariably announced himself a member of the Seventh Kansas. Every countryman who was robbed declared the robbery was committed by the Seventh Kansas "Jayhawkers." Uniting all the stories of robbery, one would conclude that the Seventh Kansas was about twenty thousand strong, and constantly in motion by fifty different roads, leading to all points of the compass.

One day a soldier of the Second Illinois Cavalry gave me an account of his experience in horse-stealing.

"Jim and I went to an old farmer's house, and told him we wanted his horses. He said he wanted to use them himself, and couldn't spare them.

"'That don't make no sort of difference,' said I; 'we want your horses more than you do.'

"'What regiment do you belong to?'

"'Seventh Kansas Jayhawkers. The whole regiment talks of coming round here. I reckon I'll bring them.'

"When I told him that," said the soldier, "he said I might take the horses, if I would only go away. He offered me a pint of whisky if I would promise not to bring the regiment there. Jim and me drank the whisky, and told him we would use our influence for him."

Before the war was ended, the entire armies of the Southwest were able to equal the "Jayhawkers" in foraging. The march of Sherman's column through Mississippi, and afterward through Georgia and South Carolina, fully proved this. Particularly in the latter State, which originated the Rebellion, were the accomplishments of the foragers most conspicuously displayed. Our army left very little for another army to use.

The desolation which was spread through the Southern States was among the most effective blows at the Rebellion. The Rebels were taught in the most practical manner, that insurrection was not to be indulged in with impunity. Those who suffered most were generally among the earliest to sue for peace. Sherman's terse answer to the mayor of Atlanta, when the latter protested against the banishment of the inhabitants, was appreciated by the Rebels after our final campaigns. "War is cruelty--you cannot refine it," speaks a volume in a few words.

When hostilities commenced, the Kansas regiments were clamorous to be led into Missouri. During the border war of '55 and '56, Missourians invaded Kansas to control the elections by force of arms, and killed, often in cold blood, many of the quiet citizens of the Territory. The tier of counties in Missouri adjoining Kansas were most anxious to make the latter a slave State, and used every possible means to accomplish their object.

The Kansas soldiers had their wish. They marched through Missouri. Those who had taken part in the outrages upon Kansas, five years earlier, were made to feel the hand of retribution. If they had burned the buildings of free-State settlers in '56, they found their own houses destroyed in '62. In the old troubles they contended for their right to make whatever warfare they chose, but were astounded and horrified in the latter days, when the tables were turned against them by those they had wronged.

Along the frontier of Missouri the old system of warfare was revived. Guerrilla bands were formed, of which Quantrel and similar men were the leaders. Various incursions were made into Kansas by these marauders, and the depredations were worse than ever.

They culminated in the burning of Lawrence and the massacre of its inhabitants.

To break up these guerrilla bands, it became necessary to depopulate the western tier of counties in Missouri, from the Missouri River down to the thirty-eighth parallel of latitude. The most wealthy of these was Jackson County. Before the war it had a slave population of not far from four thousand, and its fields were highly productive. Two years after the war broke out it contained less than three hundred slaves, and its wealth had diminished in almost as great proportion. This was before any freedom had been officially declared to the slaves in the Border States. The order of depopulation had the desired effect. It brought peace to the border, though at a terrible cost. Missouri suffered greatly, and so did Kansas.

The most prominent officer that Kansas furnished during the Rebellion, was Brigadier-General Blunt. At the beginning of the war he enlisted as a private soldier, but did not remain long in the ranks. His reputation in the field was that of a brave and reckless officer, who had little regard to military forms. His successes were due to audacity and daring, rather than to skill in handling troops, or a knowledge of scientific warfare.

The battle of Cane Hill is said to have commenced by General Blunt and his orderlies attacking a Rebel picket. The general was surveying the country with his orderlies and a company of cavalry, not suspecting the enemy was as near as he proved to be.

At the moment Blunt came upon the picket, the cavalry was looking in another direction. Firing began, and the picket was driven in and fell back to a piece of artillery, which had an infantry support. Blunt was joined by his cavalry, and the gun was taken by a vigorous charge and turned upon the Rebels. The latter were kept at bay until the main force was brought up and joined in the conflict. The Rebels believed we had a much larger number than we really possessed, else our first assault might have proved a sudden repulse. The same daring was kept up throughout the battle, and gave us the victory.

At this battle we captured four guns, two of which bore a history of more than ordinary interest. They were of the old "Bragg's Battery" that turned the scale at Buena Vista, in obedience to General Taylor's mandate, "Give them a little more grape, captain." After the Mexican war they were sent to the United States Arsenal at Baton Rouge, whence they were stolen when the insurrection commenced. They were used against us at Wilson Creek and Pea Ridge.

At another battle, whose name I have forgotten, our entire force of about two thousand men was deployed into a skirmish line that extended far beyond the enemy's flanks. The Rebels were nearly six thousand strong, and at first manifested a disposition to stand their ground. By the audacity of our stratagem they were completely deceived. So large a skirmish line was an indication of a proportionately strong force to support it. When they found us closing in upon their flanks, they concluded we were far superior in numbers, and certain to overwhelm them. With but slight resistance they fled the field, leaving much of their transportation and equipments to fall into our hands. We called in our skirmishers and pressed them in vigorous pursuit, capturing wagons and stragglers as we moved.

A year after this occurrence the Rebels played the same trick upon our own forces near Fort Smith, Arkansas, and were successful in driving us before them. With about five hundred cavalry they formed a skirmish line that outflanked our force of two thousand. We fell back several miles to the protection of the fort, where we awaited attack. It is needless to say that no assault was made.

Van Buren, Arkansas, was captured by eighteen men ten miles in advance of any support. This little force moved upon the town in a deployed line and entered at one side, while a Rebel regiment moved out at the other. Our men thought it judicious not to pursue, but established head-quarters, and sent a messenger to hurry up the column before the Rebels should discover the true state of affairs. The head of the column was five hours in making its appearance.

When the circumstance became known the next day, one of our officers found a lady crying very bitterly, and asked what calamity had befallen her.

As soon as she could speak she said, through her sobs:

"I am not crying because you have captured the place. We expected that." Then came a fresh outburst of grief.

"What *are* you crying for, then?" asked the officer.

"I am crying because you took it with only eighteen men, when we had a thousand that ran away from you!"

The officer thought the reason for her sorrow was amply sufficient, and allowed her to proceed with her weeping.

On the day of my arrival at Atchison there was more than ordinary excitement. For several months there had been much disregard of law outside of the most densely populated portions of the State. Robberies, and murders for the sake of robbery, were of frequent occurrence. In one week a dozen persons met violent deaths. A citizen remarked to me that he did not consider the times a great improvement over '55 and '56.

Ten days before my arrival, a party of ruffians visited the house of a citizen about twelve miles from Atchison, for the purpose of robbery. The man was supposed to have several hundred dollars in his possession--the proceeds of a sale of stock. He had placed his funds in a bank at Leavenworth; but his visitors refused to believe his statement to that effect. They maltreated the farmer and his wife, and ended by hanging the farmer's son to a rafter and leaving him for dead. In departing, they took away all the horses and mules they could find.

Five of these men were arrested on the following day, and taken to Atchison. The judge before whom they were brought ordered them committed for trial. On the way from the court-house to the jail the men were taken from the sheriff by a crowd of citizens. Instead of going to jail, they were carried to a grove near the town and placed on trial before a "Lynch" court. The trial was conducted with all solemnity, and with every display of impartiality to the accused. The jury decided that two of the prisoners, who had been most prominent in the outrage, should be hanged on that day, while the others were remanded to jail for a regular trial. One of the condemned was executed. The other, after having a rope around his neck, was respited and taken to jail.

On the same day two additional arrests were made, of parties concerned in the outrage. These men were tried by a "Lynch" court, as their companions had been tried on the previous day. One of them was hanged, and the other sent to jail.

For some time the civil power had been inadequate to the punishment of crime. The laws of the State were so loosely framed that offenders had excellent opportunities to escape their deserts by taking advantage of technicalities. The people determined to take the law into their own hands, and give it a thorough execution. For the good of society, it was necessary to put a stop to the outrages that had been so frequently committed. Their only course in such cases was to administer justice without regard to the ordinary forms.

A delegation of the citizens of Atchison visited Leavenworth after the arrests had been made, to confer with General Blunt, the commander of the District, on the best means of securing order. They made a full representation of the state of affairs, and requested that two of the prisoners, then in jail, should be delivered to the citizens for trial. They obtained an order to that effect, addressed to the sheriff, who was holding the prisoners in charge.

On the morning of the day following the reception of the order, people began to assemble in Atchison from all parts of the county to witness the trial. As nearly all the outrages had been committed upon the farmers who lived at distances from each other, the trial was conducted by the men from the rural districts. The residents of the city took little part in the affair. About ten o'clock in the forenoon a meeting was called to order in front of the court-house, where the following document was read:--

> HEAD-QUARTERS DISTRICT OF KANSAS,
> FORT LEAVENWORTH, *May* 22, 1863.
>
> TO THE SHERIFF OF ATCHISON COUNTY:
>
> SIR:--In view of the alarming increase of crime, the insecurity of life and property within this military district, the inefficiency of the civil law to punish offenders, and the small number of troops under my command making it impossible to give such protection to loyal and law-abiding citizens as I would otherwise desire; you will therefore deliver the prisoners, Daniel Mooney and Alexander Brewer, now in your possession, to the citizens of Atchison County, for trial and punishment by a citizens' court. This course, which in ordinary times and under different circumstances could not be tolerated, is rendered necessary for the protection of the property and lives of honest citizens against the lawless acts of thieves and assassins, who, of late, have been perpetrating their crimes with fearful impunity, and to prevent which nothing but the most severe and summary punishment will suffice. In conducting these irregular proceedings, it is to be hoped they will be controlled by men of respectability, and that cool judgment and discretion will characterize their actions, to the end that the innocent may be protected and the guilty punished.
>
> Respectfully, your obedient servant,
> JAMES G. BLUNT,
> *Major-General.*

After the reading of the above order, resolutions indorsing and sustaining the action of General Blunt were passed unanimously. The following resolutions were passed separately, their reading being greeted with loud cheers. They are examples of strength rather than of elegance.

"*Resolved,* That we pledge ourselves not to stop hanging until the thieves stop thieving.

"*Resolved,* That as this is a citizens' court, we have no use for lawyers, either for the accused or for the people."

A judge and jury were selected from the assemblage, and embraced some of the best known and most respected citizens of the county. Their selection was voted upon, just as if they had been the officers of a political gathering. As soon as elected, they proceeded to the trial of the prisoners.

The evidence was direct and conclusive, and the prisoners were sentenced to death by hanging. The verdict was read to the multitude, and a vote taken upon its acceptance or rejection. Nineteen-twentieths of those present voted that the sentence should be carried into execution.

The prisoners were taken from the court-house to the grove where the preceding executions had taken place. They were made to stand upon a high wagon while ropes were placed about their necks and attached to the limb of a large, spreading elm. When all was ready, the wagon was suddenly drawn from beneath the prisoners, and their earthly career was ended.

A half-hour later the crowd had dispersed. The following morning showed few traces of the excitement of the previous day. The executions were effectual in restoring quiet to the region which had been so much disturbed.

The Rebel sympathizers in St. Louis took many occasions to complain of the tyranny of the National Government. At the outset there was a delusion that the Government had no rights that should be respected, while every possible right belonged to the Rebels. General Lyon removed the arms from the St. Louis arsenal to a place of safety at Springfield, Illinois. "He had no constitutional right to do that," was the outcry of the Secessionists. He commenced the organization of Union volunteers for the defense of the city. The Constitution made no provision for this. He captured Camp Jackson, and took his prisoners to the arsenal. This, they declared, was a most flagrant violation of constitutional privileges. He moved upon the Rebels in the interior, and the same defiance of law was alleged. He suppressed the secession organ in St. Louis, thus trampling upon the liberties of the Rebel Press.

General Fremont declared the slaves of Rebels were free, and thus infringed upon the rights of property. Numbers of active, persistent traitors were arrested and sent to military prisons: a manifest tyranny on the part of the Government. In one way and another the unfortunate and long-suffering Rebels were most sadly abused, if their own stories are to be regarded.

It was forbidden to display Rebel emblems in public: a cruel restriction of personal right. The wealthy Secessionists of St. Louis were assessed the sum of ten thousand dollars, for the benefit of the Union refugees from Arkansas and other points in the Southwest. This was another outrage. These persons could not understand why they should be called upon to contribute to the support of Union people who had been rendered houseless and penniless by Rebels elsewhere. They made a most earnest protest, but their remonstrances were of no avail. In default of payment of the sums assessed, their superfluous furniture was seized and sold at auction. This was a violation of the laws that exempt household property from seizure.

The auction sale of these goods was largely attended. The bidding was very spirited. Pianos, ottomans, mirrors, sofas, chairs, and all the adornments of the homes of affluence, were sold for "cash in United States Treasury notes." Some of the parties assessed declared they would pay nothing on the assessment, but they reconsidered their decisions, and bought their own property at the auction-rooms, without regard to the prices they paid. In subsequent assessments they found it better to pay without hesitation whatever sums were demanded of them. They spoke and labored against the Union until they found such efforts were of no use. They could never understand why they should not enjoy the protection of the flag without being called upon to give it material aid.

In May, 1863, another grievance was added to the list. It became necessary, for the good of the city, to banish some of the more prominent Rebel sympathizers.

It was a measure which the Rebels and their friends opposed in the strongest terms. These persons were anxious to see the Confederacy established, but could not consent to live in its limits. They resorted to every device to evade the order, but were not allowed to remain. Representations of personal and financial inconvenience were of no avail; go they must.

The first exodus took place on the 13th of May. An immense crowd thronged the levee as the boat which was to remove the exiles took its departure. In all there were about thirty persons, half of them ladies. The men were escorted to the boat on foot, but the ladies were brought to the landing in carriages, and treated with every possible courtesy. A strong guard was posted at the landing to preserve order and allow no insult of any kind to the prisoners.

One of the young women ascended to the hurricane roof of the steamer and cheered for the "Confederacy." As the boat swung into the stream, this lady was joined by two others, and the trio united their sweet voices in singing "Dixie" and the "Bonnie Blue Flag." There was no cheering or other noisy demonstration at their departure, though there was a little waving of handkerchiefs, and a few tokens of farewell were given. This departure was soon followed by others, until St. Louis was cleared of its most turbulent spirits.

CHAPTER XXVII
GETTYSBURG

While in St. Louis, late in June, 1863, I received the following telegram:--

"HERALD OFFICE,
"NEW YORK, *June* 28.

"Report at Harrisburg, Pennsylvania, at the earliest possible moment."

Two hours later, I was traveling eastward as fast as an express train could carry me.

The Rebel army, under General Lee, had crossed the Potomac, and was moving toward Harrisburg. The Army of the Potomac was in rapid pursuit. A battle was imminent between Harrisburg and Baltimore.

Waiting a day at Harrisburg, I found the capital of the Keystone State greatly excited. The people were slow to move in their own behalf. Earthworks were being thrown up on the south bank of the Susquehanna, principally by the soldiers from other parts of Pennsylvania and from New York.

When it was first announced that the enemy was approaching, only seventeen men volunteered to form a local defense. I saw no such enthusiasm on the part of the inhabitants as I had witnessed at Cincinnati during the previous autumn. Pennsylvania sent many regiments to the field during the war, and her soldiers gained a fine reputation; but the best friends of the State will doubtless acknowledge that Harrisburg was slow to act when the Rebels made their last great invasion.

I was ordered to join the Army of the Potomac wherever I could find it. As I left Harrisburg, I learned that a battle was in progress. Before I could reach the field the great combat had taken place. The two contending armies had made Gettysburg historic.

I joined our army on the day after the battle. I could find no person of my acquaintance, amid the confusion that followed the termination of three days' fighting. The army moved in pursuit of Lee, whose retreat was just commencing. As our long lines stretched away toward the Potomac, I walked over the ground where the battle had raged, and studied the picture that was presented. I reproduce, in part, my letter of that occasion:--

"Gettysburg, Pennsylvania, *July* 6,1863.

"To-day I have passed along the whole ground where the lines of battle were drawn. The place bears evidence of a fierce struggle. The shocks of those two great armies surging and resurging, the one against the other, could hardly pass without leaving their traces in fearful characters. At Waterloo, at Wagram, and at Jena the wheat grows more luxuriantly, and the corn shoots its stalks further toward the sky than before the great conflicts that rendered those fields famous. The broad acres of Gettysburg and Antietam will in future years yield the farmer a richer return than he has hitherto received.

"Passing out of Gettysburg by the Baltimore turnpike, we come in a few steps to the entrance of the cemetery. Little of the inclosure remains, save the gateway, from which the gates have been torn. The neat wooden fence, first thrown down to facilitate the movement of our artillery, was used for fuel, as the soldiers made their camp on the spot. A few scattered palings are all that remain. The cemetery was such as we usually find near thrifty towns like Gettysburg. None of the monuments and adornings were highly expensive, though all were neat, and a few were elaborate. There was considerable taste displayed in the care of the grounds, as we can see from the few traces that remain. The eye is arrested by a notice, prominently posted, forbidding the destruction or mutilation of any shrub, tree, or stone about the place, under severe penalties. The defiance that war gives to the civil law is forcibly apparent as one peruses those warning lines.

"Monuments and head-stones lie everywhere overturned. Graves, which loving hands once carefully adorned, have been trampled by horses' feet until the vestiges of verdure have disappeared. The neat and well-trained shrubbery has vanished, or is but a broken and withered mass of tangled brushwood. On one grave lies the body of a horse, fast decomposing under the July sun. On another lie the torn garments of some wounded soldier, stained and saturated with blood. Across a small head-stone, bearing the words,

'To the memory of our beloved child, Mary,' lie the fragments of a musket shattered by a cannon-shot.

"In the center of a space inclosed by an iron fence, and containing a half-dozen graves, a few rails are standing where they were erected by our soldiers to form their shelter in bivouac. A family shaft has been broken in fragments by a shell. Stone after stone felt the effects of the *feu d'enfer* that was poured upon the crest of the hill. Cannon thundered, and foot and horse soldiers tramped over the resting-place of the dead. Other dead were added to those who are resting here. Many a wounded soldier lives to remember the contest above those silent graves.

"The hill on which this cemetery is located was the center of our line of battle and the key to our position. Had the Rebels been able to carry this point, they would have forced us into retreat, and the battle would have been lost. To pierce our line in this locality was Lee's great endeavor, and he threw his best brigades against it. Wave after wave of living valor rolled up that slope, only to roll back again under the deadly fire of our artillery and infantry. It was on this hill, a little to the right of the cemetery, where the 'Louisiana Tigers' made their famous charge. It was their boast that they were never yet foiled in an attempt to take a battery; but on this occasion they suffered a defeat, and were nearly annihilated. Sad and dispirited, they mourn their repulse and their terrible losses in the assault.

"From the summit of this hill a large portion of the battle-ground is spread out before the spectator. In front and at his feet lies the town of Gettysburg, containing, in quiet times, a population of four or five thousand souls. It is not more than a hundred yards to the houses in the edge of the village, where the contest with the Rebel sharp-shooters took place. To the left of the town stretches a long valley, bounded on each side by a gently-sloping ridge. The crest of each ridge is distant nearly a mile from the other. It was on these ridges that the lines of battle on the second and third days were formed, the Rebel line being on the ridge to the westward. The one stretching directly from our left hand, and occupied by our own men, has but little timber upon it, while that held by the rebels can boast of several groves of greater or less extent. In one of these the Pennsylvania College is embowered, while in another is seen the Theological Seminary. Half-way between the ridges are the ruins of a large brick building burned during the engagement. Dotted about, here and there, are various brick and frame structures. Two miles at our left rises a sharp-pointed elevation, known to the inhabitants of the region as Round Hill. Its sides are wooded, and the forest stretches from its base across the valley to the crest of the western ridge.

"It must not be supposed that the space between the ridges is an even plain, shaven with, the scythe and leveled with the roller. It rises and falls gently, and with little regularity, but in no place is it steep of ascent. Were it not for its ununiformity and for the occasional sprinkling of trees over its surface, it could be compared to a patch of rolling prairie in miniature. To the southwest of the further ridge is seen the mountain region of Western Maryland, behind which the Rebels had their line of retreat. It is not a wild, rough mass of mountains, but a region of hills of the larger and more inaccessible sort. They are traversed by roads only in a few localities, and their passage, except through, the gaps, is difficult for a single team, and impossible for an army.

"The Theological Seminary was the scene of a fierce struggle. It was beyond it where the First and Eleventh Corps contended with Ewell and Longstreet on the first day of the engagement. Afterward, finding the Rebels were too strong for them, they fell back to a new position, this building being included in the line. The walls of the Seminary were perforated by shot and shell, and the bricks are indented with numerous bullet-marks. Its windows show the effects of the musketry, and but little glass remains to shut out the cold and rain. The building is now occupied as a hospital by the Rebels. The Pennsylvania College is similarly occupied, and the instruction of its students is neglected for the present.

"In passing from the cemetery along the crest of the ridge where our line of battle stood, I first came upon the position occupied by some of our batteries. This is shown by the many dead horses lying unburied, and by the mounds which mark where others have been slightly covered up. There are additional traces of an artillery fight. Here is a broken wheel of a gun-carriage, an exploded caisson, a handspike, and some of the accoutrements of the men. In the fork of a tree I found a Testament, with the words, 'Charles Durrale, Corporal of Company G,' written on the fly-leaf. The guns and the gunners, have disappeared. Some of the latter are now with the column moving in pursuit of the enemy, others are suffering in the hospitals, and still others are resting where the bugle's reveille shall never wake them.

"Between the cemetery and the town and at the foot of the ridge where I stand, runs the road leading to Emmetsburg. It is not a turnpike, but a common dirt-road, and, as it leaves the main street leading into town, it makes a diagonal ascent of the hill. On the eastern side, this road is bordered by a stone wall for a short distance. Elsewhere on both sides there is only a rail fence. A portion of our sharp-shooters took position behind this wall, and erected traverses to protect them from a flanking fire, should the enemy attempt to move up the road from Gettysburg. These traverses are constructed at right angles to the wall, by making a 'crib' of fence-rails, two feet high and the same distance apart, and then filling the crib with dirt. Further along I find the rails from the western side of the road, piled against the fence on the east, so as to form a breast-work two or three feet in height--a few spadesful of dirt serve to fill the interstices. This defense was thrown up by the Rebels at the time they were holding the line of the roads.

"Moving to the left, I find still more severe traces of artillery fighting. Twenty-seven dead horses on a space of little more than one acre is evidence of heavy work. Here are a few scattered trees, which were evidently used as a screen for our batteries. These trees did not escape the storm of shot and shell that was rained in that direction. Some of them were perforated by cannon-shot, or have been completely cut off in that peculiar splintering that marks the course of a projectile through green wood. Near the scene of this fighting is a large pile of muskets and cartridge-boxes collected from the field. Considerable work has been done in thus gathering the débris of the battle, but it is by no means complete. Muskets, bayonets, and sabers are scattered everywhere.

"My next advance to the left carries me where the ground is thickly studded with graves. In one group I count a dozen graves of soldiers belonging to the Twentieth Massachusetts;

near them are buried the dead of the One Hundred and Thirty-seventh New York, and close at hand an equal number from the Twelfth New Jersey. Care has been taken to place a head-board at each grave, with a legible inscription thereon, showing whose remains are resting beneath. On one board the comrades of the dead soldier had nailed the back of his knapsack, which bore his name. On another was a brass plate, bearing the soldier's name in heavily stamped letters.

"Moving still to the left, I found an orchard in which the fighting appears to have been desperate in the extreme. Artillery shot had plowed the ground in every direction, and the trees did not escape the fury of the storm. The long bolts of iron, said by our officers to be a modification of the Whitworth projectile, were quite numerous. The Rebels must have been well supplied with this species of ammunition, and they evidently used it with no sparing hand. At one time I counted twelve of these bolts lying on a space not fifty feet square. I am told that many shot and shell passed over the heads of our soldiers during the action.

"A mile from our central position at the cemetery, was a field of wheat, and near it a large tract, on which corn had been growing. The wheat was trampled by the hurrying feet of the dense masses of infantry, as they changed their positions during the battle. In the cornfield artillery had been stationed, and moved about as often as the enemy obtained its range. Hardly a hill of corn is left in its pristine luxuriance. The little that escaped the hoof or the wheel, as the guns moved from place to place, was nibbled by hungry horses during the bivouac subsequent to the battle. Not a stalk of wheat is upright; not a blade of corn remains uninjured; all has fallen long before the time of harvest. Another harvest, in which Death was the reaper, has been gathered above it.

"On our extreme left the pointed summit of a hill, a thousand feet in elevation, rises toward the sky. Beyond it, the country falls off into the mountain region that extends to the Potomac and across it into Virginia. This hill is quite difficult of ascent, and formed a strong position, on which the left of our line rested. The enemy assaulted this point with great fury, throwing his divisions, one after the other, against it. Their efforts were of no avail. Our men defended their ground against every attack. It was like the dash of the French at Waterloo against the immovable columns of the English. Stubborn resistance overcame the valor of the assailants. Again and again they came to the assault, only to fall back as they had advanced. Our left held its ground, though it lost heavily.

"On this portion of the line, about midway between the crests of the ridges, is a neat farm-house. Around this dwelling the battle raged, as around Hougoumont at Waterloo. At one time it was in the possession of the Rebels, and was fiercely attacked by our men. The walls were pierced by shot and shell, many of the latter exploding within, and making a scene of devastation. The glass was shattered by rifle bullets on every side, and the wood-work bears testimony to the struggle. The sharp-shooters were in every room, and added to the disorder caused by the explosion of shells. The soldiers destroyed what the missiles spared. The Rebels were driven from the house, and the position was taken by our own men. They, in turn, were dislodged, but finally secured a permanent footing in the place.

"Retracing my steps from the extreme left, I return to the center of our position on Cemetery Hill. I do not follow the path by which I came, but take a route along the hollow, between the two ridges. It was across this hollow that the Rebels made their assaults upon our position. Much blood was poured out between these two swells of land. Most of the dead were buried where they fell, or gathered in little clusters beneath some spreading tree or beside clumps of bushes. Some of the Rebel dead are still unburied. I find one of these as I descend a low bank to the side of a small spring. The body is lying near the spring, as if the man had crawled there to obtain a draught of water. Its hands are outspread upon the earth, and clutching at the little tufts of grass beneath them. The soldier's haversack and canteen are still remaining, and his hat is lying not far away.

"A few paces distant is another corpse, with its hands thrown upward in the position the soldier occupied when he received his fatal wound. The clothing is not torn, no blood appears upon the garments, and the face, though swollen, bears no expression of anguish. Twenty yards away are the remains of a body cut in two by a shell. The grass is drenched in blood, that the rain of yesterday has not washed away. As

I move forward I find the body of a Rebel soldier, evidently slain while taking aim over a musket. The hands are raised, the left extended beyond the right, and the fingers of the former partly bent, as if they had just been grasping the stock of a gun. One foot is advanced, and the body is lying on its right side. To appearances it did not move a muscle after receiving its death-wound. Another body attracts my attention by its delicate white hands, and its face black as that of a negro.

"The farm-house on the Emmetsburg road, where General Meade held his head-quarters during the cannonade, is most fearfully cut up. General Lee masked his artillery, and opened with one hundred and thirty pieces at the same moment. Two shells in every second of time fell around those head-quarters. They tore through the little white building, exploding and scattering their fragments in every direction. Not a spot in its vicinity was safe. One shell through the door-step, another in the chimney, a third shattering a rafter, a fourth carrying away the legs of a chair in which an officer was seated; others severing and splintering the posts in front of the house, howling through the trees by which the dwelling was surrounded, and raising deep furrows in the soft earth. One officer, and another, and another were wounded. Strange to say, amid all this iron hail, no one of the staff was killed.

"Once more at the cemetery, I crossed the Baltimore turnpike to the hill that forms the extremity of the ridge, on which the main portion of our line of battle was located. I followed this ridge to the point held by our extreme right. About midway along the ridge was the scene of the fiercest attack upon that portion of the field. Tree after tree was scarred from base to limbs so thickly that it would have been impossible to place one's hand upon the trunk without covering the marks of a bullet. One tree was stripped of more than half its leaves; many of its twigs were partially severed, and hanging wilted and nearly ready to drop to the ground. The trunk of the tree, about ten inches in diameter, was cut and scarred in every part. The fire which struck these trees was that from our muskets upon the advancing Rebels. Every tree and bush for the distance of half a mile along these works was nearly as badly marked. The rocks, wherever they faced our breast-works, were thickly stippled with dots like snow-flakes. The missiles, flattened by contact with the rock, were lying among the leaves, giving little indication of their former character.

"Our sharp-shooters occupied novel positions. One of them found half a hollow log, standing upright, with a hole left by the removal of a knot, which gave him an excellent embrasure. Some were in tree-tops, others in nooks among the rocks, and others behind temporary barricades of their own construction. Owing to the excellence of our defenses, the Rebels lost heavily."

A few days after visiting this field, I joined the army in Western Maryland. The Rebels were between us and the Potomac. We were steadily pressing them, rather with a design of driving them across the Potomac without further fighting, than of bringing on an engagement. Lee effected his crossing in safety, only a few hundred men of his rear-guard being captured on the left bank of the Potomac.

The Maryland campaign was ended when Lee was driven out. Our army crossed the Potomac further down that stream, but made no vigorous pursuit. I returned to New York, and once more proceeded to the West.

Our victory in Pennsylvania was accompanied by the fall of Vicksburg and the surrender of Pemberton's army. A few days later, the capture of Port Hudson was announced. The struggle for the possession of the Mississippi was substantially ended when the Rebel fortifications along its banks fell into our hands.

CHAPTER XXVIII
IN THE NORTHWEST

Early in September, 1863, I found myself in Chicago, breathing the cool, fresh air from Lake Michigan. From Chicago to Milwaukee I skirted the shores of the lake, and from the latter city pushed across Wisconsin to the Mississippi River. Here it was really the blue Mississippi: its appearance was a pleasing contrast to the general features of the river a thousand miles below. The banks, rough and picturesque, rose abruptly from the water's edge, forming cliffs that overtopped the table-land beyond. These cliffs appeared in endless succession, as the boat on which I traveled steamed up the river toward St. Paul. Where the stream widened into Lake Pepin, they seemed more prominent and more precipitous than elsewhere, as the larger expanse of water was spread at their base. The promontory known as "Maiden's Rock" is the most conspicuous of all. The Indians relate that some daughter of the forest, disappointed in love, once leaped from its summit to the rough rocks, two hundred feet below. Her lover, learning her fate, visited the spot, gazed from the fearful height, and, after a prayer to the Great Spirit who watches over the Red Man--returned to his friends and broke the heart of another Indian maid.

Passing Lake Pepin and approaching St. Paul, the river became very shallow. There had been little rain during the summer, and the previous spring witnessed no freshet in that region. The effect was apparent in the condition of the Mississippi. In the upper waters boats moved with difficulty. The class that is said to steam wherever there is a heavy dew, was brought into active use. From St. Paul to a point forty miles below, only the lightest of the "stern-wheel" boats could make any headway. The inhabitants declared they had never before known such a low stage of water, and earnestly hoped it would not occur again. It was paralyzing much of the business of the State. Many flouring and lumber mills were lying idle. Transportation was difficult, and the rates very high. A railway was being constructed to connect with the roads from Chicago, but it was not sufficiently advanced to be of any service.

Various stories were in circulation concerning the difficulties of navigation on the Upper Mississippi in a low stage of water. One pilot declared the wheels of his boat actually raised a cloud of dust in many places. Another said his boat could run easily in the moisture on the outside of a pitcher of ice-water, but could not move to advantage in the river between Lake Pepin and St. Paul. A person interested in the railway proposed to secure a charter for laying the track in the bed of the Mississippi, but feared the company would be unable to supply the locomotives with water on many portions of the route. Many other jests were indulged in, all of which were heartily appreciated by the people of St. Paul.

The day after my arrival at St. Paul, I visited the famous Falls of the Minnehaha. I am unable to give them a minute description, my visit being very brief. Its brevity arose from the entire absence of water in the stream which supplies the fall. That fluid is everywhere admitted to be useful for purposes of navigation, and I think it equally desirable in the formation of a cascade.

The inhabitants of St. Paul have reason to bless the founders of their city for the excellent site of the future metropolis of the Northwest. Overlooking and almost overhanging the river in one part, in another it slopes gently down to the water's edge, to the levee where the steamers congregate. Back from the river the limits of the city extend for several miles, and admit of great expansion. With a hundred years of prosperity there would still be ample room for growth.

Before the financial crash in '57, this levee was crowded with merchandise from St. Louis and Chicago. Storage was not always to be had, though the construction of buildings was rapidly pushed. Business was active, speculation was carried to the furthest limit, everybody had money in abundance, and scattered it with no niggard hand. In many of the brokers' windows, placards were posted offering alluring inducements to capitalists. "Fifty per cent. guaranteed on investments," was set forth on these placards, the offers coming from parties considered perfectly sound. Fabulous sums were paid for wild land and for lots in apocryphal towns. All was prosperity and activity.

By-and-by came the crash, and this well-founded town passed through a period of mourning and fasting. St. Paul saw many of its best and heaviest houses vanish into thin air; merchants, bankers, land-speculators, lumbermen, all suffered alike. Some disappeared forever; others survived the shock, but never recovered their former footing. Large amounts of property went under the auctioneer's hammer, "to be sold without limit." Lots of land which cost two or three hundred dollars in '56, were sold at auction in '58 for five or six dollars each. Thousands of people lost their all in these unfortunate land-speculations. Others who survived the crash have clung to their acres, hoping that prosperity may return to the Northwest. At present their wealth consists mainly of Great Expectations.

Though suffering greatly, the capital and business center of Minnesota was by no means ruined. The speculators departed, but the farmers and other working classes remained. Business "touched bottom" and then slowly revived. St. Paul existed through all the calamity, and its people soon learned the actual necessities of Minnesota. While they mourn the departure of the "good times," many of them express a belief that those happy days were injurious to the permanent prosperity of the State.

St. Paul is one of the few cities of the world whose foundation furnishes the material for their construction. The limestone rock on which it is built is in layers of about a foot in thickness, and very easy to quarry. The blocks require little dressing to fit them for use. Though very soft at first, the stone soon hardens by exposure to the air, and forms a neat and durable wall. In digging a cellar one will obtain more than sufficient stone for the walls of his house.

At the time of my visit the Indian expedition of 1863 had just returned, and was camped near Fort Snelling. This expedition was sent out by General Pope, for the purpose of chastising the Sioux Indians. It was under command of General Sibley, and accomplished a march of nearly six hundred miles. As it lay in camp at Fort Snelling, the men and animals presented the finest appearance I had ever observed in an army just returned from a long campaign.

The Sioux massacres of 1862, and the campaign of General Pope in the autumn of that year, attracted much attention. Nearly all the settlers in the valley of the Minnesota above Fort Snelling were killed or driven off. Other localities suffered to a considerable extent. The murders--like nearly all murders of whites by the Indians--were of the most atrocious character. The history of those massacres is a chronicle of horrors rarely equaled during the present century. Whole counties were made desolate, and the young State, just recovering from its financial misfortunes, received a severe blow to its prosperity.

Various causes were assigned for the outbreak of hostilities on the part of the Sioux Indians. Very few residents of Minnesota, in view of the atrocities committed by the Indians, could speak calmly of the troubles. All were agreed that there could be no peace and security until the white men were the undisputed possessors of the land.

Before the difficulties began, there was for some time a growing discontent on the part of the Indians, on account of repeated grievances. Just previous to the outbreak, these Indians were summoned to one of the

Government Agencies to receive their annuities. These annuities had been promised them at a certain time, but were not forthcoming. The agents, as I was informed, had the money (in coin) as it was sent from Washington, but were arranging to pay the Indians in Treasury notes and pocket the premium on the gold. The Indians were kept waiting while the gold was being exchanged for greenbacks. There was a delay in making this exchange, and the Indians were put off from day to day with promises instead of money.

An Indian knows nothing about days of grace, protests, insolvency, expansions, and the other technical terms with which Wall Street is familiar. He can take no explanation of broken promises, especially when those promises are made by individuals who claim to represent the Great Father at Washington. In this case the Sioux lost all confidence in the agents, who had broken their word from day to day. Added to the mental annoyance, there was great physical suffering. The traders at the post would sell nothing without cash payment, and, without money, the Indians were unable to procure what the stores contained in abundance.

The annuities were not paid, and the traders refused to sell on credit. Some of the Indians were actually starving, and one day they forced their way into a store to obtain food. Taking possession, they supplied themselves with what they desired. Among other things, they found whisky, of the worst and most fiery quality. Once intoxicated, all the bad passions of the savages were let loose. In their drunken frenzy, the Indians killed one of the traders. The sight of blood made them furious. Other white men at the Agency were killed, and thus the contagion spread.

From the Agency the murderers spread through the valley of the St. Peter's, proclaiming war against the whites. They made no distinction of age or sex. The atrocities they committed are among the most fiendish ever recorded.

The outbreak of these troubles was due to the conduct of the agents who were dealing with the Indians. Knowing, as they should have known, the character of the red man everywhere, and aware that the Sioux were at that time discontented, it was the duty of those agents to treat them with the utmost kindness and generosity. I do not believe the Indians, when they plundered the store at the Agency, had any design beyond satisfying their hunger. But with one murder committed, there was no restraint upon their passions.

Many of our transactions with the Indians, in the past twenty years, have not been characterized by the most scrupulous honesty. The Department of the Interior has an interior history that would not bear investigation. It is well known that the furnishing of supplies to the Indians often enriches the agents and their political friends. There is hardly a tribe along our whole frontier that has not been defrauded. Dishonesty in our Indian Department was notorious during Buchanan's Administration. The retirement of Buchanan and his cabinet did not entirely bring this dishonesty to an end.

An officer of the Hudson Bay Company told me, in St. Paul, that it was the strict order of the British Government, enforced in letter and spirit by the Company, to keep full faith with the Indians. Every stipulation is most scrupulously carried out. The slightest infringement by a white man upon the rights of the Indians is punished with great severity. They are furnished with the best qualities of goods, and the quantity never falls below the stipulations. Consequently the Indian has no cause of complaint, and is kept on the most friendly terms. This officer said, "A white man can travel from one end to the other of our territory, with no fear of molestation. It is forty years since any trouble occurred between us and the Indians, while on your side of the line you have frequent difficulties."

The autumn of '62 witnessed the campaign for the chastisement of these Indians. Twenty-five thousand men were sent to Minnesota, under General Pope, and employed against the Sioux. In a wild country, like the interior of Minnesota, infantry cannot be used to advantage. On this account, the punishment of the Indians was not as complete as our authorities desired.

Some of the Indians were captured, some killed, and others surrendered. Thirty-nine of the captives were hanged. A hundred others were sent to prison at Davenport, Iowa, for confinement during life. The coming of Winter caused a suspension of hostilities.

The spring of 1863 opened with the outfitting of two expeditions--one to proceed through Minnesota, under General Sibley, and the other up the Missouri River, under General Sully. These expeditions were designed to unite somewhere on the Missouri River, and, by inclosing the Indians between them, to bring them to battle. If the plan was successful, the Indians would be severely chastised.

General Sibley moved across Minnesota, according to agreement, and General Sully advanced up the Missouri. The march of the latter was delayed on account of the unprecedented low water in the Missouri, which retarded the boats laden with supplies. Although the two columns failed to unite, they were partially successful in their primary object. Each column engaged the Indians and routed them with considerable loss.

After the return of General Sibley's expedition, a portion of the troops composing it were sent to the Southwest, and attached to the armies operating in Louisiana.

The Indian war in Minnesota dwindled to a fight on the part of politicians respecting its merits in the past, and the best mode of conducting it in the future. General Pope, General Sibley, and General Sully were praised and abused to the satisfaction of every resident of the State. Laudation and denunciation were poured out with equal liberality. The contest was nearly as fierce as the struggle between the whites and Indians. If epithets had been as fatal as bullets, the loss of life would have been terrible. Happily, the wordy battle was devoid of danger, and the State of Minnesota, her politicians, her generals, and her men emerged from it without harm.

Various schemes have been devised for placing the Sioux Indians where they will not be in our way. No spot of land can be found between the Mississippi and the Pacific where their presence would not be an annoyance to somebody. General Pope proposed to disarm these Indians, allot no more reservations to them, and allow no traders among them. He recommended that they be placed on Isle Royale, in Lake Superior, and there furnished with barracks, rations, and clothing, just as the same number of soldiers would be furnished. They should have no arms, and no means of escaping to the main-land. They would thus be secluded from all evil influence, and comfortably housed and cared for at Government expense. If this plan should be adopted, it would be a great relief to the people of our Northwestern frontier.

Minnesota has fixed its desires upon a railway to the Pacific. The "St. Paul and Pacific Railway" is already in operation about forty miles west of St. Paul, and its projectors hope, in time, to extend it to the shores of the "peaceful sea." It has called British capital to its aid, and is slowly but steadily progressing.

In the latter part of 1858 several enterprising citizens of St. Paul took a small steamer in midwinter from the upper waters of the Mississippi to the head of navigation, on the Red River of the North. The distance was two hundred and fifty miles, and the route lay through a wilderness. Forty yoke of oxen were required for moving the boat. When navigation was open in the spring of 1859, the boat (the *Anson Northrup*) steamed down to Fort Garry, the principal post of the Hudson Bay Company, taking all the inhabitants by surprise. None of them had any intimation of its coming, and were, consequently, as much astonished as if the steamer had dropped from the clouds.

The agents of the Hudson Bay Company purchased the steamer, a few hours after its arrival, for about four times its value. They hoped to continue their seclusion by so doing; but were doomed to disappointment. Another and larger boat was built in the following year at Georgetown, Minnesota, the spot where the *Northrup* was launched. The isolation of the fur-traders was ended. The owners of the second steamer (the *International*) were the proprietors of a stage and express line to all parts of Minnesota. They extended their line to Fort Garry, and soon established a profitable business.

From its organization in 1670, down to 1860, the Hudson Bay Company sent its supplies, and received its furs in return, by way of the Arctic Ocean and Hudson's Bay. There are only two months in the year in which a ship can enter or leave Hudson's Bay. A ship sailing from London in January, enters the Bay in August. When the cargo is delivered at York Factory, at the mouth of Nelson's River, it is too late in the season to send the goods to the great lakes of Northwestern America, where the trading posts are located. In the following May the goods are forwarded. They go by canoes where the river is navigable, and are carried on the backs of men around the frequent and sometimes long rapids. The journey requires three months.

The furs purchased with these goods cannot be sent to York Factory until a year later, and another year passes away before they leave Hudson's Bay. Thus, returns for a cargo were not received in London until four years after its shipment from that port.

Since American enterprise took control of the carrying trade, goods are sent from London to Fort Garry by way of New York and St. Paul, and are only four months in transit. Four or five months will be required to return a cargo of furs to London, making a saving of three years over the old route. Stupid as our English cousin sometimes shows himself, he cannot fail to perceive the advantages of the new route, and has promptly embraced them. The people of Minnesota are becoming well acquainted with the residents of the country on their northern boundary. Many of the Northwestern politicians are studying the policy of "annexation."

The settlement at Pembina, near Pembina Mountain, lies in Minnesota, a few miles only from the international line. The settlers supposed they were on British soil until the establishment of the boundary showed them their mistake. Every year the settlement sends a train to St. Paul, nearly seven hundred miles distant, to exchange its buffalo-robes, furs, etc., for various articles of necessity that the Pembina region does not produce. This annual train is made up of "Red River carts"--vehicles that would be regarded with curiosity in New York or Washington.

A Red River cart is about the size of a two-wheeled dray, and is built entirely of wood--not a particle of iron entering into its composition. It is propelled by a single ox or horse, generally the former, driven by a half-breed native. Sometimes, though not usually, the wheels are furnished with tires of rawhide, placed upon them when green and shrunk closely in drying. Each cart carries about a thousand pounds of freight, and the train will ordinarily make from fifteen to twenty miles a day. It was estimated that five hundred of these carts would visit St. Paul and St. Cloud in the autumn of 1863.

The settlements of which Fort Garry is the center are scattered for several miles along the Red River of the North. They have schools, churches, flouring and saw mills, and their houses are comfortably and often luxuriously furnished. They have pianos imported from St. Paul, and their principal church, has an organ. At St. Cloud I saw evidences of extreme civilization on their way to Fort Garry. These were a whisky-still, two sewing-machines, and a grain-reaper. No people can remain in darkness after adopting these modern inventions.

The monopoly which the Hudson Bay Company formerly held, has ceased to exist. Under its charter, granted by Charles II. in 1670, it had exclusive control of all the country drained by Hudson's Bay. In addition to its privilege of trade, it possessed the "right of eminent domain" and the full political management of the country. Crime in this territory was not punished by the officers of the British Government, but by the courts and officers of the Company. All settlements of farmers and artisans were discouraged, as it was the desire of the Company to maintain the territory solely as a fur preserve, from the Arctic Ocean to the United States boundary.

The profits of this fur-trade were enormous, as the Company had it under full control. The furs were purchased of the Indians and trappers at very low rates, and paid for in goods at enormous prices. An industrious trapper could earn a comfortable support, and nothing more.

Having full control of the fur market in Europe, the directors could regulate the selling prices as they chose. Frequently they issued orders forbidding the killing of a certain class of animals for several years. The fur from these animals would become scarce and very high, and at the same time the animals would increase in numbers. Suddenly, when the market was at its uppermost point, the order would be countermanded and a large supply brought forward for sale. This course was followed with all classes of fur in succession. The Company's dividends in the prosperous days would shame the best oil wells or Nevada silver mines of our time.

Though its charter was perpetual, the Hudson Bay Company was obliged to obtain once in twenty-one years a renewal of its license for exclusive trade. From 1670 to 1838 it had no difficulty in obtaining the desired renewal. The last license expired in 1859. Though a renewal was earnestly sought, it was not attained. The territory is now open to all traders, and the power of the old Company is practically extinguished.

The first explorations in Minnesota were made shortly after the discovery of the Mississippi River by Marquette and Hennepin. St. Paul was originally a French trading post, and the resort of the Indians throughout the Northwest. Fort Snelling was established by the United Suites Government in 1819, but no settlements were made until 1844. After the current of emigration began, the territory was rapidly filled.

While Minnesota was a wilderness, the American Fur Company established posts on the upper waters of the Mississippi. The old trading-house below the Falls of St. Anthony, the first frame building erected in the territory, is yet standing, though it exhibits many symptoms of decay.

At one time the emigration to Minnesota was very great, but it has considerably fallen off during the last eight years. The State is too far north to hold out great inducements to settlers. The winters are long and severe, and the productions of the soil are limited in character and quantity. In summer the climate is excellent, attracting large numbers of pleasure-seekers. The Falls of St. Anthony and the Minnehaha have a world-wide reputation.

CHAPTER XXIX
INAUGURATION OF A GREAT ENTERPRISE

I have elsewhere alluded to the orders of General Grant at Lagrange, Tennessee, in the autumn of 1862, relative to the care of the negroes where his army was then operating.

The plan was successful in providing for the negroes in Tennessee and Northern Mississippi, where the number, though large, was not excessive. At that time, the policy of arming the blacks was being discussed in various quarters. It found much opposition. Many persons thought it would be an infringement upon the "rights" of the South, both unconstitutional and unjust. Others cared nothing for the South, or its likes and dislikes, but opposed the measure on the ground of policy. They feared its adoption would breed discontent among the white soldiers of the army, and cause so many desertions and so much uneasiness that the importance of the new element would be more than neutralized. Others, again, doubted the courage of the negroes, and thought their first use under fire would result in disgrace and disaster to our arms. They opposed the experiment on account of this fear.

In South Carolina and in Kansas the negroes had been put under arms and mustered into service as Union soldiers. In engagements of a minor character they had shown coolness and courage worthy of veterans. There was no valid reason why the negroes along the Mississippi would not be just as valuable in the army, as the men of the same race in other parts of the country. Our Government determined to try the experiment, and make the *Corps d'Afrique* a recognized and important adjunct of our forces in the field.

When General Grant encamped his army at Milliken's Bend and Young's Point, preparatory to commencing the siege of Vicksburg, many of the cotton plantations were abandoned by their owners. Before our advent nearly all the white males able to bear arms had, willingly or unwillingly, gone to aid in filling the ranks of the insurgents. On nearly every plantation there was a white man not liable to military service, who remained to look after the interests of the property. When our army appeared, the majority of these white men fled to the interior of Louisiana, leaving the plantations and the negroes to the tender mercy of the invaders. In some cases the fugitives took the negroes with them, thus leaving the plantations entirely deserted.

When the negroes remained, and the plantations were not supplied with provisions, it became necessary for the Commissary Department to issue rations for the subsistence of the blacks. As nearly all the planters cared nothing for the negroes they had abandoned, there was a very large number that required the attention of the Government.

On many plantations the cotton crop of 1862 was still in the field, somewhat damaged by the winter rains; but well worth gathering at the prices which then ruled the market. General Grant gave authority for the gathering of this cotton by any parties who were willing to take the contract. The contractors were required to feed the negroes and pay them for their labor. One-half the cotton went to the Government, the balance to the contractor. There was no lack of men to undertake the collection of abandoned cotton on these terms, as the enterprise could not fail to be exceedingly remunerative.

This cotton, gathered by Government authority, was, with a few exceptions, the only cotton which could be shipped to market. There were large quantities of "old" cotton--gathered and baled in previous years--which the owners were anxious to sell, and speculators ready to buy. Numerous applications were made for shipping-permits, but nearly all were rejected. A few cases were pressed upon General Grant's attention, as deserving exception from the ordinary rule.

There was one case of two young girls, whose parents had recently died, and who were destitute of all comforts on the plantation where they lived. They had a quantity of cotton which they wished to take to Memphis, for sale in that market. Thus provided with money, they would proceed North, and remain there till the end of the war.

A speculator became interested in these girls, and plead with all his eloquence for official favor in their behalf. General Grant softened his heart and gave this man a written permit to ship whatever cotton belonged to the orphans. It was understood, and so stated in the application, that the amount was between two hundred and three hundred bales. The exact number not being known, there was no quantity specified in the permit.

The speculator soon discovered that the penniless orphans could claim two thousand instead of two hundred bales, and thought it possible they would find three thousand bales and upward. On the strength of his permit without special limit, he had purchased, or otherwise procured, all the cotton he could find in the immediate vicinity. He was allowed to make shipment of a few hundred bales; the balance was detained.

Immediately, as this transaction became known, every speculator was on the *qui vive* to discover a widow or an orphan. Each plantation was visited, and the status of the owners, if any remained, became speedily known. Orphans and widows, the former in particular, were at a high premium. Never in the history of Louisiana did the children of tender years, bereft of parents, receive such attention from strangers. A spectator might have imagined the Millennium close at hand, and the dealers in cotton about to be humbled at the feet of babes and sucklings. Widows, neither young nor comely, received the warmest attention from men of Northern birth. The family of John Rodgers, had it then lived at Milliken's Bend, would have been hailed as a "big thing." Everywhere in that region there were men seeking "healthy orphans for adoption."

The majority of the speculators found the widows and orphans of whom they were in search. Some were able to obtain permits, while others were not. Several officers of the army became interested in these speculations, and gave their aid to obtain shipping privileges. Some who were innocent were accused of dealing in the forbidden fiber, while others, guilty of the transaction, escaped without suspicion. The temptation was great. Many refused to be concerned in the traffic; but there were some who yielded.

The contractors who gathered the abandoned cotton were enabled to accumulate small fortunes. Some of them acted honestly, but others made use of their contracts to cover large shipments of purchased or stolen cotton, baled two or three years before. The ordinary yield of an acre of ground is from a bale to a bale and a half. The contractors were sometimes able to show a yield of ten or twenty bales to the acre.

About the first of April, Adjutant-General Thomas arrived at Milliken's Bend, bringing, as he declared, authority to regulate every thing as he saw fit. Under his auspices, arrangements were made for putting the able-bodied male negroes into the army. In a speech delivered at a review of the troops at Lake Providence, he announced the determination of the Government to use every just measure to suppress the Rebellion.

The Rebels indirectly made use of the negroes against the Government, by employing them in the production of supplies for their armies in the field. "In this way," he said, "they can bring to bear against us all the power of their so-called Confederacy. At the same time we are compelled to retain at home a portion of our fighting force to furnish supplies for the men at the front. The Administration has determined to take the negroes belonging to disloyal men, and make them a part of the army. This is the policy that has been fixed and will be fully carried out."

General Thomas announced that he brought authority to raise as many regiments as possible, and to give commissions to all proper persons who desired them. The speech was listened to with attention, and loudly cheered at its close. The general officers declared themselves favorable to the new movement, and gave it their co-operation. In a few days a half-dozen regiments were in process of organization. This was the beginning of the scheme for raising a large force of colored soldiers along the Mississippi.

The disposition to be made of the negro women and children in our lines, was a subject of great importance. Their numbers were very large, and constantly increasing. Not a tenth of these persons could find employment in gathering abandoned cotton. Those that found such employment were only temporarily provided for. It would be a heavy burden upon the Government to support them in idleness during the entire summer. It would be manifestly wrong to send them to the already overcrowded camps at Memphis and Helena. They were upon our hands by the fortune of war, and must be cared for in some way.

The plantations which their owners had abandoned were supposed to afford the means of providing homes for the negroes, where they could be sheltered, fed, and clothed without expense to the Government. It was proposed to lease these plantations for the term of one year, to persons who would undertake the production of a crop of cotton. Those negroes who were unfit for military service were to be distributed on these plantations, where the lessees would furnish them all needed supplies, and pay them for their labor at certain stipulated rates.

The farming tools and other necessary property on the plantations were to be appraised at a fair valuation, and turned over to the lessees. Where the plantations were destitute of the requisite number of mules for working them, condemned horses and mules were loaned to the lessees, who should return them whenever called for. There were promises of protection against Rebel raids, and of all assistance that the Government could consistently give. General Thomas announced that the measure was fully decided upon at Washington, and should receive every support.

The plantations were readily taken, the prospects being excellent for enormous profits if the scheme proved successful. The cost of producing cotton varies from three to eight cents a pound. The staple would find ready sale at fifty cents, and might possibly command a higher figure. The prospects of a large percentage on the investment were alluring in the extreme. The plantations, the negroes, the farming utensils, and the working stock were to require no outlay. All that was demanded before returns would be received, were the necessary expenditures for feeding and clothing the negroes until the crop was made and gathered. From five to thirty thousand dollars was the estimated yearly expense of a plantation of a thousand acres. If successful, the products for a year might be set down at two hundred thousand dollars; and should cotton appreciate, the return would be still greater.

CHAPTER XXX
COTTON-PLANTING IN 1863

It was late in the season before the plantations were leased and the work of planting commenced. The ground was hastily plowed and the seed as hastily sown. The work was prosecuted with the design of obtaining as much as possible in a single season. In their eagerness to accumulate fortunes, the lessees frequently planted more ground than they could care for, and allowed much of it to run to waste.

Of course, it could not be expected the Rebels would favor the enterprise. They had prophesied the negro would not work when free, and were determined to break up any effort to induce him to labor. They were not even willing to give him a fair trial. Late in June they visited the plantations at Milliken's Bend and vicinity.

They stripped many of the plantations of all the mules and horses that could be found, frightened some of the negroes into seeking safety at the nearest military posts, and carried away others. Some of the lessees were captured; others, having timely warning, made good their escape. Of those captured, some were released on a regular parole not to take up arms against the "Confederacy." Others were liberated on a promise to go North and remain there, after being allowed a reasonable time for settling their business. Others were carried into captivity and retained as prisoners of war until late in the summer. A Mr. Walker was taken to Brownsville, Texas, and there released, with the privilege of crossing to Matamoras, and sailing thence to New Orleans. It was six months from the time of his capture before he reached New Orleans on his return home.

The Rebels made a fierce attack upon the garrison at Milliken's Bend. For a few moments during the fight the prospects of their success were very good. The negroes composing the garrison had not been long under arms, and their discipline was far from perfect. The Rebels obtained possession of a part of our works, but were held at bay by the garrison, until the arrival of a gun-boat turned the scale in our favor. The odds were against us at the outset, but we succeeded in putting the enemy to flight.

In this attack the Rebels made use of a movable breast-work, consisting of a large drove of mules, which they kept in their front as they advanced upon the fort. This breast-work served very well at first, but grew unmanageable as our fire became severe. It finally broke and fled to the rear, throwing the Rebel lines into confusion. I believe it was the first instance on record where the defenses ran away, leaving the defenders uncovered. It marked a new, but unsuccessful, phase of war. An officer who was present at the defense of Milliken's Bend vouches for the truth of the story.

The Rebels captured a portion of the garrison, including some of the white officers holding commissions in negro regiments. The negro prisoners were variously disposed of. Some were butchered on the spot while pleading for quarter; others were taken a few miles on the retreat, and then shot by the wayside. A few were driven away by their masters, who formed a part of the raiding force, but they soon escaped and returned to our lines. Of the officers who surrendered as prisoners of war, some were shot or hanged within a short distance of their place of capture. Two were taken to Shreveport and lodged in jail with one of the captured lessees. One night these officers were taken from the jail by order of General Kirby Smith, and delivered into the hands of the provost-marshal, to be shot for the crime of accepting commissions in negro regiments. Before morning they were dead.

Similar raids were made at other points along the river, where plantations were being cultivated under the new system. At all these places the mules were stolen and the negroes either frightened or driven away. Work was suspended until the plantations could be newly stocked and equipped. This suspension occurred at the busiest time in the season. The production of the cotton was, consequently, greatly retarded. On some plantations the weeds grew faster than the cotton, and refused to be put down. On others, the excellent progress the weeds had made, during the period of idleness, rendered the yield of the cotton-plant very small. Some of the plantations were not restocked after the raid, and speedily ran to waste.

In 1863, no lessee made more than half an ordinary crop of *cotton*, and very few secured even this return. Some obtained a quarter or an eighth of a bale to the acre, and some gathered only one bale where they should have gathered twelve or twenty. A few lost money in the speculation. Some made a fair profit on their investment, and others realized their expectations of an enormous reward. Several parties united their interest on three or four plantations in different localities, so that a failure in one quarter was offset by success in another.

The majority of the lessees were unprincipled men, who undertook the enterprise solely as a speculation. They had as little regard for the rights of the negro as the most brutal slaveholder had ever shown. Very few of them paid the negroes for their labor, except in furnishing them small quantities of goods, for which they charged five times the value. One man, who realized a profit of eighty thousand dollars, never paid his negroes a penny. Some of the lessees made open boast of having swindled their negroes out of their summer's wages, by taking advantage of their ignorance.

The experiment did not materially improve the condition of the negro, save in the matter of physical treatment. As a slave the black man received no compensation for his labor. As a free man, he received none.

He was well fed, and, generally, well clothed. He received no severe punishment for non-performance of duty, as had been the case before the war. The difference between working for nothing as a slave, and working for the same wages under the Yankees, was not always perceptible to the unsophisticated negro.

Several persons leased plantations that they might use them as points for shipping purchased or stolen cotton. Some were quite successful in this, while others were unable to find any cotton to bring out. Various parties united with the plantation-owners, and agreed to obtain all facilities from the Government officials, if their associates would secure protection against Rebel raids. In some cases this experiment was successful, and the plantations prospered, while those around them were repeatedly plundered. In others, the Rebels were enraged at the plantation-owners for making any arrangements with "the Yankees," and treated them with merciless severity. There was no course that promised absolute safety, and there was no man who could devise a plan of operations that would cover all contingencies.

Every thing considered, the result of the free-labor enterprise was favorable to the pockets of the avaricious lessees, though it was not encouraging to the negro and to the friends of justice and humanity. All who had been successful desired to renew their leases for another season. Some who were losers were willing to try again and hope for better fortune.

All the available plantations in the vicinity of Vicksburg, Milliken's Bend, and other points along that portion of the Mississippi were applied for before the beginning of the New Year. Application for these places were generally made by the former lessees or their friends. The prospects were good for a vigorous prosecution of the free-labor enterprise during 1864.

In the latter part of 1863, I passed down the Mississippi, *en route* to New Orleans. At Vicksburg I met a gentleman who had been investigating the treatment of the negroes under the new system, and was about making a report to the proper authorities. He claimed to have proof that the agents appointed by General Thomas had not been honest in their administration of affairs.

One of these agents had taken five plantations under his control, and was proposing to retain them for another year. It was charged that he had not paid his negroes for their labor, except in scanty supplies of clothing, for which exorbitant prices were charged. He had been successful with his plantations, but delivered very little cotton to the Government agents.

The investigations into the conduct of agents and lessees were expected to make a change in the situation. Up to that time the War Department had controlled the whole system of plantation management. The Treasury Department was seeking the control, on the ground that the plantations were a source of revenue to the Government, and should be under its financial and commercial policy. If it could be proved that the system pursued was an unfair and dishonest one, there was probability of a change.

I pressed forward on my visit to New Orleans. On my return, two weeks later, the agents of General Thomas were pushing their plans for the coming year. There was no indication of an immediate change in the management. The duties of these agents had been enlarged, and the region which they controlled extended from Lake Providence, sixty miles above Vicksburg, to the mouth of Red River, nearly two hundred miles below. One of the agents had his office at Lake Providence, a second was located at Vicksburg, while the third was at Natchez.

Nearly all the plantations near Lake Providence had been leased or applied for. The same was the case with most of those near Vicksburg. In some instances, there were several applicants for the same plantation. The agents announced their determination to sell the choice of plantations to the highest bidder. The competition for the best places was expected to be very active.

There was one pleasing feature. Some of the applicants for plantations were not like the sharp-eyed speculators who had hitherto controlled the business. They seemed to be men of character, desirous of experimenting with free labor for the sake of demonstrating its feasibility when skillfully and honestly managed. They hoped and believed it would be profitable, but they were not undertaking the enterprise solely with a view to money-making. The number of these men was not large, but their presence, although in small force, was exceedingly encouraging.

I regret to say that these men were outstripped in the struggle for good locations by their more unscrupulous competitors. Before the season was ended, the majority of the honest men abandoned the field.

During 1863, many negroes cultivated small lots of ground on their own account. Sometimes a whole family engaged in the enterprise, a single individual having control of the matter. In other cases, two, three, or a half-dozen negroes would unite their labor, and divide the returns. One family of four persons sold twelve bales of cotton, at two hundred dollars per bale, as the result of eight months' labor. Six negroes who united their labor were able to sell twenty bales. The average was about one and a half or two bales to each of those persons who attempted the planting enterprise on their own account. A few made as high as four bales each, while others did not make more than a single bale. One negro, who was quite successful in planting on his own account, proposed to take a small plantation in 1864, and employ twenty or more colored laborers. How he succeeded I was not able to ascertain.

The commissioners in charge of the freedmen gave the negroes every encouragement to plant on their own account. In 1864 there were thirty colored lessees near Milliken's Bend, and about the same number at Helena. Ten of these persons at Helena realized $31,000 for their year's labor. Two of them planted forty acres in cotton; their expenses were about $1,200; they sold their crop for $8,000. Another leased twenty-four acres. His expenses were less than $2,000, and he sold his crop for $6,000. Another leased seventeen acres. He earned by the season's work enough to purchase a good house, and leave him a cash balance of $300. Another leased thirteen and a half acres, expended about $600 in its cultivation, and sold his crop for $4,000.

At Milliken's Bend the negroes were not as successful as at Helena-- much of the cotton crop being destroyed by the "army worm." It is possible that the return of peace may cause a discontinuance of the policy of leasing land to negroes.

The planters are bitterly opposed to the policy of dividing plantations into small parcels, and allowing them to be cultivated by freedmen. They believe in extensive tracts of land under a single management, and endeavor to make the production of cotton a business for the few rather than the many. It has always been the rule to discourage small planters. No aristocratic proprietor, if he could avoid it, would sell any portion of his estate to a man of limited means. In the hilly portions of the South, the rich men were unable to carry out their policy. Consequently, there were many who cultivated cotton on a small scale. On the lower Mississippi this was not the case.

When the Southern States are fairly "reconstructed," and the political control is placed in the hands of the ruling race, every effort will be made to maintain the old policy. Plantations of a thousand or of three thousand acres will be kept intact, unless the hardest necessity compels their division. If possible, the negroes will not be permitted to possess or cultivate land on their own account. To allow them to hold real estate will be partially admitting their claim to humanity. No true scion of chivalry can permit such an innovation, so long as he is able to make successful opposition.

I have heard Southern men declare that a statute law should, and would, be made to prevent the negroes holding real estate. I have no doubt of the disposition of the late Rebels in favor of such enactment, and believe they would display the greatest energy in its enforcement. It would be a labor of love on their part, as well as of duty. Its success would be an obstacle in the way of the much-dreaded "negro equality."

CHAPTER XXXI
AMONG THE OFFICIALS

In my visit to Vicksburg I was accompanied by my fellow-journalist, Mr. Colburn, of *The World*. Mr. Colburn and myself had taken more than an ordinary interest in the free-labor enterprise. We had watched its inception eight months before, with many hopes for its success, and with as many fears for the result. The experiment of 1863, under all its disadvantages, gave us convincing proof that the production of cotton and sugar by free labor was both possible and profitable. The negro had proved the incorrectness of the slaveholders' assertion that no black man would labor on a plantation except as a slave. So much we had seen accomplished. It was the result of a single year's trial. We desired to see a further and more extensive test.

While studying the new system in the hands of others, we were urged to bring it under our personal observation. Various inducements were held out. We were convinced of the general feasibility of the enterprise, wherever it received proper attention. As a philanthropic undertaking, it was commendable. As a financial experiment, it promised success. We looked at the matter in all its aspects, and finally decided to gain an intimate knowledge of plantation life in war-time. Whether we succeeded or failed, we would learn more about the freedmen than we had hitherto known, and would assist, in some degree, to solve the great problem before the country. Success would be personally profitable, while failure could not be disastrous.

We determined to lease a plantation, but had selected none. In her directions for cooking a hare, Mrs. Glass says: "First, catch your hare." Our animal was to be caught, and the labor of securing it proved greater than we anticipated.

All the eligible locations around Vicksburg had been taken by the lessees of the previous season, or by newly-arrived persons who preceded us. There were several residents of the neighboring region who desired persons from the North to join them in tilling their plantations. They were confident of obtaining Rebel protection, though by no means certain of securing perfect immunity. In each case they demanded a cash advance of a few thousands, for the purpose of hiring the guerrillas to keep the peace. As it was evident that the purchase of one marauding band would require the purchase of others, until the entire "Confederacy" had been bought up, we declined all these proposals.

Some of these residents, who wished Northern men to join them, claimed to have excellent plantations along the Yazoo, or near some of its tributary bayous. These men were confident a fine cotton crop could be made, "if there were some Northern man to manage the niggers." It was the general complaint with the people who lived in that region that, with few exceptions, no Southern man could induce the negroes to continue at work. One of these plantation proprietors said his location was such that no guerrilla could get near it without endangering his life. An investigation showed that no other person could reach the plantation without incurring a risk nearly as great. Very few of these owners of remote plantations were able to induce strangers to join them.

We procured a map of the Mississippi and the country bordering its banks. Whenever we found a good location and made inquiry about it at the office of the leasing agents, we were sure to ascertain that some one had already filed an application. It was plain that Vicksburg was not the proper field for our researches. We shook its dust from our feet and went to Natchez, a hundred and twenty-five miles below, where a better prospect was afforded.

In the spring of 1863, the Rebels felt confident of retaining permanent possession of Vicksburg and Port Hudson, two hundred and fifty miles apart. Whatever might be the result elsewhere, this portion of the Mississippi should not be abandoned. In the belief that the progress of the Yankees had been permanently stopped, the planters in the locality mentioned endeavored to make as full crops as possible of the great staple of the South. Accordingly, they plowed and planted, and tended the growing cotton until midsummer came. On the fourth of July, Vicksburg surrendered, and opened the river to Port Hudson. General Herron's Division was sent to re-enforce General Banks, who was besieging the latter place. In a few days, General Gardner hauled down his flag and gave Port Hudson to the nation. "The Father of Waters went unvexed to the Sea."

The rich region that the Rebels had thought to hold was, by the fortune of war, in the possession of the National army. The planters suspended their operations, through fear that the Yankees would possess the land.

Some of them sent their negroes to the interior of Louisiana for safety. Others removed to Texas, carrying all their human property with them. On some plantations the cotton had been so well cared for that it came to maturity in fine condition. On others it had been very slightly cultivated, and was almost choked out of existence by weeds and grass. Nearly every plantation could boast of more or less cotton in the field--the quantity varying from twenty bales to five hundred. On some plantations cotton had been neglected, and a large crop of corn grown in its place. Everywhere the Rebel law had been obeyed by the production of more corn than usual. There was enough for the sustenance of our armies for many months.

Natchez was the center of this newly-opened region. Before the war it was the home of wealthy slave-owners, who believed the formation of a Southern Confederacy would be the formation of a terrestrial paradise. On both banks of the Mississippi, above and below Natchez, were the finest cotton plantations of the great valley. One family owned nine plantations, from which eight thousand bales of cotton were annually sent to market. Another family owned seven plantations, and others were the owners of from three to six, respectively.

The plantations were in the care of overseers and agents, and rarely visited by their owners. The profits were large, and money was poured out in profusion. The books of one of the Natchez banks showed a daily business, in the picking season, of two or three million dollars, generally on the accounts of planters and their factors.

Prior to the Rebellion, cotton was usually shipped to New Orleans, and sold in that market. There were some of the planters who sent their cotton to Liverpool or Havre, without passing it through the hands of New Orleans factors. A large balance of the proceeds of such shipments remained to the credit of the shippers when the war broke out, and saved them from financial ruin. The business of Natchez amounted, according to the season, from a hundred thousand to three hundred thousand bales. This included a great quantity that was sent to New Orleans from plantations above and below the city, without touching at all upon the levee at Natchez.

Natchez consists of Natchez-on-the-Hill and Natchez-under-the-Hill. A bluff, nearly two hundred feet high, faces the Mississippi, where there is an eastward bend of the stream. Toward the river this bluff is almost perpendicular, and is climbed by three roads cut into its face like inclined shelves. The French established a settlement at this point a hundred and fifty years ago, and erected a fortification for its defense. This work, known as Fort Rosalie, can still be traced with distinctness, though it has fallen into extreme decay. It was evidently a rectangular, bastioned work, and the location of the bastions and magazine can be readily made out.

Natchez-under-the-Hill is a small, straggling village, having a few commission houses and stores, and dwellings of a suspicious character.

It was once a resort of gamblers and other *chevaliers d'industrie*, whose livelihood was derived from the travelers along the Mississippi. At present it is somewhat shorn of its glory.

Natchez-on-the-Hill is a pleasant and well-built city, of about ten thousand inhabitants. The buildings display wealth and good taste, the streets are wide and finely shaded, and the abundance of churches speaks in praise of the religious sentiment of the people. Near the edge of the bluff there was formerly a fine park, commanding a view of the river for several miles in either direction, and overlooking the plantations and cypress forests on the opposite shore. This pleasure-ground was reserved for the white people alone, no negro being allowed to enter the inclosure under severe penalties. A regiment of our soldiers encamped near this park, and used its fence for fuel. The park is now free to persons of whatever color.

Natchez suffered less from the war than most other places of its size along the Mississippi. The Rebels never erected fortifications in or around Natchez, having relied upon Vicksburg and Port Hudson for their protection. When Admiral Farragut ascended the river, in 1862, after the fall of New Orleans, he promised that Natchez should not be disturbed, so long as the people offered no molestation to our gun-boats or army transports. This neutrality was carefully observed, except on one occasion. A party which landed from the gun-boat *Essex* was fired upon by a militia company that desired to distinguish itself. Natchez was shelled for two hours, in retaliation for this outrage. From that time until our troops occupied the city there was no disturbance.

When we arrived at Natchez, we found several Northern men already there, whose business was similar to our own. Some had secured plantations, and were preparing to take possession. Others were watching the situation and surveying the ground before making their selections. We found that the best plantations in the vicinity had been taken by the friends of Adjutant-General Thomas, and were gone past our securing. At Vidalia, Louisiana, directly opposite Natchez, were two fine plantations, "Arnuldia" and "Whitehall," which had been thus appropriated. Others in their vicinity had been taken in one way or another, and were out of our reach. Some of the lessees declared they had been forced to promise a division with certain parties in authority before obtaining possession, while others maintained a discreet silence on the subject. Many plantations owned by widows and semi-loyal persons, would not be placed in the market as "abandoned property." There were many whose status had not been decided, so that they were practically out of the market. In consequence of these various drawbacks, the number of desirable locations that were open for selection was not large.

One of the leasing agents gave us a letter to a young widow who resided in the city, and owned a large plantation in Louisiana, fifteen miles from Natchez. We lost no time in calling upon the lady.

Other parties had already seen her with a view to leasing her plantation. Though she had promised the lease to one of these visitors, she had no objections to treating with ourselves, provided she could make a more advantageous contract.

In a few days we repeated our visit. Our rival had urged his reasons for consideration, and was evidently in favor. He had claimed to be a Secessionist, and assured her he could obtain a safeguard from the Rebel authorities. The lady finally consented to close a contract with him, and placed us in the position of discarded suitors. We thought of issuing a new edition of "The Rejected Addresses."

CHAPTER XXXII
A JOURNEY OUTSIDE THE LINES

Mr. Colburn went to St. Louis, on business in which both were interested, and left me to look out a plantation. I determined to make a tour of exploration in Louisiana, in the region above Vidalia. With two or three gentlemen, who were bound on similar business, I passed our pickets one morning, and struck out into the region which was dominated by neither army. The weather was intensely cold, the ground frozen solid, and a light snow falling.

Cold weather in the South has one peculiarity: it can seem more intense than the same temperature at the North. It is the effect of the Southern climate to unfit the system for any thing but a warm atmosphere. The chill penetrates the whole body with a severity I have never known north of the Ohio River. In a cold day, the "Sunny South" possesses very few attractions in the eyes of a stranger.

In that day's ride, and in the night which followed, I suffered more than ever before from cold. I once passed a night in the open air in the Rocky Mountains, with the thermometer ten degrees below zero. I think it was more endurable than Louisiana, with the mercury ten degrees above zero. On my plantation hunt I was thickly clad, but the cold *would* penetrate, in spite of every thing. An hour by a fire might bring some warmth, but the first step into the open air would drive it away. Fluid extract of corn failed to have its ordinary effect. The people of the vicinity said the weather was unusually severe on that occasion. For the sake of those who reside there hereafter, I hope their statement was true.

Our party stopped for the night at a plantation near Waterproof, a small village on the bank of the river, twenty-two miles from Natchez. Just as we were comfortably seated by the fire in the overseer's house, one of the negroes announced that a person at the door wished to see us.

I stepped to the door, and found a half-dozen mounted men in blue uniforms. Each man had a carbine or revolver drawn on me. One of my companions followed me outside, and found that the strange party had weapons enough to cover both of us. It had been rumored that several guerrillas, wearing United States uniforms, were lurking in the vicinity. Our conclusions concerning the character of our captors were speedily made.

Resistance was useless, but there were considerations that led us to parley as long as possible. Three officers, and as many soldiers, from Natchez, had overtaken us in the afternoon, and borne us company during the latter part of our ride. When we stopped for the night, they concluded to go forward two or three miles, and return in the morning. Supposing ourselves fairly taken, we wished to give our friends opportunity to escape. With this object in view, we endeavored, by much talking, to consume time.

I believe it does not make a man eloquent to compel him to peer into the muzzles of a half-dozen cocked revolvers, that may be discharged at any instant on the will of the holders. Prevarication is a difficult task, when time, place, and circumstances are favorable. It is no easy matter to convince your hearers of the truth of a story you know to be false, even when those hearers are inclined to be credulous. Surrounded by strangers, and with your life in peril, the difficulties are greatly increased. I am satisfied that I made a sad failure on that particular occasion.

My friend and myself answered, indiscriminately, the questions that were propounded. Our responses did not always agree. Possibly we might have done better if only one of us had spoken.

"Come out of that house," was the first request that was made.

We came out.

"Tell those soldiers to come out."

"There are no soldiers here," I responded.

"That's a d--d lie."

"There are none here."

"Yes, there are," said the spokesman of the party. "Some Yankee soldiers came here a little while ago."

"We have been here only a few minutes."

"Where did you come from?"

This was what the lawyers call a leading question. We did not desire to acknowledge we were from Natchez, as that would reveal us at once. We did not wish to say we were from Shreveport, as it would soon be proved we were not telling the truth. I replied that we had come from a plantation a few miles below. Simultaneously my companion said we had just crossed the river.

Here was a lack of corroborative testimony which our captors commented upon, somewhat to our discredit. So the conversation went on, our answers becoming more confused each time we spoke. At last the leader of the group dismounted, and prepared to search the house. He turned us over to the care of his companions, saying, as he did so:

"If I find any soldiers here, you may shoot these d--d fellows for lying."

During all the colloquy we had been carefully covered by the weapons of the group. We knew no soldiers could be found about the premises, and felt no fear concerning the result of the search.

Just as the leader finished his search, a lieutenant and twenty men rode up.

"Well," said our captor, "you are saved from shooting. I will turn you over to the lieutenant."

I recognized in that individual an officer to whom I had received introduction a day or two before. The recognition was mutual.

We had fallen into the hands of a scouting party of our own forces. Each mistook the other for Rebels. The contemplated shooting was indefinitely postponed. The lieutenant in command concluded to encamp near us, and we passed the evening in becoming acquainted with each other.

On the following day the scouting party returned to Natchez. With my two companions I proceeded ten miles further up the river-bank, calling, on the way, at several plantations. All the inhabitants supposed we were Rebel officers, going to or from Kirby Smith's department. At one house we found two old gentlemen indulging in a game of chess. In response to a comment upon their mode of amusement, one of them said:

"We play a very slow and cautious game, sir. Such a game as the Confederacy ought to play at this time."

To this I assented.

"How did you cross the river, gentlemen?" was the first interrogatory.

"We crossed it at Natchez."

"At Natchez! We do not often see Confederates from Natchez. You must have been very fortunate to get through."

Then we explained who and what we were. The explanation was followed by a little period of silence on the part of our new acquaintances. Very soon, however, the ice was broken, and our conversation became free. We were assured that we might travel anywhere in that region as officers of the Rebel army, without the slightest suspicion of our real character. They treated us courteously, and prevailed upon us to join them at dinner. Many apologies were given for the scantiness of the repast. Corn-bread, bacon, and potatoes were the only articles set before us. Our host said he was utterly unable to procure flour, sugar, coffee, or any thing else not produced upon his plantation. He thought the good times would return when the war ended, and was particularly anxious for that moment to arrive. He pressed us to pass the night at his house, but we were unable to do so. On the following day we returned to Natchez.

Everywhere on the road from Vidalia to the farthest point of our journey, we found the plantations running to waste. The negroes had been sent to Texas or West Louisiana for safety, or were remaining quietly in their quarters. Some had left their masters, and were gone to the camps of the National army at Vicksburg and Natchez. The planters had suspended work, partly because they deemed it useless to do any thing in the prevailing uncertainty, and partly because the negroes were unwilling to perform any labor. Squads of Rebel cavalry had visited some of the plantations, and threatened punishment to the negroes if they did any thing whatever toward the production of cotton. Of course, the negroes would heed such advice if they heeded no other.

On all the plantations we found cotton and corn, principally the latter, standing in the field. Sometimes there were single inclosures of several hundred acres. The owners were desirous of making any arrangement that would secure the tilling of their soil, while it did not involve them in any trouble with their neighbors or the Rebel authorities.

They deplored the reverses which the Rebel cause had suffered, and confessed that the times were out of joint. One of the men we visited was a judge in the courts of Louisiana, and looked at the question in a legal light. After lamenting the severity of the storm which was passing over the South, and expressing his fear that the Rebellion would be a failure, he referred to his own situation.

"I own a plantation," said he, "and have combined my planting interest with the practice of law. The fortune of war has materially changed my circumstances. My niggers used to do as I told them, but that time is passed. Your Northern people have made soldiers of our servants, and will, I presume, make voters of them. In five years, if I continue the practice of law, I suppose I shall be addressing a dozen negroes as gentlemen of the jury."

"If you had a negro on trial," said one of our party, "that would be correct enough. Is it not acknowledged everywhere that a man shall be tried by his peers?"

The lawyer admitted that he never thought of that point before. He said he would insist upon having negroes admitted into court as counsel for negroes that were to be tried by a jury of their race. He did not believe they would ever be available as laborers in the field if they were set free, and thought so many of them would engage in theft that negro courts would be constantly busy.

Generally speaking, the planters that I saw were not violent Secessionists, though none of them were unconditional Union men. All said they had favored secession at the beginning of the movement, because they thought it would strengthen and perpetuate slavery. Most of them had lost faith in its ultimate success, but clung to it as their only hope. The few Union men among them, or those who claimed to be loyal, were friends of the nation with many conditions. They desired slavery to be restored to its former status, the rights of the States left intact, and a full pardon extended to all who had taken part in the Rebellion. Under these conditions they would be willing to see the Union restored. Otherwise, the war must go on.

We visited several plantations on our tour of observation, and compared their respective merits. One plantation contained three thousand acres of land, but was said to be very old and worn out. Near it was one of twelve hundred acres, three-fourths covered with corn, but with no standing cotton. One had six hundred acres of cotton in the field. This place belonged to a Spaniard, who would not be disturbed by Government, and who refused to allow any work done until after the end of the war. Another had four hundred acres of standing cotton, but the plantation had been secured by a lessee, who was about commencing work.

All had merits, and all had demerits. On some there was a sufficient force for the season's work, while on others there was scarcely an able field-hand. On some the gin-houses had been burned, and on others they were standing, but disabled. A few plantations were in good order, but there was always some drawback against our securing them. Some were liable to overflow during the expected flood of the Mississippi; others were in the hands of their owners, and would not be leased by the Government. Some that had been abandoned were so thoroughly abandoned that we would hesitate to attempt their cultivation. There were several plantations more desirable than others, and I busied myself to ascertain the status of their owners, and the probabilities concerning their disposal.

Some of the semi-loyal owners of plantations were able to make very good speculations in leasing their property. There was an earnest competition among the lessees to secure promising plantations. One owner made a contract, by which he received five thousand dollars in cash and half the product of the year's labor.

A week after the lessee took possession, he was frightened by the near approach of a company of Rebel cavalry. He broke his contract and departed for the North, forfeiting the five thousand dollars he had advanced. Another lessee was ready to make a new contract with the owner, paying five thousand dollars as his predecessor had done. Four weeks later, this lessee abandoned the field, and the owner was at liberty to begin anew.

To widows and orphans the agents of the Government displayed a commendable liberality. Nearly all of these persons were allowed to retain control of their plantations, leasing them as they saw fit, and enjoying the income. Some were required to subscribe to the oath of allegiance, and promise to show no more sympathy for the crumbling Confederacy. In many cases no pledge of any kind was exacted.

I knew one widow whose disloyalty was of the most violent character. On a visit to New Orleans she was required to take the oath of allegiance before she could leave the steamboat at the levee. She signed the printed oath under protest. A month later, she brought this document forward to prove her loyalty and secure the control of her plantation.

CHAPTER XXXIII
OH THE PLANTATION

Parties who proposed to lease and cultivate abandoned plantations were anxious to know what protection would be afforded them. General Thomas and his agents assured them that proper military posts would soon be established at points within easy distance of each other along the river, so that all plantations in certain limits would be amply protected. This would be done, not as a courtesy to the lessees, but as a part of the policy of providing for the care of the negroes. If the lessees would undertake to feed and clothe several thousand negroes, besides paying them for their labor, they would relieve the Government authorities of a great responsibility. They would demonstrate the feasibility of employing the negroes as free laborers. The cotton which they would throw into market would serve to reduce the prices of that staple, and be a partial supply to the Northern factories. All these things considered, the Government was anxious to foster the enterprise, and would give it every proper assistance. The agents were profuse in their promises of protection, and assured us it would be speedily forthcoming.

There was a military post at Vidalia, opposite Natchez, which afforded protection to the plantations in which General Thomas's family and friends were interested. Another was promised at Waterproof, twenty miles above, with a stockade midway between the two places. There was to be a force of cavalry to make a daily journey over the road between Vidalia and Waterproof. I selected two plantations about two miles below Waterproof, and on the bank of the Mississippi. They were separated by a strip of wood-land half a mile in width, and by a small bayou reaching from the river to the head of Lake St. John. Both plantations belonged to the same person, a widow, living near Natchez.

The authorities had not decided what they would do with these plantations--whether they would hold them as Government property, or allow the owner to control them. In consideration of her being a widow of fifteen years' standing, they at length determined upon the latter course. It would be necessary to take out a lease from the authorities after obtaining one from the owner. I proceeded at once to make the proper negotiations.

Another widow! My first experience in seeking to obtain a widow's plantation was not encouraging. The first widow was young, the second was old. Both were anxious to make a good bargain. In the first instance I had a rival, who proved victorious. In the second affair I had no rival at the outset, but was confronted with one when my suit was fairly under way. Before he came I obtained a promise of the widow's plantations. My rival made her a better offer than I had done. At this she proposed to desert me. I caused the elder Weller's advice to be whispered to him, hoping it might induce his withdrawal. He did not retire, and we, therefore, continued our struggle. *He* was making proposals on his own behalf; I was proposing for myself and for Mr. Colburn, who was then a thousand miles away.

My widow (I call her mine, for I won at last) desired us to give her all the corn and cotton then on the plantations, and half of what should be produced under our management. I offered her half the former and one-fourth the latter. These were the terms on which nearly all private plantations were being leased. She agreed to the offer respecting the corn and cotton then standing in the field, and demanded a third of the coming year's products. After some hesitation, we decided upon "splitting the difference." Upon many minor points, such as the sale of wood, stock, wool, etc., she had her own way.

A contract was drawn up, which gave Colburn and myself the lease of the two plantations, "Aquasco" and "Monono," for the period of one year. We were to gather the crops then standing in the field, both cotton and corn, selling all the former and such portion of the latter as was not needed for the use of the plantations. We were to cultivate the plantations to the best of our abilities, subject to the fortunes of flood, fire, and pestilence, and the operations of military and marauding forces. We agreed to give up the plantations at the end of the year in as good condition as we found them in respect to stock, tools, etc., unless prevented by circumstances beyond our control. We were to have full supervision of the plantations, and manage them as we saw fit. We were to furnish such stock and tools as might be needed, with the privilege of removing the same at the time of our departure.

Our widow (whom I shall call Mrs. B.) was to have one-half the proceeds of the corn and cotton then on the plantations, and seven twenty-fourths of such as might be produced during the year. She was to have the privilege of obtaining, once a week, the supplies of butter, chickens, meal, vegetables, and similar articles she might need for her family use. There were other provisions in the contract, but the essential points were those I have mentioned. The two plantations were to be under a single management. I shall have occasion to speak of them jointly, as "the plantation."

With this contract duly signed, sealed, and stamped, I went to the "Agent for Abandoned Plantations." After some delay, and a payment of liberal fees, I obtained the Government lease. These preliminaries concluded, I proceeded to the locality of our temporary home. Colburn had not returned from the North, but was expected daily.

The bayou which I have mentioned, running through the strip of woods which separated the plantations, formed the dividing line between the parishes "Concordia" and "Tensas," in the State of Louisiana. Lake St. John lay directly in rear of "Monono," our lower plantation. This lake was five or six miles long by one in width, and was, doubtless, the bed of the Mississippi many years ago.

On each plantation there were ten dwelling-houses for the negroes. On one they were arranged in a double row, and on the other in a single row. There was a larger house for the overseer, and there were blacksmith shops, carpenter shops, stables, corn-cribs, meat-houses, cattle-yards, and gin-houses.

On Aquasco there was a dwelling-house containing five large rooms, and having a wide veranda along its entire front. This dwelling-house was in a spacious inclosure, by the side of a fine garden. Inside this inclosure, and not far from the dwelling, were the quarters for the house-servants, the carriage-house and private stable, the smoke-house and the kitchen, which lay detached from the main building, according to the custom prevailing in the South.

Our garden could boast of fig and orange trees, and other tropical productions. Pinks and roses we possessed in abundance. Of the latter we had enough in their season to furnish all the flower-girls on Broadway with a stock in trade. Our gardener "made his garden" in February. By the middle of March, his potatoes, cabbages, beets, and other vegetables under his care were making fine progress. Before the jingle of sleigh-bells had ceased in the Eastern States, we were feasting upon delicious strawberries from our own garden, ripened in the open air. The region where plowing begins in January, and corn is planted in February or early March, impresses a New Englander with its contrast to his boyhood home.

When I took possession of our new property, the state of affairs was not the most pleasing. Mrs. B. had sent the best of her negroes to Texas shortly after the fall of Vicksburg. Those remaining on the plantations were not sufficient for our work. There were four mules where we needed fifty, and there was not a sufficient supply of oxen and wagons. Farming tools, plows, etc., were abundant, but many repairs must be made. There was enough of nearly every thing for a commencement. The rest would be secured in due season.

Cotton and corn were in the field. The former was to receive immediate attention. On the day after my arrival I mustered thirty-four laborers of all ages and both sexes, and placed them at work, under the superintendence of a foreman. During the afternoon I visited them in the field, to observe the progress they were making. It was the first time I had ever witnessed the operation, but I am confident I did not betray my inexperience in the presence of my colored laborers. The foreman asked my opinion upon various points of plantation management, but I deferred making answer until a subsequent occasion. In every case I told him to do for the present as they had been accustomed, and I would make such changes as I saw fit from time to time.

Cotton-picking requires skill rather than strength. The young women are usually the best pickers, on account of their superior dexterity. The cotton-stalk, or bush, is from two to five or six feet high. It is unlike any plant with which we are familiar in the North. It resembles a large currant-bush more nearly than any thing else I can think of. Where the branches are widest the plant is three or four feet from side to side. The lowest branches are the longest, and the plant, standing by itself, has a shape similar to that of the Northern spruce. The stalk is sometimes an inch and a half in diameter where it leaves the ground. Before the leaves have fallen, the rows in a cotton-field bear a strong resemblance to a series of untrimmed hedges.

When fully opened, the cotton-bolls almost envelop the plant in their snow-white fiber. At a distance a cotton-field ready for the pickers forcibly reminds a Northerner of an expanse covered with snow. Our Northern expression, "white as snow," is not in use in the Gulf States. "White as cotton" is the form of comparison which takes its place.

The pickers walk between the rows, and gather the cotton from the stalks on either side. Each one gathers half the cotton from the row on his right, and half of that on his left. Sometimes, when the stalks are low, one person takes an entire row to himself, and gathers from both sides of it. A bag is suspended by a strap over the shoulder, the end of the bag reaching the ground, so that its weight may not be an inconvenience. The open boll is somewhat like a fully bloomed water-lily. The skill in picking lies in thrusting the fingers into the boll so as to remove all the cotton with a single motion. Ordinary-pickers grasp the boll with one hand and pluck out the cotton with the other. Skillful pickers work with both hands, never touching the bolls, but removing the cotton by a single dextrous twist of the fingers. They can thus operate with great rapidity.

As fast as the bags are filled, they are emptied into large baskets, which are placed at a corner of the field or at the ends of the rows. When the day's work is ended the cotton is weighed. The amount brought forward by each person is noted on a slate, from which it is subsequently recorded on the account-book of the plantation.

From one to four hundred pounds, according to the state of the plants, is the proper allowance for each hand per day.

In the days of slavery the "stint" was fixed by the overseer, and was required to be picked under severe penalties. It is needless to say that this stint was sufficiently large to allow of no loitering during the entire day. If the slave exceeded the quantity required of him, the excess was sometimes placed to his credit and deducted from a subsequent day. This was by no means the universal custom. Sometimes he received a small present or was granted some especial favor. By some masters the stint was increased by the addition of the excess. The task was always regulated by the condition of the cotton in the field. Where it would sometimes be three hundred pounds, at others it would not exceed one hundred.

At the time I commenced my cotton-picking, the circumstances were not favorable to a large return. The picking season begins in August or September, and is supposed to end before Christmas. In my case it was late in January, and the winter rain had washed much of the cotton from the stalks. Under the circumstances I could not expect more than fifty or seventy-five pounds per day for each person engaged.

During the first few days I did not weigh the cotton. I knew the average was not more than fifty pounds to each person, but the estimates which the negroes made fixed it at two hundred pounds. One night I astonished them by taking the weighing apparatus to the field and carefully weighing each basket. There was much disappointment among all parties at the result. The next day's picking showed a surprising improvement. After that time, each day's work was tested and the result announced. The "tell-tale," as the scales were sometimes called, was an overseer from whom there was no escape. I think the negroes worked faithfully as soon as they found there was no opportunity for deception.

I was visited by Mrs. B.'s agent a few days after I became a cotton-planter. We took an inventory of the portable property that belonged to the establishment, and arranged some plans for our mutual advantage. This agent was a resident of Natchez. He was born in the North, but had lived so long in the slave States that his sympathies were wholly Southern. He assured me the negroes were the greatest liars in the world, and required continual watching. They would take every opportunity to neglect their work, and were always planning new modes of deception. They would steal every thing of which they could make any use, and many articles that they could not possibly dispose of. Pretending illness was among the most frequent devices for avoiding labor, and the overseer was constantly obliged to contend against such deception. In short, as far as I could ascertain from this gentleman, the negro was the embodiment of all earthly wickedness. Theft, falsehood, idleness, deceit, and many other sins which afflict mortals, were the especial heritage of the negro.

In looking about me, I found that many of these charges against the negro were true. The black man was deceptive, and he was often dishonest. There can be no effect without a cause, and the reasons for this deception and dishonesty were apparent, without difficult research. The system of slavery necessitated a constant struggle between the slave and his overseer. It was the duty of the latter to obtain the greatest amount of labor from the sinews of the slave. It was the business of the slave to perform as little labor as possible. It made no difference to him whether the plantation produced a hundred or a thousand bales. He received nothing beyond his subsistence and clothing. His labor had no compensation, and his balance-sheet at the end of the month or year was the same, whether he had been idle or industrious. It was plainly to his personal interest to do nothing he could in any way avoid. The negro displayed his sagacity by deceiving the overseer whenever he could do so. The best white man in the world would have shunned all labor under such circumstances. The negro evinced a pardonable weakness in pretending to be ill whenever he could hope to make the pretense successful.

Receiving no compensation for his services, beyond his necessary support, the negro occasionally sought to compensate himself. He was fond of roasted pork, but that article did not appear on the list of plantation rations. Consequently some of the negroes would make clandestine seizure of the fattest pigs when the chance of detection was not too great. It was hard to convince them that the use of one piece of property for the benefit of another piece, belonging to the same person, was a serious offense.

"You see, Mr. K----," said a negro to me, admitting that he had sometimes stolen his master's hogs, "you see, master owns his saddle-horse, and he owns lots of corn. Master would be very mad if I didn't give the horse all the corn he wanted. Now, he owns me, and he owns a great many hogs. I like hog, just as much as the horse likes corn, but when master catches me killing the hogs he is very mad, and he makes the overseer whip me."

Corn, chickens, flour, meal, in fact, every thing edible, became legitimate plunder for the negroes when the rations furnished them were scanty.

I believe that in nine cases out of ten the petty thefts which the negroes committed were designed to supply personal wants, rather than for any other purpose. What the negro stole was usually an article of food, and it was nearly always stolen from the plantation where he belonged.

Sometimes there was a specially bad negro--one who had been caught in some extraordinary dishonesty. One in my employ was reported to have been shot at while stealing from a dwelling-house several years before. Among two hundred negroes, he was the only noted rascal. I did not attribute his dishonesty to his complexion alone. I have known worse men than he, in whose veins there was not a drop of African blood. The police records everywhere show that wickedness of heart "dwells in white and black the same."

With his disadvantages of position, the absence of all moral training, and the dishonesty which was the natural result of the old system of labor, the negro could not be expected to observe all the rules prescribed for his guidance, but which were never explained. Like ignorant and degraded people everywhere, many of the negroes believed that guilt lay mainly in detection. There was little wickedness in stealing a pig or a chicken, if the theft were never discovered, and there was no occasion for allowing twinges of conscience to disturb the digestion.

I do not intend to intimate, by the above, that all were dishonest, even in these small peculations. There were many whose sense of right and wrong was very clear, and whose knowledge of their duties had been derived from the instructions of the white preachers. These negroes "obeyed their masters" in every thing, and considered it a religious obligation to be always faithful. They never avoided their tasks, in the field or elsewhere, and were never discovered doing any wrong. Under the new system of labor at the South, this portion of the negro population will prove of great advantage in teaching their kindred the duties they owe to each other. When all are trained to think and act for themselves, the negroes will, doubtless, prove as correct in morals as the white people around them.

Early in the present year, the authorities at Davies' Bend, below Vicksburg, established a negro court, in which all petty cases were tried. The judge, jury, counsel, and officers were negroes, and no white man was allowed to interfere during the progress of a trial. After the decisions were made, the statement of the case and the action thereon were referred to the superintendent of the Government plantations at that point.

It was a noticeable feature that the punishments which the negroes decreed for each other were of a severe character. Very frequently it was necessary for the authorities to modify the sentences after the colored judge had rendered them. The cases tried by the court related to offenses of a minor character, such as theft, fraud, and various delinquencies of the freed negroes.

The experiment of a negro court is said to have been very successful, though it required careful watching. It was made in consequence of a desire of the authorities to teach the freedmen how to govern themselves. The planters in the vicinity were as bitterly opposed to the movement as to any other effort that lifts the negro above his old position.

At the present time, several parties in Vicksburg have leased three plantations, in as many localities, and are managing them on different plans. On the first they furnish the negroes with food and clothing, and divide the year's income with them. On the second they pay wages at the rate of ten dollars per month, furnishing rations free, and retaining half the money until the end of the year. On the third they pay daily wages of one dollar, having the money ready at nightfall, the negro buying his own rations at a neighboring store.

On the first plantation, the negroes are wasteful of their supplies, as they are not liable for any part of their cost. They are inclined to be idle, as their share in the division will not be materially affected by the loss of a few days' labor. On the second they are less wasteful and more industrious, but the distance of the day of payment is not calculated to develop notions of strict economy. On the third they generally display great frugality, and are far more inclined to labor than on the other plantations.

The reason is apparent. On the first plantation their condition is not greatly changed from that of slavery, except in the promise of compensation and the absence of compulsory control. In the last case they are made responsible both for their labor and expenses, and are learning how to care for themselves as freemen.

CHAPTER XXXIV
RULES AND REGULATIONS UNDER
THE OLD AND NEW SYSTEMS

Nearly every planter in the South required the manager of his plantation to keep a record of all events of importance. Books were prepared by a publishing house in New Orleans, with special reference to their use by overseers. These books had a blank for every day in the year, in which the amount and kind of work performed were to be recorded by the overseer. There were blanks for noting the progress during the picking season, and the amount picked by each person daily. There were blanks for monthly and yearly inventories of stock, tools, etc., statements of supplies received and distributed, lists of births and deaths (there were no blanks for marriages), time and amount of shipments of cotton, and for all the ordinary business of a plantation. In the directions for the use of this book, I found the following:--

> "On the pages marked I, the planter himself will make a careful record of all the negroes upon the plantation, stating their ages as nearly as possible, and their cash value, at the commencement of the year. At the close, he will again enter their individual value at that time, adding the year's increase, and omitting those that may have died. The difference can then be transferred to the balance-sheet. The year's crop is chargeable with any depreciation in the value of the negroes, occasioned by overwork and improper management, in the effort, perhaps, to make an extra crop independent of every other consideration. On the other hand, should the number of children have greatly increased during the year; the strength and usefulness of the old been sustained by kind treatment and care; the youngsters taught to be useful, and, perhaps, some of the men instructed in trades and the women in home manufactures, the increased value of the entire force will form a handsome addition to the side of *profits*."

On the pages where the daily incidents of the plantation were recorded, I frequently discovered entries that illustrated the "peculiar institution." Some of them read thus:--

June 5th. Whipped Harry and Sarah to-day, because they didn't keep up their rows.

July 7th. Aleck ran away to the woods, because I threatened to whip him.

July 9th. Got Mr. Hall's dogs and hunted Aleck. Didn't find him. Think he is in the swamp back of Brandon's.

July 12th. Took Aleck out of Vidalia jail. Paid $4.50 for jail fees. Put him in the stocks when we got home.

July 30th. Moses died this morning. Charles and Henry buried him. His wife was allowed to keep out of the field until noon.

August 10th. Sent six mules and four negroes down to the lower plantation. They will come back to-morrow.

September 9th. John said he was sick this morning, but I made him go to the field. They brought him in before noon. He has a bad fever. Am afraid he won't be able to go out again soon.

September 20th. Whipped Susan, because she didn't pick as much cotton as she did yesterday.

September 29th. Put William in the stocks and kept him till sunset, for telling Charles he wanted to run away.

October 8th. William and Susan want to be married. Told them I should not allow it, but they might live together if they wanted to.

(The above memorandum was explained to me by one of the negroes. The owner of the plantation did not approve of marriages, because they were inconvenient in case it was desired to sell a portion of the working force.)

October 1st. Took an inventory of the negroes and stock. Their value is about the same as when the last inventory was taken.

December 3d. Finished picking. Gave the negroes half a holiday.

Nearly every day's entry shows the character and amount of work performed. Thus we have:--

February 10th. Fifteen plows running, five hands piling logs, four hands ditching, six hands in trash-gang.

In the planting, hoeing, and picking seasons, the result of the labor was recorded in the same manner. Whippings were more or less frequent, according to the character of the overseer. Under one overseer I found that whippings were rare. Under other overseers they were of common occurrence.

The individual who prepared the "*Plantation Record*" for the publishers, gave, in addition to directions for its use, instructions for the overseer's general conduct.

I copy them below, preserving the author's language throughout.

THE DUTIES OF AN OVERSEER.

It is here supposed that the overseer is not immediately under his employer's eye, but is left for days or weeks, perhaps months, to the exercise of his own judgment in the management of the plantation. To him we would say--

Bear in mind, that you have engaged for a stated sum of money, to devote your time and energies, for an entire year, *to one object*--to carry out the orders of your employer, strictly, cheerfully, and to the best of your ability; and, in all things, to study his interests--requiring something more than your mere presence on the plantation, and that at such times as suits your own pleasure and convenience.

On entering upon your duties, inform yourself thoroughly of the condition of the plantation, negroes, stock, implements, etc. Learn the views of your employer as to the general course of management he wishes pursued, and make up your mind to carry out these views fully, as far as in your power. If any objections occur to you, state them distinctly, that they may either be yielded to or overcome.

Where full and particular directions are not given to you, but you are left, in a great measure, to the exercise of your own judgment, you will find the following hints of service. They are compiled from excellent sources--from able articles in the agricultural journals of the day, from Washington's Directions to his Overseers, and from personal experience.

"I do, in explicit terms, enjoin it upon you to remain constantly at home (unless called off by unavoidable business, or to attend Divine worship), and to be constantly with your people when there. There is no other sure way of getting work well done, and quietly, by negroes; for when an overlooker's back is turned the most of them will slight their work, or be idle altogether. In which case correction cannot retrieve either, but often produces evils which are worse than the disease. Nor is there any other mode than this to prevent thieving and other disorders, the consequences of opportunities. You will recollect that your time is paid for by me, and if I am deprived of it, it is worse even than robbing my purse, because it is also a breach of trust, which every honest man ought to hold most sacred. You have found me, and you will continue to find me, faithful to my part of the agreement which was made with you, whilst you are attentive to your part; but it is to be remembered that a breach on one side releases the obligation on the other."

Neither is it right that you should entertain a constant run of company at your house, incurring unnecessary expense, taking up your own time and that of the servants beyond what is needful for your own comfort--a woman to cook and wash for you, milk, make butter, and so on. More than this you have no claim to.

Endeavor to take the same interest in every thing upon the place, as if it were your own; indeed, the responsibility in this case is greater than if it were all your own--having been intrusted to you by another. Unless you feel thus, it is impossible that you can do your employer justice.

The health of the negroes under your charge is an important matter. Much of the usual sickness among them is the result of carelessness and mismanagement. Overwork or unnecessary exposure to rain, insufficient clothing, improper or badly-cooked food, and night rambles, are all fruitful causes of disease. A great majority of the cases you should be yourself competent to manage, or you are unfit for the place you hold; but whenever you find that the case is one you do not understand, send for a physician, if such is the general order of the owner. By exerting yourself to have their clothing ready in good season; to arrange profitable in-door employment in wet weather; to see that an abundant supply of wholesome, *well-cooked food*, including plenty of vegetables, be supplied to them *at regular hours*; that the sick be cheered and encouraged, and some extra comforts allowed them, and the convalescent not exposed to the chances of a relapse; that women, whilst nursing, be kept as near to the nursery as possible, but at no time allowed to suckle their children when overheated; that the infant be nursed three times during the day, in addition to the morning and evening; that no whisky be allowed upon the place at any time or under any circumstances; but that they have, whilst heated and at work, plenty of pure, *cool* water; that care be taken to prevent the hands from carrying their baskets full of cotton on their head--a most injurious practice; and, in short, that such means be used for their comfort as every judicious, humane man will readily think of, you will find the amount of sickness gradually lessened.

Next to the negroes, the stock on the place will require your constant attention. You can, however, spare yourself much trouble by your choice of a stock-minder, and by adopting and enforcing a strict system in the care of the stock. It is a part of their duty in which overseers are generally most careless.

The horse and mule stock are first in importance. Unless these are kept in good condition, it is impossible that the work can go on smoothly, or your crop be properly tended. Put your stable in good order; and, if possible, inclose it so that it can be kept under lock. Place a steady, careful old man there as hostler, making him responsible for every thing, and that directly to yourself. The foreman of the plow-gang, and the hands under his care, should be made answerable to the hostler--whose business it is to have the feed cut up, ground, and ready; the stalls well littered and cleaned out at proper intervals; to attend to sick or maimed animals; to see that the gears are always hung in their proper place, kept in good order, and so on.

It is an easy matter to keep horses or mules fat, with a full and open corn-crib and abundance of fodder. But that overseer shows his good management who can keep his teams fat at the least expense of corn and fodder. The waste of those articles in the South, through shameful carelessness and neglect, is immense; as food for stock, they are most expensive articles. Oats, millet, peas (vine and all), broadcast corn, Bermuda and crab-grass hay, are all much cheaper and equally good. Any one of these crops, fed whilst green--the oats and millet as they begin to shoot, the peas to blossom, and the corn when tasseling--with a feed of dry oats, corn, or corn-chop at noon, will keep a plow-team in fine order all the season. In England, where they have the finest teams in the world, this course *is invariably pursued*, for its economy. From eight to nine hours per day is as long as the team should be at actual work. They will perform more upon less feed, and keep in better order for a *push* when needful, worked briskly in that way, than when kept dragging a plow all day long at a slow pace. And the hands have leisure to rest, to cut up feed, clean and repair gears, and so on.

Oxen. No more work oxen should be retained than can be kept at all times in good order. An abundant supply of green feed during spring and summer, cut and fed as recommended above, and in winter well-boiled cotton-seed, with a couple of quarts of meal in it per head; turnips, raw or cooked; corn-cobs soaked twenty-four hours in salt and water; shucks, pea-vines, etc., passed through a cutting-box--any thing of the kind, in short, is cheaper food for them in winter, and will keep them in better order than dry corn and shucks or fodder.

Indeed, the fewer cattle are kept on any place the better, unless the range is remarkably good. When young stock of any kind are stinted of their proper food, and their growth receives a check, they never can wholly recover it. Let the calves have a fair share of milk, and also as much of the cooked food prepared for the cows and oxen as they will eat; with at times a little dry meal to lick. When cows or oxen show symptoms of failing, from age or otherwise, fatten them off at once; and if killed for the use of the place, *save the hide carefully*--rubbing at least two quarts of salt upon it; then roll up for a day or two, when it may be stretched and dried.

Hogs are generally sadly mismanaged. Too many are kept, and kept badly. One good brood sow for every five hands on a place, is amply sufficient--indeed, more pork will be cured from these than from a greater number. Provide at least two good grazing lots for them, with Bermuda, crab-grass, or clover, which does as well at Washington, Miss., as anywhere in the world, with two bushels of ground plaster to the acre, sowed over it. Give a steady, trusty hand no other work to do but to feed and care for them. With a large set kettle or two, an old mule and cart to haul his wood for fuel, cotton-seed, turnips, etc., for feed, and leaves for bedding, he can do full justice to one hundred head, old and young. They will increase and thrive finely, with good grazing, and a full mess, twice a day, of swill prepared as follows: Sound cotton-seed, with a gallon of corn-meal to the bushel, a quart of oak or hickory ashes, a handful of salt, and a good proportion of turnips or green food of any kind, even clover or peas; the whole thoroughly--mind you, *thoroughly* cooked--then thrown into a large trough, and there allowed *to become sour before being fed.*

Sheep may be under the charge of the stock-minder; from ten to twenty to the hand may be generally kept with advantage.

Sick animals require close and judicious attention. Too frequently they are either left to get well or to die of themselves, or are bled and dosed with nauseous mixtures indiscriminately. Study the subject of the diseases of animals during your leisure evenings, which you can do from some of the many excellent works on the subject. *Think* before you *act.* When your animal has fever, nature would dictate that all stimulating articles of diet or medicine should be avoided. Bleeding may be necessary to reduce the force of the circulation; purging, to remove irritating substances from the bowels; moist, light, and easily-digested food, that his weakened digestion may not be oppressed; cool drinks, to allay his thirst, and, to some extent, compensate for diminished secretions; rest and quiet, to prevent undue excitement in his system, and so on through the whole catalogue of diseases--but do nothing without a reason. Carry out this principle, and you will probably do much good--hardly great harm; go upon any other, and your measures are more likely to be productive of injury than benefit.

The implements and tools require a good deal of looking after. By keeping a memorandum of the distribution of any set of tools, they will be much more likely to be forthcoming at the end of the month. Axes, hoes, and other small tools, of which every hand has his own, should have his number marked upon it with a steel punch. The strict enforcement of one single rule will keep every thing straight: "Have a place for every thing, and see that every thing is in its place."

Few instances of good management will better please an employer than that of having all of the winter clothing spun and woven on the place. By having a room devoted to that purpose, under charge of some one of the old women, where those who may be complaining a little, or convalescent after sickness, may be employed in some light work, and where all of the women may be sent in wet weather, more than enough of both cotton and woolen yarn can be spun for the supply of the place.

Of the principal staple crop of the plantation, whether cotton, sugar, or rice, we shall not here speak.

Of the others--the provision crops--there is most commonly enough made upon most plantations for their own supply. Rarely, however, is it saved without great and inexcusable waste, and fed out without still greater. And this, to their lasting shame be it said, is too often the case to a disgraceful extent, when an overseer feels satisfied that he will not remain another year upon the place. His conduct should be the very opposite of this--an honorable, right-thinking man will feel a particular degree of pride in leaving every thing in thorough order, and especially an abundant supply of all kinds of feed. He thus establishes a character for himself which *must* have its effect.

Few plantations are so rich in soil as not to be improved by manure. Inform yourself of the best means, suited to the location and soil of the place under, your charge, of improving it in this and in every other way. When an opportunity offers, carry out these improvements. Rely upon it there are few employers who will not see and reward such efforts. Draining, ditching, circling, hedging, road-making, building, etc., may all be effected to a greater or less extent every season.

During the long evenings of winter improve your own mind and the knowledge of your profession by reading and study. The many excellent agricultural periodicals and books now published afford good and cheap opportunities for this.

It is indispensable that you exercise judgment and consideration in the management of the negroes under your charge. Be *firm*, and, at the same time, *gentle* in your control. Never display yourself before them in a passion; and even if inflicting the severest punishment, do so in a mild, cool manner, and it will produce a tenfold effect. When you find it necessary to use the whip--and desirable as it would be to dispense with it entirely, it *is* necessary at times-- apply it slowly and deliberately, and to the extent you had determined, in your own mind, to be needful before you began. The indiscriminate, constant, and excessive use of the whip is altogether unnecessary and inexcusable. When it can be done without a too great loss of time, the stocks offer a means of punishment greatly to be preferred. So secured, in a lonely, quiet place, where no communication can be held with any one, nothing but bread and water allowed, and the confinement extending from Saturday, when they drop work, until Sabbath evening, will prove much more effectual in preventing a repetition of the offense, than any amount of whipping. Never threaten a negro, but if you have occasion to punish, do it at once, or say nothing until ready to do so. A violent and passionate threat will often scare the best-disposed negro to the woods. Always keep your word with them, in punishments as well as in rewards. If you have named the penalty for any certain offense, inflict it without listening to a word of excuse. Never forgive that in one that you would punish in another, but treat all alike, showing no favoritism. By pursuing such a course, you convince them that you act from principle and not from impulse, and will certainly enforce your rules. Whenever an opportunity is afforded you for rewarding continued good behavior, do not let it pass--occasional rewards have a much better effect than frequent punishments.

Never be induced by a course of good behavior on the part of the negroes to relax the strictness of your discipline; but, when you have by judicious management brought them to that state, keep them so by the same means. By taking frequent strolls about the premises, including of course the quarter and stock yards, during the evening, and at least twice a week during the night, you will put a more effectual stop to any irregularities than by the most severe punishments. The only way to keep a negro honest, is not to trust him. This seems a harsh assertion; but it is, unfortunately, too true.

You will find that an hour devoted, every Sabbath morning, to their moral and religious instruction, would prove a great aid to you in bringing about a better state of things among the negroes. It has been thoroughly tried, and with the most satisfactory results, in many parts of the South. As a mere matter of interest it has proved to be advisable--to say nothing of it as a point of duty. The effect upon their general good behavior, their cleanliness, and good conduct on the Sabbath, is such as alone to recommend it to both planter and overseer.

In conclusion:--Bear in mind that *a fine crop* consists, first, in an increase in the number, and a marked improvement in the condition and value, of the negroes; second, an abundance of provision of all sorts for man and beast, carefully saved and properly housed; third, both summer and winter clothing made at home; also leather tanned, and shoes and harness made, when practicable; fourth, an improvement in the productive qualities of the land, and in the general condition of the plantation; fifth, the team and stock generally, with the farming implements and the buildings, in fine order at the close of the year; and young hogs more than enough for next year's killing; *then,* as heavy a crop of cotton, sugar, or rice as could possibly be made under these circumstances, sent to market in good season, and of prime quality. The time has passed when the overseer is valued solely upon the number of bales of cotton, hogsheads of sugar, or tierces of rice he has made, without reference to other qualifications.

In contrast with the instructions to overseers under the old management, I present the proclamation of General Banks, regulating the system of free labor in the Department of the Gulf. These regulations were in force, in 1864, along the Mississippi, from Helena to New Orleans. They were found admirably adapted to the necessities of the case. With a few changes, they have been continued in operation during the present year:--

HEAD-QUARTERS DEPARTMENT OF THE GULF, NEW ORLEANS, *February 3,* 1864.

GENERAL ORDERS, NO. 23.

The following general regulations are published for the information and government of all interested in the subject of compensated plantation labor, public or private, during the present year, and in continuation of the system established January 30, 1863:--

I. The enlistment of soldiers from plantations under cultivation in this department having been suspended by order of the Government, will not be resumed except upon direction of the same high authority.

II. The Provost-Marshal-General is instructed to provide for the division of parishes into police and school districts, and to organize from invalid soldiers a competent police for the preservation of order.

III. Provision will be made for the establishment of a sufficient number of schools, one at least for each of the police and school districts, for the instruction of colored children under twelve years of age, which, when established, will be placed under the direction of the Superintendent of Public Education.

IV. Soldiers will not be allowed to visit plantations without the written consent of the commanding officer of the regiment or post to which they are attached, and never with arms, except when on duty, accompanied by an officer.

V. Plantation hands will not be allowed to pass from one place to another, except under such regulations as may be established by the provost-marshal of the parish.

VI. Flogging and other cruel or unusual punishments are interdicted.

VII. Planters will be required, as early as practicable after the publication of these regulations, to make a roll of persons employed upon their estates, and to transmit the same to the provost marshal of the parish. In the employment of hands, the unity of families will be secured as far as possible.

VIII. All questions between the employer and the employed, until other tribunals are established, will be decided by the provost-marshal of the parish.

IX. Sick and disabled persons will be provided for upon the plantations to which they belong, except such as may be received in establishments provided for them by the Government, of which one will be established at Algiers and one at Baton Rouge.

X. The unauthorized purchase of clothing, or other property, from laborers, will be punished by fine and imprisonment. The sale of whisky or other intoxicating drinks to them, or to other persons, except under regulations established by the Provost-Marshal-General, will be followed by the severest punishment.

XL The possession of arms, or concealed or dangerous weapons, without authority, will be punished by fine and imprisonment.

XII. Laborers shall render to their employer, between daylight and dark, *ten* hours in summer, and *nine* hours in winter, of respectful, honest, faithful labor, and receive therefor, in addition to just treatment, healthy rations, comfortable clothing, quarters, fuel, medical attendance, and instruction for children, wages per month as follows, payment of one-half of which, at least, shall be reserved until the end of the year:--

For first-class hands	$8.00	per month.
For second-class hands	6.00	" "
For third-class hands	5.00	" "
For fourth-class hands	3.00	" "

Engineers and foremen, when faithful in the discharge of their duties, will be paid $2 per month extra. This schedule of wages may be commuted, by consent of both parties, at the rate of one-fourteenth part of the net proceeds of the crop, to be determined and paid at the end of the year. Wages will be deducted in case of sickness, and rations, also, when sickness is feigned. Indolence, insolence, disobedience of orders, and crime will be suppressed by forfeiture of pay, and such punishments as are provided for similar offenses by Army Regulations. Sunday work will be avoided when practicable, but when necessary will be considered as extra labor, and paid at the rates specified herein.

XIII. Laborers will be permitted to choose their employers, but when the agreement is made they will be held to their engagement for one year, under the protection of the Government. In cases of attempted imposition, by feigning sickness, or stubborn refusal of duty, they will be turned over to the provost-marshal of the parish, for labor upon the public works, without pay.

XIV. Laborers will be permitted to cultivate land on private account, as herein specified, as follows:

First and second class hands, 1 acre each.
with families

First and second class hands, 1/2 " "
without families

Second and third class hands, 1/2 " "
with families

Second and third class hands, 1/4 " "
without families

To be increased for good conduct at the discretion of the employer. The encouragement of independent industry will strengthen all the advantages which capital derives from labor, and enable the laborer to take care of himself and prepare for the time when he can render so much labor for so much money, which is the great end to be attained. No exemption will be made in this apportionment, except upon imperative reasons; and it is desirable that for good conduct the quantity be increased until faithful hands can be allowed to cultivate extensive tracts, returning to the owner an equivalent of product for rent of soil.

XV. To protect the laborer from possible imposition, no commutation of his supplies will be allowed, except in clothing, which may be commuted at the rate of $3 per month for first-class hands, and in similar proportion for other classes. The crops will stand pledged, wherever found, for the wages of labor.

XVI. It is advised, as far as practicable, that employers provide for the current wants of their hands, by perquisites for extra labor, or by appropriation of land for share cultivation; to discourage monthly-payments so far as it can be done without discontent, and to reserve till the full harvest the yearly wages.

XVII. A FREE-LABOR BANK will be established for the safe deposit of all accumulations of wages and other savings; and in order to avoid a possible wrong to depositors, by official defalcation, authority will be asked to connect the bank with the Treasury of the United States in this department.

XVIII. The transportation of negro families to other countries will not be approved. All propositions for this privilege have been declined, and application has been made to other departments for surplus negro families for service in this department.

XIX. The last year's experience shows that the planter and the negro comprehend the revolution. The overseer, having little interest in capital, and less sympathy with labor, dislikes the trouble of thinking, and discredits the notion that any thing new has occurred. He is a relic of the past, and adheres to its customs. His stubborn refusal to comprehend the condition of things, occasioned most of the embarrassments of the past year. Where such incomprehension is chronic, reduced wages, diminished rations, and the mild punishments imposed by the army and navy, will do good.

XX. These regulations are based upon the assumption that labor is a public duty, and idleness and vagrancy a crime. No civil or military officer of the Government is exempt from the operation of this universal rule. Every enlightened community has enforced it upon all classes of people by the severest penalties. It is especially necessary in agricultural pursuits. That portion of the people identified with the cultivation of the soil, however changed in condition by the revolution through which we are passing, is not relieved from the necessity of toil, which is the condition of existence with all the children of God. The revolution has altered its tenure, but not its law. This universal law of labor will be enforced, upon just terms, by the Government under whose protection the laborer rests secure in his rights. Indolence, disorder, and crime will be suppressed. Having exercised the highest right in the choice and place of employment, he must be held to the fulfillment of his engagements, until released therefrom by the Government. The several provost-marshals are hereby invested with plenary powers upon all matters connected with labor, subject to the approval of the Provost-Marshal-General and the commanding officer of the department. The most faithful and discreet officers will be selected for this duty, and the largest force consistent with the public service detailed for their assistance.

XXI. Employers, and especially overseers, are notified, that undue influence used to move the marshal from his just balance between the parties representing labor and capital, will result in immediate change of officers, and thus defeat that regular and stable system upon which the interests of all parties depend.

XXII. Successful industry is especially necessary at the present time, when large public debts and onerous taxes are imposed to maintain and protect the liberties of the people and the integrity of the Union. All officers, civil or military, and all classes of citizens who assist in extending the profits of labor, and increasing the product of the soil upon which, in the end, all national prosperity and power depends, will render to the Government a service as great as that derived from the terrible sacrifices of battle. It is upon such consideration only that the planter is entitled to favor. The Government has accorded to him, in a period of anarchy, a release from the disorders resulting mainly from insensate and mad resistance to sensible reforms, which can never be rejected without revolution, and the criminal surrender of his interests and power to crazy politicians, who thought by metaphysical abstractions to circumvent the laws of God. It has restored to him in improved, rather than impaired condition, his due privileges, at a moment when, by his own acts, the very soil was washed from beneath his feet.

XXIII. A more majestic and wise clemency human history does not exhibit. The liberal and just conditions that attend it cannot be disregarded. It protects labor by enforcing the performance of its duty, and it will assist capital by compelling just contributions to the demands of the Government. Those who profess allegiance to other Governments will be required, as the condition of residence in this State, to acquiesce, without reservation, in the demands presented by Government as a basis of permanent peace. The non-cultivation of the soil, without just reason, will be followed by temporary forfeiture to those who will secure its improvement. Those who have exercised or are entitled to the rights of citizens of the United States, will be required to participate in the measures necessary for the re-establishment of civil government. War can never cease except as civil governments crush out contest, and secure the supremacy of moral over physical power. The yellow harvest must wave over the crimson field of blood, and the representatives of the people displace the agents of purely military power.

XXIV. The amnesty offered for the past is conditioned upon an unreserved loyalty for the future, and this condition will be enforced with an iron hand. Whoever is indifferent or hostile, must choose between the liberty which foreign lands afford, the poverty of the Rebel States, and the innumerable and inappreciable blessings which our Government confers upon its people.

May God preserve the Union of the States!

By order of Major-General Banks.

Official:

GEORGE B. DRAKE,

Assistant Adjutant-General.

The two documents have little similarity. Both are appropriate to the systems they are intended to regulate. It is interesting to compare their merits at the present time. It will be doubly interesting to make a similar comparison twenty years hence.

While I was in Natchez, a resident of that city called my attention to one of the "sad results of this horrid, Yankee war."

"Do you see that young man crossing the street toward ----'s store?"

I looked in the direction indicated, and observed a person whom I supposed to be twenty-five years of age, and whose face bore the marks of dissipation. I signified, by a single word, that I saw the individual in question.

"His is a sad case," my Southern friend remarked.

"Whisky, isn't it?"

"Oh, no, I don't mean that. He does drink some, I know, but what I mean is this: His father died about five years ago. He left his son nothing but fourteen or fifteen niggers. They were all smart, young hands, and he has been able to hire them out, so as to bring a yearly income of two thousand dollars. This has supported him very comfortably. This income stopped a year ago. The niggers have all run away, and that young man is now penniless, and without any means of support. It is one of the results of your infernal Abolition war."

I assented that it was a very hard case, and ought to be brought before Congress at the earliest moment. That a promising young man should be deprived of the means of support in consequence of this Abolition war, is unfortunate--for the man.

CHAPTER XXXV
OUR FREE-LABOR ENTERPRISE IN PROGRESS

On each of the plantations the negroes were at work in the cotton-field. I rode from one to the other, as circumstances made it necessary, and observed the progress that was made. I could easily perceive they had been accustomed to performing their labor under fear of the lash. Some of them took advantage of the opportunity for carelessness and loitering under the new arrangement. I could not be in the field at all times, to give them my personal supervision. Even if I were constantly present, there was now no lash to be feared. I saw that an explanation of the new state of affairs would be an advantage to all concerned. On the first Sunday of my stay on the plantation, I called all the negroes together, in order to give them an understanding of their position.

I made a speech that I adapted as nearly as possible to the comprehension of my hearers. My audience was attentive throughout. I made no allusions to Homer, Dante, or Milton; I did not quote from Gibbon or Macaulay, and I neglected to call their attention to the spectacle they were presenting to the crowned heads of Europe. I explained to them the change the war had made in their condition, and the way in which it had been effected. I told them that all cruel modes of punishment had been abolished. The negroes were free, but they must understand that freedom did not imply idleness. I read to them the regulations established by the commissioners, and explained each point as clearly as I was able. After I had concluded, I offered to answer any questions they might ask.

There were many who could not understand why, if they were free, they should be restricted from going where they pleased at all times. I explained that it was necessary, for the successful management of the plantation, that I should always be able to rely upon them. I asked them to imagine my predicament if they should lose half their time, or go away altogether, in the busiest part of the season. They "saw the point" at once, and readily acknowledged the necessity of subordination.

I found no one who imagined that his freedom conferred the right of idleness and vagrancy. All expected to labor in their new condition, but they expected compensation for their labor, and did not look for punishment. They expected, further, that their families would not be separated, and that they could be allowed to acquire property for themselves. I know there were many negroes in the South who expected they would neither toil nor spin after being set free, but the belief was by no means universal. The story of the negro at Vicksburg, who expected his race to assemble in New York after the war, "and have white men for niggers," is doubtless true, but it would find little credence with the great majority of the freedmen of the South.

The schedule of wages, as established by the commissioners, was read and explained. The negroes were to be furnished with house-rent, rations, fuel, and medical attendance, free of charge. Able-bodied males were to receive eight dollars a month. Other classes of laborers would be paid according to the proportionate value of their services. We were required to keep on hand a supply of clothing, shoes, and other needed articles, which would be issued as required and charged on account. All balances would be paid as soon as the first installment of the cotton crop was sent to market.

This was generally satisfactory, though some of the negroes desired weekly or monthly payments. One of them thought it would be better if they could be paid at the end of each day, and suggested that silver would be preferable to greenbacks or Confederate money. Most of them thought the wages good enough, but this belief was not universal. One man, seventy years old, who acted as assistant to the "hog-minder," thought he deserved twenty-five dollars per month, in addition to his clothing and rations. Another, of the same age, who carried the breakfast and dinner to the field, was of similar opinion. These were almost the only exceptions. Those whose services were really valuable acquiesced in the arrangement.

On our plantation there was an old negress named "Rose," who attended the women during confinement. She was somewhat celebrated in her profession, and received occasional calls to visit white ladies in the neighborhood. After I had dismissed the negroes and sent them to their quarters, I was called upon by Rose, to ascertain the rate at which she would be paid. As she was regularly employed as one of the house-servants, I allowed her the same wages that the other women received. This was satisfactory, so far, but it was not entirely so. She wished to understand the matter of perquisites.

"When I used to go out to 'tend upon white ladies," said Rose, "they gave me ten dollars. Mistress always took half and let me keep the other half."

"Well, hereafter, you may keep the ten dollars yourself."

"Thank you."

After a pause, she spoke again:

"Didn't you say the black people are free?"

"Yes."

"White people are free, too, ain't they?"

"Yes."

"Then why shouldn't you pay me ten dollars every time I 'tend upon the black folks on the plantation?"

The question was evidently designed as a "corner." I evaded it by assuring Rose that though free, the negroes had not attained all the privileges that pertained to the whites, and I should insist on her professional services being free to all on the plantation.

The negroes were frequently desirous of imitating the customs of white people in a manner that should evince their freedom. Especially did they desire to have no distinction in the payment of money, on account of the color of the recipient.

After this Sunday talk with the negroes, I found a material improvement. Occasionally I overheard some of them explaining to others their views upon various points. There were several who manifested a natural indolence, and found it difficult to get over their old habits. These received admonitions from their comrades, but could not wholly forget the laziness which was their inheritance. With these exceptions, there was no immediate cause for complaint.

During the earlier part of my stay in that region, I was surprised at the readiness with which the negroes obeyed men from the North, and believed they would fulfill their promises, while they looked with distrust on all Southern white men. Many owners endeavored in vain to induce their negroes to perform certain labor. The first request made by a Northern man to the same effect would be instantly complied with. The negroes explained that their masters had been in the habit of making promises which they never kept, and cited numerous instances to prove the truth of their assertion. It seemed to have been a custom in that region to deceive the negroes in any practicable manner. To make a promise to a negro, and fail to keep it, was no worse than to lure a horse into a stable-yard, by offering him a choice feed of corn, which would prove but a single mouthful. That the negroes had any human rights was apparently rarely suspected by their owners and overseers. The distrust which many of the negroes entertained for their former masters enabled the lessees to gain, at once, the confidence of their laborers. I regret to say that this confidence was abused in a majority of cases.

I gave the negroes a larger ration of meat, meal, and potatoes than had been previously issued. As soon as possible, I procured a quantity of molasses, coffee, and tobacco. These articles had not been seen on the plantation for many months, and were most gladly received. As there was no market in that vicinity where surplus provisions could be sold, I had no fear that the negroes would resort to stealing, especially as their daily supply was amply sufficient for their support. It was the complaint of many overseers and owners that the negroes would steal provisions on frequent occasions. If they committed any thefts during my time of management, they were made so carefully that I never detected them. It is proper to say that I followed the old custom of locking the store-houses at all times.

Very soon after commencing labor I found that our working force must be increased. Accordingly, I employed some of the negroes who were escaping from the interior of the State and making their way to Natchez. As there were but few mules on the plantation, I was particularly careful to employ those negroes who were riding, rather than walking, from slavery. If I could not induce these mounted travelers to stop with us, I generally persuaded them to sell their saddle animals. Thus, hiring negroes and buying mules, I gradually put the plantation in a presentable condition. While the cotton was being picked the blacksmith was repairing the plows, the harness-maker was fitting up the harnesses for the mules, and every thing was progressing satisfactorily. The gin-house was cleaned and made ready for the last work of preparing cotton for the market. Mr. Colburn arrived from the North after I had been a planter of only ten days' standing. He was enthusiastic at the prospect, and manifested an energy that was the envy of his neighbors.

It required about three weeks to pick our cotton. Before it was all gathered we commenced "ginning" the quantity on hand, in order to make as little delay as possible in shipping our "crop" to market.

The process of ginning cotton is pretty to look upon, though not agreeable to engage in. The seed-cotton (as the article is called when it comes from the field) is fed in a sort of hopper, where it is brought in contact with a series of small and very sharp saws. From sixty to a hundred of these saws are set on a shaft, about half an inch apart. The teeth of these saws tear the fiber from the seed, but do not catch the seed itself. A brush which revolves against the saws removes the fiber from them at every revolution. The position of the gin is generally at the end of a large room, and into this room the detached fiber is thrown from the revolving brush.

This apartment is technically known as the "lint-room," and presents an interesting scene while the process of ginning is going on. The air is full of the flying lint, and forcibly reminds a Northerner of a New England snow-storm. The lint falls, like the snow-flakes, with most wonderful lightness, but, unlike the snow-flakes, it does not melt. When the cotton is picked late in the season, there is usually a dense cloud of dust in the lint-room, which settles in and among the fiber. The person who watches the lint-room has a position far from enviable. His lungs become filled with dust, and, very often, the fine, floating fiber is drawn into his nostrils. Two persons are generally permitted to divide this labor. There were none of the men on our plantation who craved it. Some of the mischievous boys would watch their opportunity to steal into the lint-room, where they greatly enjoyed rolling upon the soft cotton. Their amusement was only stopped by the use of a small whip.

The machinery of a cotton-gin is driven by steam or horse power; generally the former. There is no water-power in the State of Louisiana, but I believe some of the lakes and bayous might be turned to advantage in the same way that the tide is used on the sea-coast.

All the larger plantations are provided with steam-engines, the chimneys of which are usually carried to a height sufficient to remove all danger from sparks. There is always a corn-mill, and frequently a saw-mill attached to the gin, and driven by the same power. On every plantation, one day in the week is set apart for grinding a seven-days' supply of corn. This regulation is never varied, except under the most extraordinary circumstances. There is a universal rule in Louisiana, forbidding any person, white or black, smoking in the inclosure where the gin-house stands. I was told there was a legal enactment to this effect, that affixed heavy penalties to its infringement. For the truth of this latter statement I cannot vouch.

With its own corn-mill, saw-mill, and smithery, each plantation is almost independent of the neighborhood around it. The chief dependence upon the outside world is for farming tools and the necessary paraphernalia for the various branches of field-work. I knew one plantation, a short distance from ours, whose owner had striven hard to make it self-sustaining. He raised all the corn and all the vegetables needed. He kept an immense drove of hogs, and cured his own pork. Of cattle he had a goodly quantity, and his sheep numbered nearly three hundred. Wool and cotton supplied the raw material for clothing. Spinning-wheels and looms produced cloth in excess of what was needed. Even the thread for making the clothing for the negroes was spun on the plantation. Hats were made of the palmetto, which grew there in abundance. Shoes were the only articles of personal wear not of home production. Plows, hoes, and similar implements were purchased in the market, but the plantation was provided with a very complete repair-shop, and the workmen were famous for their skill.

The plantation, thus managed, yielded a handsome profit to its owner. The value of each year's cotton crop, when delivered on the bank of the river, was not less than forty thousand dollars. Including wages of the overseer, and all outlays for repairs and purchase of such articles as were not produced at home, the expenses would not exceed five or six thousand dollars. Cotton-planting was very profitable under almost any management, and especially so under a prudent and economical owner. Being thus profitable with slave labor, it was natural for the planters to think it could prosper under no other system. "You can't raise cotton without niggers, and you must own the niggers to raise it," was the declaration in all parts of the South.

CHAPTER XXXVI
WAR AND AGRICULTURE

Our cotton having been ginned and baled, we made preparations for shipping it to market. These preparations included the procurement of a permit from the Treasury agent at Natchez, a task of no small magnitude. An application for the permit required, in addition to my own signature, the names of two property-owning citizens, as security for payment of the duties on the cotton. This application being placed in the hands of the Treasury agent, I was requested to call in two hours. I did so, and was then put off two hours longer. Thus I spent two whole days in frequent visits to that official. His memory was most defective, as I was obliged to introduce myself on each occasion, and tell him the object of my call.

A gentleman who had free access to the agent at all times hinted that he could secure early attention to my business on payment for his trouble. Many persons asserted that they were obliged to pay handsomely for official favors. I do not *know* this to be true. I never paid any thing to the Treasury agent at Natchez or elsewhere, beyond the legitimate fees, and I never found any man who would give me a written statement that he had done so. Nevertheless, I had much circumstantial evidence to convince me that the Treasury officials were guilty of dishonorable actions. The temptation was great, and, with proper care, the chances of detection were small.

Armed with my permit, I returned to the plantation. Mr. Colburn, in my absence, had organized our force, lately engaged in cotton-picking, into suitable parties for gathering corn, of which we had some three hundred acres standing in the field. In New England I fear that corn which had remained ungathered until the middle of February, would be of comparatively little value. In our case it was apparently as sound as when first ripened.

Corn-gathering in the South differs materially from corn-gathering in the North. The negroes go through the field breaking the ears from the stalks without removing the husk. The ears are thrown into heaps at convenient distances from each other, and in regular rows. A wagon is driven between these rows, and the corn gathered for the crib. Still unhusked, it is placed in the crib, to be removed when needed. It is claimed that the husk thus remaining on the corn, protects it from various insects, and from the effect of the weather.

Every body of laborers on a plantation is called a "gang." Thus we had "the picking-gang," "the corn-gang," "the trash-gang," "the hoe-gang," "the planting-gang," "the plow-gang," and so on through the list. Each gang goes to the field in charge of a head negro, known as the driver. This driver is responsible for the work of his gang, and, under the old *régime*, was empowered to enforce his orders with the whip, if necessary. Under our new dispensation the whip was laid aside, and a milder policy took its place. It was satisfactory with the adults; but there were occasions when the smaller boys were materially benefited by applications of hickory shrubs. Solomon's words about sparing the rod are applicable to children of one race as well as to those of another. We did not allow our drivers to make any bodily punishment in the field, and I am happy to say they showed no desire to do so.

As I have before stated, our first organization was the picking-gang. Then followed the gin-gang and the press-gang. Our gin-gang was organized on principles of total abstinence, and, therefore, differed materially from the gin-gangs of Northern cities. Our press-gang, unlike the press-gangs of New York or Chicago, had nothing to do with morning publications, and would have failed to comprehend us had we ordered the preparation of a sensation leader, or a report of the last great meeting at Union Square. Our press-gang devoted its time and energies to putting our cotton into bales of the proper size and neatness.

The corn-gang, the trash-gang, and the plow-gang were successively organized by Mr. Colburn. Of the first I have spoken. The duties of the second were to gather the corn-stalks or cotton-stalks, as the case might be, into proper heaps for burning. As all this débris came under the generic name of "trash," the appellation of the gang is readily understood. Our trash-gang did very well, except in a certain instance, when it allowed the fire from the trash to run across a field of dead grass, and destroy several hundred feet of fence. In justice to the negroes, I should admit that the firing of the grass was in obedience to our orders, and the destruction of the fence partly due to a strong wind which suddenly sprang up. The trash-gang is usually composed of the younger children and the older women. The former gather and pile the stalks which the latter cut up. They particularly enjoy firing the heaps of dry trash.

It was on Saturday, the 13th of February, that our press-gang completed its labors. On the afternoon of that day, as we were hauling our cotton to the landing, the garrison at Waterproof, two miles distant, suddenly opened with its artillery upon a real or supposed enemy. A gun-boat joined in the affair, and for half an hour the cannonade was vigorous. We could see the flashes of the guns and the dense smoke rising through the trees, but could discover nothing more. When the firing ceased we were somewhat anxious to know the result. Very soon a white man, an Irishman, who had been a short time in the vicinity to purchase cotton, reached our place in a state of exhaustion. He told a frightful story of the surprise and massacre of the whole garrison, and was very certain no one but himself had escaped. He had fortunately concealed himself under a very small bridge while the fight was going on. He called attention to his clothes, which were covered with mud, to prove the truth of his statement.

For a short time the situation had an unpleasant appearance. While we were deliberating upon the proper measures for safety, one of our negroes, who was in Waterproof during the firing, came to us with *his* story. The fight had been on our side, some guerrillas having chased one of our scouting parties to a point within range of our guns. Our men shelled them with artillery, and this was the extent of the battle. The story of the Irishman, in connection with the true account of the affair, forcibly reminded me of the famous battle of Piketon, Kentucky, in the first year of the war.

On the next day (Sunday) I rode to Waterproof, leaving Colburn on the plantation. Just as I arrived within the lines, I ascertained that an attack was expected. The most stringent orders had been issued against allowing any person to pass out. Ten minutes later a scout arrived, saying that a force of Rebels was advancing to attack the post. The gun-boat commenced shelling the woods in the rear of Waterproof, and the artillery on land joined in the work. The Rebels did not get near enough to make any serious demonstration upon the town. The day passed with a steady firing from the gun-boat, relieved by an occasional interval of silence. Toward night the small garrison was re-enforced by the arrival of a regiment from Natchez. On the following day a portion of General Ellet's Marine Brigade reached Waterproof, and removed all possibility of further attack.

In the garrison of Waterproof, at the commencement of this fight, there was a certain officer who could have sat for the portrait of Falstaff with very little stuffing, and without great change of character. Early in the war he belonged to an Eastern regiment, but on that occasion he had no commission, though this fact was not generally known. Nearly as large as Hackett's Falstaff, he was as much a gascon as the hero of the Merry Wives of Windsor. He differed from Falstaff in possessing a goodly amount of bravery, but this bravery was accompanied with an entire absence of judgment.

In the early part of the fight, and until he was too drunk to move, this *preux chevalier* dashed about Waterproof, mounted on a small horse, which he urged to the top of his speed. In one hand he flourished a cane, and in the other a revolver. He usually allowed the reins to lie on his horse's neck, except when he wished to change his direction. With his abdomen protruding over the pommel of the saddle, his stirrups several inches too short, one boot-leg outside his pantaloons and the other inside, a very large hat pressed nearly to his eyes, and a face flushed with excitement and whisky, he was a study John Leech would have prized. Frequent and copious draughts of the cup which cheers and inebriates placed him *hors de combat* before the close of the day.

From the crest of the levee, he could at any time discover several lines of battle approaching the town. Frequently he informed the commandant that the Rebels were about to open upon us with a dozen heavy batteries, which they were planting in position for a long siege. If the enemy had been in the force that this man claimed, they could not have numbered less than fifty thousand. When unhorsed for the last time during the day, he insisted that I should listen to the story of his exploits.

"I went," said he, "to the colonel, this morning, and told him, sir, to give me ten men, and I would go out and feel the enemy's position. He gave me the men, and I went. We found the enemy not less than a thousand strong, sir, behind Mrs. Miller's gin-house. They were the advance of the whole Rebel army, sir, and I saw they must be driven back. We charged, and, after a desperate fight, drove them. They opposed us, sir, every inch of the way for two miles; but we routed them. We must have killed at least a hundred of them, sir, and wounded as many more. They didn't hurt a man of us; but the bullets flew very thick, sir--very. I myself killed twelve of them with my own hand, sir. This is the way it was, sir. This revolver, you see, sir, has six barrels. I emptied it once, sir; I reloaded; I emptied it again, sir. Two times six are twelve, sir. I killed twelve of them with my own hand. Let it be recorded.

"On my way back, sir, I set fire to the gin-house, so that it should no more be a shelter for those infernal Rebels. You yourself, sir, saw that building in flames, and can testify to the truth of my story."

In this strain the warrior gave the history of his moments of glory. The portion I have written was true in some points. He found three men (instead of a thousand), and pursued them a few hundred yards. He discharged his revolver at very long range, but I could not learn that his shots were returned. He fired the gin-house "to cover his retreat," and gained the fortifications without loss. I do not know his locality at the present time, but presume he remained, up to the close of the war, where storms of shot and shell continually darkened the air, and where lines of battle were seen on every side.

The siege being raised, I returned to the plantation. From Waterproof, during the fight, I could see our buildings with perfect distinctness. I had much fear that some Rebel scouting party might pay the plantation a visit while the attack was going on. I found, on my return, that Colburn had taken the matter very coolly, and prevented the negroes becoming alarmed. He declared that he considered the plantation as safe as Waterproof, and would not have exchanged places with me during the fight. The negroes were perfectly quiet, and making preparations for plowing. While the fight was in progress, my associate was consulting with the drivers about the details of work for the ensuing week, and giving his orders with the utmost *sang froid*. In consideration of the uncertainty of battles in general, and the possibility of a visit at any moment from a party of Rebel scouts, my partner's conduct was worthy of the highest commendation.

Before leaving Waterproof I had arranged for a steamer to call for our cotton, which was lying on the river bank. Waterproof lay at one side of the neck of a peninsula, and our plantation was at the other side. It was two miles across this peninsula, and sixteen miles around it, so that I could start on horseback, and, by riding very leisurely, reach the other side, long in advance of a steamboat. The steamer came in due time. After putting our cotton on board, I bade Mr. Colburn farewell, and left him to the cares and perplexities of a planter's life. I was destined for New Orleans, to sell our cotton, and to purchase many things needed for the prosecution of our enterprise.

On my way down the river, I found that steamboat traveling was not an entirely safe amusement. The boat that preceded me was fired upon near Morganzia, and narrowly escaped destruction. A shell indented her steam-pipe, and passed among the machinery, without doing any damage. Had the pipe been cut, the steam would have filled every part of the boat.

I was not disturbed by artillery on the occasion of my journey, but received a compliment from small-arms. On the morning after leaving Natchez, I was awakened by a volley of musketry from the river-bank. One of the bullets penetrated the thin walls of the cabin and entered my state-room, within two inches of my head. I preserved the missile as a souvenir of travel.

On the next day the Rebels brought a battery of artillery to the spot. A steamer received its greeting, but escaped with a single passenger wounded.

A gentleman who was on this boat had a very narrow escape. He told me that he was awakened by the first shot, which passed through the upper works of the steamer. He was occupying the upper berth in a state-room on the side next the locality of the Rebels. His first impulse was to spring from his resting-place, and throw himself at full length upon the floor. He had hardly done so, when a shell entered the state-room, and traversed the berth in the exact position where my friend had been lying.

Having narrowly escaped death, he concluded not to run a second risk. He returned to St. Louis by way of New York. Wishing to visit New Orleans some time later, he sailed from New York on the *Electric Spark,* and enjoyed the luxury of a capture by the pirates of the "Confederate" steamer *Florida.* After that occurrence, he concluded there was little choice between the ocean and river routes.

CHAPTER XXXVII
IN THE COTTON MARKET

The first impression that New Orleans gives a stranger is its unlikeness to Northern cities. It is built on ground that slopes downward from the Mississippi. As one leaves the river and walks toward the center of the city, he finds himself descending. New Orleans is a hundred miles from the mouth of the Mississippi and only six miles from Lake Pontchartrain, which is an arm of the sea. The river at the city is ten feet above Lake Pontchartrain, so that New Orleans is washed by water from the Mississippi and drained into the lake. The water in the gutters always runs from the river, no matter what may be its height. The steamers at the foot of Canal Street appear above the spectator, when he stands a mile or two from the landing.

There is no earthy elevation of any kind, except of artificial construction, in the vicinity of New Orleans. The level surface of the streets renders the transportation of heavy bodies a work of the utmost ease. The greatest amount of merchandise that can be loaded upon four wheels rarely requires the efforts of more than two animals. The street-cars, unlike those of Northern cities, are drawn by a single mule to each car, and have no conductors. The cemeteries are above ground, and resemble the pigeon-holes of a post-office, magnified to a sufficient size for the reception of coffins. There is not a cellar in the entire city of New Orleans.

Musquitos flourish during the entire winter. In the summer there are two varieties of these insects. The night-musquito is similar to the insect which disturbs our slumbers in Northern latitudes. The day-musquito relieves his comrade at sunrise and remains on duty till sunset. He has no song, but his bite is none the less severe. He disappears at the approach of winter, but his tuneful brother remains. Musquito nettings are a necessity all the year round.

The public walks of New Orleans are justly the pride of the inhabitants. Canal Street is probably the prettiest street in America. Along its center is a double row of shade-trees, a promenade, and the tracks of the street railway. These shade-trees are inclosed so as to form a series of small parks for the entire length of the street. On each side of these parks is a carriage-way, as wide as the great thoroughfare of New York. Canal Street is the fashionable promenade of New Orleans. In the days of glory, before the Rebellion, it presented a magnificent appearance.

Among the prettiest of the parks of New Orleans is Jackson Square, containing a fine equestrian statue of General Jackson. The pedestal of the statue is emblazoned with the words:

"THE UNION--IT MUST AND SHALL BE PRESERVED."

The French element in New Orleans is apparent on every side. The auctioneers cry their wares in mingled French and English, and the negroes and white laborers on the levee converse in a hybrid language. In the French quarter, every thing is French. The signs on the shops and the street corners, the conversation of the inhabitants and the shouts of the boys who play on the sidewalks, are in the vernacular of *La Belle France*. In Jackson Square, notices to warn visitors not to disturb the shrubbery, are posted in two languages, the French being first. On one poster I saw the sentence: "*Ne touche pas à les fleurs*," followed by the literal translation into English: "Don't touch to the flowers." I was happy to observe that the caution was very generally heeded.

Before the war, New Orleans was a city of wonderful wealth. Situated at the outlet of the great valley, its trade in cotton, sugar, and other products of the West and South, was immense. Boats, which had descended from all points along the navigable portion of the Mississippi, discharged their cargoes upon its levee. Ships of all nations were at the wharves, receiving the rich freight that the steamers had brought down. The piles of merchandise that lay along the levee were unequaled in any other city of the globe. Money was abundant, and was lavishly scattered in all directions.

With the secession of the Gulf States, the opening of hostilities, and the blockade of the Mississippi at its mouth and at Cairo, the prosperity of New Orleans disappeared. The steamers ceased to bring cotton and sugar to its wharves, and its levee presented a picture of inactivity. Many of the wealthy found themselves in straitened circumstances, and many of the poor suffered and died for want of food. For a whole year, while the Rebel flag floated over the city, the business of New Orleans was utterly suspended.

With the passage of the forts and the capture of New Orleans by Admiral Farragut, the Rebel rule was ended. Very slowly the business of the city revived, but in its revival it fell into the hands of Northern men, who had accompanied our armies in their advance. The old merchants found themselves crowded aside by the ubiquitous Yankees. With the end of the war, the glory of the city will soon return, but it will not return to its old channels. More than any other city of the South, New Orleans will be controlled by men of Northern birth and sentiments. The day of slave-auctions in the rotunda of the St. Charles has passed away forever.

New Orleans has a class of men peculiar to the South, whose business it is to sell cotton for the planters. These gentlemen are known as "factors," and, in former times, were numerous and successful. Whatever a planter needed, from a quire of paper to a steam-engine, he ordered his factor to purchase and forward. The factor obeyed the order and charged the amount to the planter, adding two and a half per cent, for commission.

If the planter wanted money, he drew upon the factor, and that individual honored the draft. At the end of the season, it often occurred that the planter was largely in debt to the factor. But the cotton crop, when gathered, being consigned to the factor, canceled this indebtedness, and generally left a balance in the planter's favor.

The factor charged a good commission for selling the cotton, and sometimes required interest upon the money he advanced. In the happy days before the war, the factor's business was highly lucrative. The advances to the planters, before the maturity of the cotton crop, often required a heavy capital, but the risk was not great. Nearly every planter was considerably indebted to his factor before his cotton went forward. In many cases the proceeds of the entire crop would but little more than cover the advances which had been made.

In New Orleans nearly all cotton is sold "by sample." Certain men are licensed to "sample" cotton, for which they charge a specified sum per bale. A hole is cut in the covering of each bale, and from this hole a handful of cotton is pulled. Every bale is thus "sampled," without regard to the size of the lot. The samples are taken to the sales-room of the commission house, where they are open to the inspection of buyers. The quality of the cotton is carefully noted, the length of the fiber or staple, the whiteness of the sample, and its freedom from dust or fragments of cotton-stalks. Not one bale in twenty is ever seen by the buyers until after its purchase. Frequently the buyers transfer their cotton to other parties without once looking upon it Sometimes cotton is sold at auction instead of being offered at private sale, but the process of "sampling" is carried out in either case.

In '63 and '64, New Orleans could boast of more cotton factors than cotton. The principal business was in the hands of merchants from the North, who had established themselves in the city soon after its occupation by the National forces. Nearly all cotton sent to market was from plantations leased by Northern men, or from purchases made of planters by Northern speculators. The patronage naturally fell into the hands of the new possessors of the soil, and left the old merchants to pine in solitude. The old cotton factors, most of them Southern men, who could boast of ten or twenty years' experience, saw their business pass into the hands of men whose arrival in New Orleans was subsequent to that of General Butler. Nearly all the old factors were Secessionists, who religiously believed no government could exist unless founded on raw cotton and slavery. They continually asserted that none but themselves could sell cotton to advantage, and wondered why those who had that article to dispose of should employ men unaccustomed to its sale. They were doomed to find themselves false prophets. The new and enterprising merchants monopolized the cotton traffic, and left the slavery-worshiping factors of the olden time to mourn the loss of their occupation.

At the time I visited New Orleans, cotton was falling. It had been ninety cents per pound. I could only obtain a small fraction above seventy cents, and within a week the same quality sold for sixty. Three months afterward, it readily brought a dollar and a quarter per pound. The advices from New York were the springs by which the market in New Orleans was controlled. A good demand in New York made a good demand in New Orleans, and *vice versâ*. The New York market was governed by the Liverpool market, and that in turn by the demand at Manchester. Thus the Old World and the New had a common interest in the production of cotton. While one watched the demand, the other closely observed the supply.

Some of the factors in New Orleans were fearful lest the attention paid to cotton-culture in other parts of the world would prove injurious to the South after the war should be ended. They had abandoned their early belief that their cotton was king, and dreaded the crash that was to announce the overthrow of all their hopes.

In their theory that cotton-culture was unprofitable, unless prosecuted by slave labor, these men could only see a gloomy picture for years to come. Not so the new occupants of the land. Believing that slavery was not necessary to the production of sugar and cotton; believing that the country could show far more prosperity under the new system of labor than was ever seen under the old; and believing that commerce would find new and enlarged channels with the return of peace, they combated the secession heresies of the old residents, and displayed their faith by their works. New Orleans was throwing off its old habits and adopting the ideas and manners of Northern civilization.

Mrs. B., the owner of our plantation, was in New Orleans at the time of my arrival. As she was to receive half the proceeds of the cotton we had gathered, I waited upon her to tell the result of our labors. The sale being made, I exhibited the account of sales to her agent, and paid him the stipulated amount. So far all was well; but we were destined to have a difference of opinion upon a subject touching the rights of the negro.

Early in 1863 the Rebel authorities ordered the destruction of all cotton liable to fall into the hands of the National forces. The order was very generally carried out. In its execution, some four hundred bales belonging to Mrs. B. were burned. The officer who superintended the destruction, permitted the negroes on the plantation to fill their beds with cotton, but not to save any in bales. When we were making our shipment, Mr. Colburn proposed that those negroes who wished to do so, could sell us their cotton, and fill their beds with moss or husks. As we paid them a liberal price, they accepted our offer, and we made up three bales from our purchase. We never imagined that Mrs. B. would lay any claim to this lot, and did not include it in the quantity for which we paid her half the proceeds.

After I had made the payment to her factor, I received a note from the lady in reference to the three bales above mentioned. She said the cotton in question was entirely her property; but, in consideration of our careful attention to the matter, she would consent to our retaining half its value. She admitted that she would have never thought to bring it to market; but since we had collected and baled it, she demanded it as her own. I "respectfully declined" to comply with her request. I believed the negroes had a claim to what was saved from the burning, and given to them by the Rebel authorities. Mrs. B. was of the opinion that a slave could own nothing, and therefore insisted that the cotton belonged to herself.

Very soon after sending my reply, I was visited by the lady's factor. A warm, though courteous, discussion transpired. The factor was a Secessionist, and a firm believer in the human and divine right of slavery. He was a man of polished exterior, and was, doubtless, considered a specimen of the true Southern gentleman. In our talk on the subject in dispute, I told him the Rebels had allowed the negroes to fill their beds with cotton, and it was this cotton we had purchased.

"The negroes had no right to sell it to you," said the factor; "neither had you any right to purchase it."

"If it was given to them," I asked, "was it not theirs to sell?"

"Certainly not. The negroes own nothing, and can own nothing. Every thing they have, the clothes they wear and the dishes they use, belongs to their owners. When we 'give' any thing to a negro, we merely allow it to remain in his custody, nothing more."

"But in this case," said I, "the gift was not made by the owner. The cotton was to be destroyed by order of your Confederate Government. That order took it from Mrs. B.'s possession. When the officer came to burn the cotton, and gave a portion to the negroes to fill their beds, he made no gift to Mrs. B."

"Certainly he did. The cotton became hers, when it was given to her negroes. If you give any thing to one of my negroes, that article becomes my property as much as if given to me."

"But how is it when a negro, by working nights or Saturdays, manages to make something for himself?"

"That is just the same. Whatever he makes in that way belongs to his master. Out of policy we allow him to keep it, but we manage to have him expend it for his own good. The negro is the property of his master, and can own nothing for himself."

"But in this case," I replied, "I have promised to pay the negroes for the cotton. It would be unjust to them to fail to do so."

"You must not pay them any thing for it. Whatever you have promised makes no difference. It is Mrs. B.'s property, not theirs. If you pay them, you will violate all our customs, and establish a precedent very bad for us and for yourself."

I assured the gentleman I should feel under obligation to deal justly with the negroes, even at the expense of violating Southern precedent. "You may not be aware," I remarked, "of the magnitude of the change in the condition of the Southern negro during the two years just closed. The difference of opinion between your people and ourselves is, no doubt, an honest one. We shall be quite as persistent in pushing our views at the present time as you have been in enforcing yours in the past. We must try our theory, and wait for the result."

We separated most amiably, each hoping the other would eventually see things in their true light. From present indications, the weight of public opinion is on my side, and constantly growing stronger.

My sales having been made, and a quantity of plantation supplies purchased, I was ready to return. It was with much difficulty that I was able to procure permits from the Treasury agent at New Orleans to enable me to ship my purchases. Before leaving Natchez, I procured all the documents required by law. Natchez and New Orleans were not in the same "district," and consequently there was much discord. For example, the agent at Natchez gave me a certain document that I should exhibit at New Orleans, and take with me on my return to Natchez. The agent at New Orleans took possession of this document, and, on my expostulating, said the agent at Natchez "had no right" to give me instructions to retain it. He kept the paper, and I was left without any defense against seizure of the goods I had in transit. They were seized by a Government officer, but subsequently released. On my arrival at Natchez, I narrated the occurrence to the Treasury agent at that point. I was informed that the agent at New Orleans "could not" take my papers from me, and I should not have allowed him to do so.

I was forcibly reminded of the case of the individual who was once placed in the public stocks. On learning his offense, a lawyer told him, "Why, Sir, they can't put you in the stocks for *that*."

"But they have."

"I tell you they can't do it."

"But, don't you see, they have."

"I tell you again they can't do any such thing."

In my own case, each Treasury agent declared the other "could not" do the things which had been done. In consequence of the inharmony of the "regulations," the most careful shipper would frequently find his goods under seizure, from which they could generally be released on payment of liberal fees and fines. I do not know there was any collusion between the officials, but I could not rid myself of the impression there was something rotten in Denmark. The invariable result of these little quarrels was the plundering of the shippers. The officials never suffered. Like the opposite sides of a pair of shears, though cutting against each other, they only injured whatever was between them.

Not a hundredth part of the official dishonesty at New Orleans and other points along the Mississippi will ever be known. Enough has been made public to condemn the whole system of permits and Treasury restrictions. The Government took a wise course when it abolished, soon after the suppression of the Rebellion, a large number of the Treasury Agencies in the South. As they were managed during the last two years of the war, these agencies proved little else than schools of dishonesty. There may have been some honest men in those offices, but they contrived to conceal their honesty.

To show the variety of charges which attach to a shipment of cotton, I append the sellers' account for the three bales about which Mrs. B. and myself had our little dispute. These bales were not sold with the balance of our shipment. The cotton of which they were composed was of very inferior quality.

Account Sales of Three Bales of Cotton for Knox & Colburn.
By PARSLEY & WILLIAMS.

Mark,	3 bales.				
"K. C."	Weight,　} 1,349 @..............	$0	60	$809	40
	533--406--410 }				
	Auctioneers' commission, 1 pr. ct.....	8	09		
	Sampling		30		
	Weighing		50		
	Watching.............................		50		
	Tarpaulins		50		
	Freight, $10 pr. bale	30	00		
	Insurance, $2.50 pr. bale	7	50		
	4 c. pr. lb. (tax) on 1,349 lb	53	96		
	1/2 c. " " " "	6	74		
	Permit and stamps		65		
	Hospital fees, $5 pr. bale...........	15	00		
	Factors' commission, 1 pr. ct.........	8	09		
		--	--	131	83
				------	------
E.O.E.	Net proceeds.....................			$677	57
NEW ORLEANS, La., February 22, 1864.					

It will be seen by the above that the charges form an important portion of the proceeds of a sale. The heaviest items are for Government and hospital taxes. The latter was levied before the war, but the former is one of the fruits of the Rebellion. It is likely to endure for a considerable time.

I knew several cases in which the sales of cotton did not cover the charges, but left a small bill to be paid by the owner. Frequently, cotton that had been innocently purchased and sent to market was seized by Government officials, on account of some alleged informality, and placed in the public warehouses. The owner could get no hearing until he made liberal presents of a pecuniary character to the proper authorities.

After much delay and many bribes, the cotton would be released. New charges would appear, and before a sale could be effected the whole value of the cotton would be gone.

A person of my acquaintance was unfortunate enough to fall into the hands of the Philistines in the manner I have described above. At the end of the transaction he found himself a loser to the extent of three hundred dollars. He has since been endeavoring to ascertain the amount of traffic on a similar scale that would be needed to make him a millionaire. At last accounts he had not succeeded in solving the problem.

CHAPTER XXXVIII
SOME FEATURES OF PLANTATION LIFE

On my return from New Orleans to the plantation, I found that Colburn had been pushing our business with a rapidity and skill that secured the admiration of everyone around us. He had increased our working force, and purchased a goodly number of mules. We had seventeen plows in operation, and two teams engaged in gathering corn, on the day before my arrival. The "trash-gang" was busy, and other working parties were occupied with their various duties. We were looking to a brilliant future, and echoed the wish of Jefferson Davis, to be "let alone."

The enterprise of a lessee at that time, and in that locality, was illustrated by his ability to supply his plantation with mules. There were many who failed in the effort, but my associate was not of the number. There were but few mules in the Natchez market--not enough to meet a tenth of the demand. Nearly every plantation had been stripped of working animals by one army or the other. Before our arrival the Rebels plundered all men suspected of lukewarmness in the cause. When the National army obtained possession, it took nearly every thing the Rebels had left. All property believed to belong to the Rebel Government was passed into the hands of our quartermaster.

A planter, named Caleb Shields, had a large plantation near Natchez, which had not been disturbed by the Rebels. His mules were branded with the letters "C.S.," the initials of their owner. As these letters happened to be the same that were used by the Confederate Government, Mr. Shields found his mules promptly seized and "confiscated." Before he could explain the matter and obtain an order for their return, his animals were sent to Vicksburg and placed in the Government corral. If the gentleman had possessed other initials, it is possible (though not certain) he might have saved his stock.

Mules being very scarce, the lessees exercised their skill in supplying themselves with those animals. On my first arrival at the plantation, I took care to hire those negroes who were riding from the interior, or, at all events, to purchase their animals. In one day I obtained two horses and four mules. An order had been issued for the confiscation of beasts of burden (or draught) brought inside the lines by negroes. We obtained permission to purchase of these runaway negroes whatever mules they would sell, provided we could make our negotiations before they reached the military lines.

Immediately after my departure, Mr. Colburn stationed one of our men on the road near our house, with orders to effect a trade with every mounted negro on his way to Natchez. The plan was successful. From two to a half-dozen mules were obtained daily. During the two weeks of my absence nearly fifty mules were purchased, placing the plantation in good order for active prosecution of our planting enterprise. At the same time many lessees in our vicinity were unable to commence operations, owing to their inability to obtain working stock.

The negroes discovered that the mule market was not well supplied, and some of the more enterprising and dishonest sons of Ham endeavored to profit by the situation. Frequently mules would be offered at a suspiciously low price, with the explanation that the owner was anxious to dispose of his property and return home. Some undertook nocturnal expeditions, ten or twenty miles into the interior, where they stole whatever mules they could find. A few of the lessees suffered by the loss of stock, which was sold an hour after it was stolen, and sometimes to the very party from whom it had been taken. We took every care to avoid buying stolen property, but were sometimes deceived.

On one occasion I purchased a mule of a negro who lived at Waterproof. The purchase was made an hour before sunset, and the animal was stolen during the night. On the following morning, Colburn bought it again of the same party with whom I had effected my trade. After this occurrence, we adopted the plan of branding each mule as soon as it came into our hands. All the lessees did the same thing, and partially protected each other against fraud.

White men were the worst mule-thieves, and generally instructed the negroes in their villainy. There were several men in Natchez who reduced mule-stealing to a science, and were as thoroughly skilled in it as Charley Bates or the Artful Dodger in the science of picking pockets. One of them had four or five white men and a dozen negroes employed in bringing stock to market. I think he retired to St. Louis, before the end of May, with ten or twelve thousand dollars as the result of three months' industry.

Some of the lessees resorted to questionable methods for supplying their plantations with the means for plowing and planting. One of them occupied a plantation owned by a man who refused to allow his own stock to be used. He wished to be neutral until the war was ended.

This owner had more than sixty fine mules, that were running loose in the field. One day the lessee told the owner that he had purchased a lot of mules at Natchez, and would bring them out soon. On the following night, while the owner slept, the lessee called some trusty negroes to his aid, caught seventeen mules from the field, sheared and branded them, and placed them in a yard by themselves. In the morning he called the owner to look at the "purchase."

"You have bought an excellent lot," said the latter individual. "Where were they from?"

"All from St. Louis." was the response. "They were brought down two days ago. I don't know what to do about turning them out. Do you think, if I put them with yours, there is any danger of their straying, on account of being on a strange place?"

"None at all. I think there is no risk."

The lessee took the risk, and expressed much delight to find that the new mules showed themselves at home on the plantation.

Several days later the owner of the plantation discovered the loss of his mules, but never suspected what had become of them. Two weeks afterward, the Rebels came and asked him to designate the property of the lessee, that they might remove it. He complied by pointing out the seventeen mules, which the Rebels drove away, leaving the balance unharmed.

I landed at the plantation one Sunday evening, with the goods I had purchased in New Orleans. I was met with the unwelcome information that the small force at Waterproof, after committing many depredations on the surrounding country, had been withdrawn, leaving us exposed to the tender mercies of the indignant chivalry. We were liable to be visited at any moment. We knew the Rebels would not handle us very tenderly, in view of what they had suffered from our own men. A party of guerrillas was reported seven miles distant on the day previous, and there was nothing to hinder their coming as near as they chose.

Accordingly, we determined to distribute the goods among the negroes as early as possible. On Monday morning we commenced. There was some delay, but we succeeded in starting a very lively trade before seven o'clock.

Shoes were in great demand, as the negroes had not been supplied with these articles for nearly three years. A hundred pairs were speedily issued, when the balance was laid aside for future consideration. There were some of the negroes whose feet were too large for any shoes we had purchased. It was a curious fact that these large-footed negroes were not above the ordinary stature. I remember one in particular who demanded "thirteens," but who did not stand more than five feet and five inches in his invisible stockings.

After the shoes, came the material for clothing. For the men we had purchased "gray denims" and "Kentucky jeans;" for the women, "blue denims" and common calico. These articles were rapidly taken, and with them the necessary quantity of thread, buttons, etc. A supply of huge bandana kerchiefs for the head was eagerly called for. I had procured as many of these articles as I thought necessary for the entire number of negroes on the plantation; but found I had sadly miscalculated. The kerchiefs were large and very gaudy, and the African taste was at once captivated by them. Instead of being satisfied with one or two, every negro desired from six to a dozen, and was much disappointed at the refusal. The gaudy colors of most of the calicoes created a great demand, while a few pieces of more subdued appearance were wholly discarded. White cotton cloth, palm-leaf hats, knives and forks, tin plates, pans and dishes, and other articles for use or wear, were among the distributions of the day.

Under the slave-owner's rule, the negro was entitled to nothing beyond his subsistence and coarse clothing. Out of a large-hearted generosity the master gave him various articles, amounting, in the course of a year, to a few dollars in value. These articles took the name of "presents," and their reception was designed to inspire feelings of gratitude in the breast of the slave.

Most of the negroes understood that the new arrangements made an end of present-giving. They were to be paid for all their labor, and were to pay for whatever they received. When the plan was first announced, all were pleased with it; but when we came to the distribution of the goods, many of the negroes changed their views. They urged that the clothing, and every thing else we had purchased, should be issued as "presents," and that they should be paid for their labor in addition. Whatever little advantages the old system might have, they wished to retain and ingraft upon their new life. To be compensated for labor was a condition of freedom which they joyfully accepted. To receive "presents" was an apparent advantage of slavery which they did not wish to set aside.

The matter was fully explained, and I am confident all our auditors understood it. Those that remained obstinate had an eye to their personal interests. Those who had been sick, idle, absent, or disabled, were desirous of liberal gifts, while the industrious were generally in favor of the new system, or made no special opposition to it.

One negro, who had been in our employ two weeks, and whose whole labor in that time was less than four days, thought he deserved a hundred dollars' worth of presents, and compensation in money for a fortnight's toil. All were inclined to value their services very highly; but there were some whose moderation knew no bounds.

A difficulty arose on account of certain promises that had been made to the negroes by the owner of the plantation, long before our arrival. Mrs. B. had told them (according to their version) that the proceeds of the cotton on the plantation should be distributed in the form of presents, whenever a sale was effected. She did not inform us of any such promise when we secured the lease of the plantation. If she made any agreement to that effect, it was probably forgotten. Those who claimed that this arrangement had been made desired liberal presents in addition to payment for their labor. Our non-compliance with this demand was acknowledged to be just, but it created considerable disappointment.

One who had been her mistress's favorite argued the question with an earnestness that attracted my attention. Though past sixty years of age, she was straight as an arrow, and her walk resembled that of a tragedy queen. In her whole features she was unlike those around her, except in her complexion, which was black as ink. There was a clear, silvery tone to her voice, such as I have rarely observed in persons of her race. In pressing her claim, she grew wonderfully eloquent, and would have elicited the admiration of an educated audience. Had there been a school in that vicinity for the development of histrionic talent in the negro race, I would have given that woman a recommendation to its halls.

During my absence, Mr. Colburn employed an overseer on our smaller plantation, and placed him in full charge of the work. This overseer was a mulatto, who had been fifteen years the manager of a large plantation about seven miles distant from ours. In voice and manner he was a white man, but his complexion and hair were those of the subject race. There was nothing about the plantation which he could not master in every point. Without being severe, he was able to accomplish all that had been done under the old system. He imitated the customs of the white man as much as possible, and it was his particular ambition to rank above those of his own color. As an overseer he was fully competent to take charge of any plantation in that locality. During all my stay in the South, I did not meet a white overseer whom I considered the professional equal of this negro.

"Richmond" was the name to which our new assistant answered. His master had prevented his learning to read, but allowed him to acquire sufficient knowledge of figures to record the weight of cotton in the field. Richmond could mark upon the slate all round numbers between one hundred and four hundred; beyond this he was never able to go. He could neither add nor subtract, nor could he write a single letter of the alphabet. He was able, however, to write his own name very badly, having copied it from a pass written by his master. He had possessed himself of a book, and, with the help of one of our negroes who knew the alphabet, he was learning to read. His house was a model of neatness. I regret to say that he was somewhat tyrannical when superintending the affairs of his domicile.

As the day of our distribution of goods was a stormy one, Richmond was called from the plantation to assist us. Under his assistance we were progressing fairly, interrupted occasionally by various causes of delay. Less than half the valuable articles were distributed, when our watches told us it was noon. Just as we were discussing the propriety of an adjournment for dinner, an announcement was made that banished all thoughts of the mid-day meal.

One of our boys had been permitted to visit Waterproof during the forenoon. He returned, somewhat breathless, and his first words dropped like a shell among the assembled negroes:

"The Rebels are in Waterproof."

"How do you know?"

"I saw them there, and asked a lady what they were. She said they were Harrison's Rebels."

We told the negroes to go to their quarters. Richmond mounted his horse and rode off toward the plantation of which he had charge. In two minutes, there was not a negro in the yard, with the exception of the house-servants. Our goods were lying exposed. We threw some of the most valuable articles into an obscure closet.

At the first alarm we ordered our horses brought out. When the animals appeared we desisted from our work.

"The Rebels are coming down the road," was the next bulletin from the front.

We sprang upon our horses and rode a hundred yards along the front of our "quarter-lot," to a point where we could look up the road toward Waterproof. There they were, sure enough, thirty or more mounted men, advancing at a slow trot. They were about half a mile distant, and, had we been well mounted, there was no doubt of our easy escape. "Now comes the race," said Colburn. "Twenty miles to Natchez. A single heat, with animals to go at will."

We turned our horses in the direction of Natchez.

"Stop," said I, as we reached the house again. "They did not see us, and have not quickened their pace. Strategy, my boy, may assist us a little."

Throwing my bridle into Colburn's hand, I slid from my saddle and bounded into the dwelling. It was the work of a moment to bring out a jug and a glass tumbler, but I was delayed longer than I wished in finding the key of our closet. The jug contained five gallons of excellent whisky (so pronounced by my friends), and would have been a valuable prize in any portion of the Confederacy.

Placing the jug and tumbler side by side on the veranda, in full view from the road, I remounted, just as the Rebels reached the corner of our quarter-lot.

"We have pressing engagements in Natchez," said Colburn.

"So we have," I replied; "I had nearly forgotten them. Let us lose no time in meeting them."

As we rode off, some of the foremost Rebels espied us and quickened their pace. When they reached the house they naturally looked toward it to ascertain if any person was there. They saw the jug, and were at once attracted. One man rode past the house, but the balance stopped. The minority of one was prudent, and returned after pursuing us less than fifty yards. The whisky which the jug contained was quickly absorbed. With only one tumbler it required some minutes to drain the jug. These minutes were valuable.

Whisky may have ruined many a man, but it saved us. Around that seductive jug those thirty guerrillas became oblivious to our escape. We have reason to be thankful that we disobeyed the rules of strict teetotalers by "keeping liquor in the house."

I was well mounted, and could have easily kept out of the way of any ordinary chase. Colburn was only fairly mounted, and must have been run down had there been a vigorous and determined pursuit. As each was resolved to stand by the other, the capture of one would have doubtless been the capture of both.

CHAPTER XXXIX
VISITED BY GUERRILLAS

As soon as satisfied we were not followed we took a leisurely pace, and in due time reached Natchez. Four hours later we received the first bulletin from the plantation. About thirty guerrillas had been there, mainly for the purpose of despoiling the plantation next above ours. This they had accomplished by driving off all the mules. They had not stolen *our* mules, simply because they found as much cloth and other desirable property as they wished to take on that occasion. Besides, our neighbor's mules made as large a drove as they could manage. They promised to come again, and we believed they would keep their word. We ascertained that my strategy with the whisky saved us from pursuit.

On the next day a messenger arrived, saying all was quiet at the plantation. On the second day, as every thing continued undisturbed, I concluded to return. Colburn had gone to Vicksburg, and left me to look after our affairs as I thought best. We had discussed the propriety of hiring a white overseer to stay on the plantation during our absence. The prospect of visits from guerrillas convinced us that *we* should not spend much of our time within their reach. We preferred paying some one to risk his life rather than to risk our own lives. The prospect of getting through the season without serious interruption had become very poor, but we desired to cling to the experiment a little longer. Once having undertaken it, we were determined not to give it up hastily.

I engaged a white man as overseer, and took him with me to the plantation. The negroes had been temporarily alarmed at the visit of the guerrillas, but, as they were not personally disturbed, their excitement was soon allayed. I found them anxiously waiting my return, and ready to recommence labor on the following day.

The ravages of the guerrillas on that occasion were not extensive. They carried off a few bolts of cloth and some smaller articles, after drinking the whisky I had set out for their entertainment. The negroes had carefully concealed the balance of the goods in places where a white man would have much trouble in finding them. In the garden there was a row of bee-hives, whose occupants manifested much dislike for all white men, irrespective of their political sentiments. Two unused hives were filled with the most valuable articles on our invoice, and placed at the ends of this row. In a clump of weeds under the bench on which the hives stood, the negroes secreted several rolls of cloth and a quantity of shoes. More shoes and more cloth were concealed in a hen-house, under a series of nests where several innocent hens were "sitting." Crockery was placed among the rose-bushes and tomato-vines in the garden; barrels of sugar were piled with empty barrels of great age; and two barrels of molasses had been neatly buried in a freshly-ploughed potato-field. Obscure corners in stables and sheds were turned into hiding-places, and the cunning of the negro was well evinced by the successful concealment of many bulky articles.

It was about two o'clock in the afternoon when I arrived at the plantation. I immediately recommenced the issue of goods, which was suspended so hastily three days before. From two o'clock until dark the overseer and myself were busily engaged, and distributed about two-thirds of our remaining stock. Night came. We suspended the distribution and indulged in supper. After giving the overseer directions for the morrow, I recollected an invitation to spend the night at the house of a friend, three miles away, on the road to Natchez.

I ordered my horse, and in a few moments the animal was ready, at the door. I told the overseer where I was going, and bade him good-night.

"Where are you going, Mr. K----?" said the negro who had brought out the horse, as he delivered the bridle into my hands.

"If any one calls to see me," said I, "you can say I have gone to Natchez."

With that I touched a spur to my horse and darted off rapidly toward my friend's house. A half-dozen negroes had gathered to assist in saddling and holding the horse. As I sprang into the saddle I heard one of them say:

"I don't see why Mr. K---- starts off to Natchez at this time of night."

Another negro explained the matter, but I did not hear the explanation. If he gave a satisfactory reason, I think he did better than I could have done.

Immediately after my departure the overseer went to bed. He had been in bed about fifteen minutes when he heard a trampling of horses' feet around the house. A moment later there was a loud call for the door to be opened. Before the overseer could comply with the request, the door was broken in. A dozen men crowded into the house, demanding that a light be struck instantly. As the match gave its first flash of light, one of the visitors said:

"Well, K----, we've got you this time."

"That," said another, "is no K----; that is Walter Owen, who used to be overseer on Stewart's plantation."

"What are you doing here?" demanded another.

Mr. Owen, trembling in his night-clothes, replied that he had been engaged to stay there as overseer.

"Where is K----, and where is Colburn?"

"Mr. Colburn hasn't been here since last Monday. Mr. K---- has gone to Natchez."

"That's a ---- lie," said one of the guerrillas. "We know he came here at two o'clock this afternoon, and was here at dark. He is somewhere around this house."

In vain did Owen protest I was not there. Every room and every closet in the house was searched. A pile of bagging in a garret was overhauled, in the expectation that I was concealed within it. Even the chimneys were not neglected, though I doubt if the smallest of professional sweeps could pass through them. One of the guerrillas opened a piano, to see if I had not taken refuge under its cover. They looked into all possible and impossible nooks and corners, in the hope of finding me somewhere. At last they gave up the search, and contented themselves with promising to catch both Colburn and myself before long.

"We want to go through those d--d Abolitionists, and we will do it, too. They may dodge us for a while, but we will have them by-and-by."

Not being privileged to "go through" me as they had anticipated, the gentlemanly guerrillas went through the overseer. They took his money, his hat, his pantaloons, and his saddle. His horse was standing in the stable, and they took that also. They found four of our mules, and appropriated them to their own use. They frightened one of the negroes into telling where certain articles were concealed, and were thus enabled to carry off a goodly amount of plunder. They threatened Mr. Owen with the severest punishment, if he remained any longer on the plantation. They possessed themselves of a "protection" paper which Mrs. B. had received from the commander at Natchez several months before, and were half inclined to burn her buildings as a punishment for having sought the favor of the Yankees. Their stay was of only an hour's duration.

From our plantation the robbers went to the one next above, where they were more fortunate in finding the lessees at home. They surrounded the house in the same manner they had surrounded ours, and then burst open the doors. The lessees were plundered of every thing in the shape of money, watches, and knives, and were forced to exchange hats and coats with their captors. One of the guerrillas observed an ivory-headed pencil, which he appropriated to his own use, with the remark:

"They don't make these things back here in the woods. When they do, I will send this one back."

These lessees were entertaining some friends on that evening, and begged the guerrillas to show them some distinction.

"D--n your friends," said the guerrilla leader; "I suppose they are Yankees?"

"Yes, they are; we should claim friendship with nobody else."

"Then we want to see what they have, and go through them if it is worth the while."

The strangers were unceremoniously searched. Their united contributions to the guerrilla treasury were two watches, two revolvers, three hundred dollars in money, and their hats and overcoats. Their horses and saddles were also taken. In consideration of their being guests of the house, these gentlemen were allowed to retain their coats. They were presented with five dollars each, to pay their expenses to Natchez. No such courtesy was shown to the lessees of the plantation.

On the following morning, I was awakened at an early hour by the arrival of a negro from our plantation, with news of the raid. A little later, Mr. Owen made his appearance, wearing pantaloons and hat that belonged to one of the negroes. The pantaloons were too small and the hat too large; both had long before seen their best days. He was riding a mule, on which was tied an old saddle, whose cohesive powers were very doubtful. I listened to the story of the raid, and was convinced another visit would be made very soon. I gave directions for the overseer to gather all the remaining mules and take them to Natchez for safety.

I stopped with my friend until nearly noon, and then accompanied him to Natchez. On the next morning, I learned that the guerrillas returned to our plantation while I was at my friend's house. They carried away what they were unable to take on the previous night They needed a wagon for purposes of transportation, and took one of ours, and with it all the mules they could find. Our house was stripped of every thing of any value, and I hoped the guerrillas would have no occasion to make subsequent visits. Several of our mules were saved by running them into the woods adjoining the plantation. These were taken to Natchez, and, for a time, all work on the prospective cotton crop came to an end.

For nearly three weeks, the guerrillas had full and free range in the vicinity of the leased plantations. One after another of the lessees were driven to seek refuge at Natchez, and their work was entirely suspended. The only plantations undisturbed were those within a mile or two of Vidalia. As the son of Adjutant-General Thomas was interested in one of these plantations, and intimate friends of that official were concerned in others, it was proper that they should be well protected. The troops at Vidalia were kept constantly on the look-out to prevent raids on these favored localities.

Nearly every day I heard of a fresh raid in our neighborhood, though, after the first half-dozen visits, I could not learn that the guerrillas carried away any thing, for the simple reason there was nothing left to steal. Some of the negroes remained at home, while others fled to the military posts for protection. The robbers showed no disposition to maltreat the negroes, and repeatedly assured them they should not be disturbed as long as they remained on the plantations and planted nothing but corn. It was declared that cotton should not be cultivated under any circumstances, and the negroes were threatened with the severest punishment if they assisted in planting that article.

CHAPTER XL
PECULIARITIES OF PLANTATION LABOR

On the 24th of March a small post was established at Waterproof, and on the following day we recommenced our enterprise at the plantation. We were much crippled, as nearly all our mules were gone, and the work of replacing them could not be done in a day. The market at Natchez was not supplied with mules, and we were forced to depend upon the region around us. Three days after the establishment of the post we were able to start a half-dozen plows, and within two weeks we had our original force in the field. The negroes that had left during the raid, returned to us. Under the superintendence of our overseer the work was rapidly pushed. Richmond was back again on our smaller plantation, whence he had fled during the disturbances, and was displaying an energy worthy of the highest admiration.

Our gangs were out in full force. There was the trash-gang clearing the ground for the plows, and the plow-gang busy at its appropriate work. The corn-gang, with two ox-teams, was gathering corn at the rate of a hundred bushels daily, and the fence-gang was patting the fences in order. The shelling-gang (composed of the oldest men and women) was husking and shelling corn, and putting it in sacks for market. The gardener, the stock-tenders, the dairy-maids, nurserymaids, hog-minders, and stable-keepers were all in their places, and we began to forget our recent troubles in the apparent prospect of success.

One difficulty of the new system presented itself. Several of the negroes began to feign sickness, and cheat the overseer whenever it could be done with impunity. It is a part of the overseer's duty to go through the quarters every morning, examine such as claim to be sick, determine whether their sickness be real or pretended, and make the appropriate prescriptions. Under the old system the pretenders were treated to a liberal application of the lash, which generally drove away all fancied ills. Sometimes, one who was really unwell, was most unmercifully flogged by the overseer, and death not unfrequently ensued from this cause.

As there was now no fear of the lash, some of the lazily-inclined negroes would feign sickness, and thus be excused from the field. The trouble was not general, but sufficiently prevalent to be annoying. We saw that some course must be devised to overcome this evil, and keep in the field all who were really able to be there.

We procured some printed tickets, which the overseer was to issue at the close of each day. There were three colors--red, yellow, and white. The first were for a full day's work, the second for a half day, and the last for a quarter day. On the face of each was the following:--

AQUASCO & MONONO
PLANTATIONS.
1864.

These tickets were given each day to such as deserved them. They were collected every Saturday, and proper credit given for the amount of labor performed during the week. The effect was magical. The day after the adoption of our ticket system our number of sick was reduced one-half, and we had no further trouble with pretended patients. Colburn and myself, in our new character of "doctors," found our practice greatly diminished in consequence of our innovations. Occasionally it would happen that one who was not really able to work, would go to the field through a fear of diminished wages.

One Saturday night, a negro whom we had suspected of thievish propensities, presented eight full-day tickets as the representative of his week's work.

"Did you earn all these this week?" I asked.

"Yes, sir," was the reply; "Mr. Owen gave them to me. I worked every day, straight along."

"Can you tell me on which days he gave you each ticket?"

"Oh, yes. I knows every one of them," said the negro, his countenance expressing full belief in his ability to locate each ticket.

As I held the tickets in my hand, the negro picked them out. "Mr. Owen gave me this one Monday, this one Tuesday," and so on, toward the end of the week. As he reached Friday, and saw three tickets remaining, when there was only another day to be accounted for, his face suddenly fell. I pretended not to notice his embarrassment.

"Which one did he give you to-day?"

There was a stammer, a hesitation, a slight attempt to explain, and then the truth came out. He had stolen the extra tickets from two fellow-laborers only a few minutes before, and had not reflected upon the difficulties of the situation. I gave him some good advice, required him to restore the stolen tickets, and promise he would not steal any more. I think he kept the promise during the remainder of his stay on the plantation, but am by no means certain.

Every day, when the weather was favorable, our work was pushed. Every mule that could be found was put at once into service, and by the 15th of April we had upward of five hundred acres plowed and ready for planting. We had planted about eighty acres of corn during the first week of April, and arranged to commence planting cotton on Monday, the 18th of the month. On the Saturday previous, the overseer on each plantation organized his planting-gangs, and placed every thing in readiness for active work.

The ground, when plowed for cotton, is thrown into a series of ridges by a process technically known as "four-furrowing." Two furrows are turned in one direction and two in another, thus making a ridge four or five feet wide. Along the top of this ridge a "planter," or "bull-tongue," is drawn by a single mule, making a channel two or three inches in depth. A person carrying a bag of cotton seed follows the planter and scatters the seed into the channel. A small harrow follows, covering the seed, and the work of planting is complete.

A planting-gang consists of drivers for the planters, drivers for the harrows, persons who scatter the seed, and attendants to supply them with seed. The seed is drawn from the gin-house to the field in ox-wagons, and distributed in convenient piles of ten or twenty bushels each.

Cotton-seed has never been considered of any appreciable value, and consequently the negroes are very wasteful in using it. In sowing it in the field, they scatter at least twenty times as much as necessary, and all advice to use less is unheeded. It is estimated that there are forty bushels of seed to every bale of cotton produced. A plantation that sends a thousand bales of cotton to market will thus have forty thousand bushels of seed, for which there was formerly no sale.

With the most lavish use of the article, there was generally a surplus at the end of the year. Cattle and sheep will eat cotton-seed, though not in large quantities. Boiled cotton-seed is fed to hogs on all plantations, but it is far behind corn in nutritious and fattening qualities. Cotton-seed is packed around the roots of small trees, where it is necessary to give them warmth or furnish a rich soil for their growth. To some extent it is used as fuel for steam-engines, on places where the machinery is run by steam. When the war deprived the Southern cities of a supply of coal for their gasworks, many of them found cotton seed a very good substitute. Oil can be extracted from it in large quantities. For several years, the Cotton-Seed Oil Works of Memphis carried on an extensive business. Notwithstanding the many uses to which cotton-seed can be applied, its great abundance makes it of little value.

The planting-gang which we started on that Monday morning, consisted of five planters and an equal number of harrows, sowers, etc. Each planter passed over about six acres daily, so that every day gave us thirty acres of our prospective cotton crop. At the end of the week we estimated we had about a hundred and seventy acres planted. On the following week we increased the number of planters, but soon reduced them, as we found we should overtake the plows earlier than we desired. By the evening of Monday, May 2d, we had planted upward of four hundred acres. A portion of it was pushing out of the ground, and giving promise of rapid growth.

During this period the business was under the direct superintendence of our overseers, Mr. Owen being responsible for the larger plantation, and Richmond for the smaller. Every day they were visited by Colburn or myself--sometimes by both of us--and received directions for the general management, which they carried out in detail. Knowing the habits of the guerrillas, we did not think it prudent to sleep in our house at the plantation. Those individuals were liable to announce their presence at any hour of the night, by quietly surrounding the house and requesting its inmates to make their appearance.

When I spent the night at the plantation, I generally slept on a pile of cotton-seed, in an out-building to which I had secretly conveyed a pair of blankets and a flour-bag. This bag, filled with seed, served as my pillow, and though my bed lacked the elasticity of a spring mattress, it was really quite comfortable. My sleeping-place was at the foot of a huge pile of seed, containing many hundred bushels. One night I amused myself by making a tunnel into this pile in much the same way as a squirrel digs into a hillside. With a minute's warning I could have "hunted my hole," taking my blankets with me. By filling the entrance with seed, I could have escaped any ordinary search of the building. I never had occasion to use my tunnel.

Generally, however, we staid in Waterproof, leaving there early in the morning, taking breakfast at the upper plantation, inspecting the work on both plantations, and, after dinner, returning to Waterproof. We could obtain a better dinner at the plantation than Waterproof was able to furnish us. Strawberries held out until late in the season, and we had, at all times, chickens, eggs, and milk in abundance. Whenever we desired roast lamb, our purveyor caused a good selection to be made from our flock. Fresh pork was much too abundant for our tastes, and we astonished the negroes and all other natives of that region, by our seemingly Jewish propensities. Pork and corn-bread are the great staples of life in that hot climate, where one would naturally look for lighter articles of food.

Once I was detained on the plantation till after dark. As I rode toward Waterproof, expecting the negro sentinel to challenge and halt me, I was suddenly brought to a stand by the whistling of a bullet close to my ear, followed by several others at wider range.

"Who comes there?"

"A friend, with the countersign."

"If that's so, come in. We thought you was the Rebels."

As I reached the picket, the corporal of the guard explained that they were on duty for the first time, and did not well understand their business. I agreed with him fully on the latter point. To fire upon a solitary horseman, advancing at a walk, and challenge him afterward, was something that will appear ridiculous in the eyes of all soldiers. The corporal and all his men promised to do better next time, and begged me not to report them at headquarters. When I reached the center of the town, I found the garrison had been alarmed at the picket firing, and was turning out to repel the enemy. On my assurance that I was the "enemy," the order to fall into line of battle was countermanded.

CHAPTER XLI
THE NEGROES AT A MILITARY POST

The soldiers forming the garrison at Waterproof, at that time, were from a regiment raised by Colonel Eaton, superintendent of contrabands at Vicksburg. They were recruited in the vicinity of Vicksburg and Milliken's Bend, especially for local defense. They made, as the negro everywhere has made, excellent material for the army. Easily subordinate, prompt, reliable, and keenly alert when on duty (as their shooting at me will evince), they completely gave the lie to the Rebel assertion that the negro would prove worthless under arms.

On one point only were they inclined to be mutinous. Their home ties were very strong, and their affection for their wives and children could not be overcome at once. It appeared that when this regiment was organized it was expected to remain at Milliken's Bend, where the families of nearly all the men were gathered. The order transferring them to Waterproof was unlooked for, and the men made some complaint. This was soon silenced, but after the regiment had been there three or four weeks, a half-dozen of the men went out of the lines one night, and started to walk to Milliken's Bend. They were brought back, and, after several days in the guardhouse, returned to duty. Others followed their example in attempting to go home, and for a while the camp was in a disturbed condition. Desertions were of daily occurrence.

It was difficult to make them understand they were doing wrong. The army regulations and the intricacies of military law were unknown to them. They had never studied any of General Halleck's translations from the French, and, had they done so, I doubt if they would have been much enlightened. None of them knew what "desertion" meant, nor the duties of a soldier to adhere to his flag at all times. All intended to return to the post after making a brief visit to their families. Most of them would request their comrades to notify their captains that they would only be absent a short time. Two, who succeeded in eluding pursuit, made their appearance one morning as if nothing had happened, and assured their officers that others would shortly be back again. Gradually they came to understand the wickedness of desertion, or absence without leave, but this comprehension of their obligations was not easily acquired.

A captain, commanding a company at Waterproof, told me an amusing story of a soldier "handing in his resignation." As the captain was sitting in front of his quarters, one of his men approached him, carrying his musket and all his accoutrements. Without a word the man laid his entire outfit upon the ground, in front of the captain, and then turned to walk away.

"Come back here," said the officer; "what do you mean by this?"

"I'se tired of staying here, and I'se going home," was the negro's answer, and he again attempted to move off.

"Come back here and pick these things up," and the captain spoke in a tone that convinced the negro he would do well to obey.

The negro told his story. He was weary of the war; he had been four weeks a soldier; he wanted to see his family, and had concluded to go home. If the captain desired it, he, would come back in a little while, but he was going home then, "*any how.*"

The officer possessed an amiable disposition, and explained to the soldier the nature of military discipline. The latter was soon convinced he had done wrong, and returned without a murmur to his duty. Does any soldier, who reads this, imagine himself tendering his resignation in the above manner with any prospect of its acceptance?

When the first regiment of colored volunteers was organized in Kansas, it was mainly composed of negroes who had escaped from slavery in Missouri. They were easily disciplined save upon a single point, and on this they were very obstinate. Many of the negroes in Missouri, as in other parts of the South, wear their hair, or wool, in little knots or braids. They refused to submit to a close shearing, and threatened to return to their masters rather than comply with the regulation. Some actually left the camp and went home. The officers finally carried their point by inducing some free negroes in Leavenworth, whose heads were adorned with the "fighting cut," to visit the camp and tell the obstinate ones that long locks were a badge of servitude.

The negroes on our plantation, as well as elsewhere, had a strong desire to go to Waterproof to see the soldiers. Every Sunday they were permitted to go there to attend church, the service being conducted by one of their own color. They greatly regretted that the soldiers did not parade on that day, as they missed their opportunities for witnessing military drills. To the negroes from plantations in the hands of disloyal owners, the military posts were a great attraction, and they would suffer all privations rather than return home. Some of them declared they would not go outside the lines under any consideration. We needed more assistance on our plantation, but it was next to impossible to induce negroes to go there after they found shelter at the military posts. Dread of danger and fondness for their new life were their reasons for remaining inside the lines. A portion were entirely idle, but there were many who adopted various modes of earning their subsistence.

At Natchez, Vicksburg, and other points, dealers in fruit, coffee, lemonade, and similar articles, could be found in abundance. There were dozens of places where washing was taken in, though it was not always well done. Wood-sawing, house-cleaning, or any other kind of work requiring strength, always found some one ready to perform it. Many of those who found employment supported themselves, while those who could not or would not find it, lived at the expense of Government. The latter class was greatly in the majority.

I have elsewhere inserted the instructions which are printed in every "Plantation Record," for the guidance of overseers in the olden time. "Never trust a negro," is the maxim given by the writer of those instructions. I was frequently cautioned not to believe any statements made by negroes. They were charged with being habitual liars, and entitled to no credence whatever. Mrs. B. constantly assured me the negroes were great liars, and I must not believe them. This assurance would be generally given when I cited them in support of any thing she did not desire to approve. *Per contrâ*, she had no hesitation in referring to the negroes to support any of her statements which their testimony would strengthen. This was not altogether feminine weakness, as I knew several instances in which white persons of the sterner sex made reference to the testimony of slaves. The majority of Southern men refuse to believe them on all occasions; but there are many who refer to them if their statements are advantageous, yet declare them utterly unworthy of credence when the case is reversed.

I have met many negroes who could tell falsehoods much easier than they could tell the truth. I have met others who saw no material difference between truth and its opposite; and I have met many whose statements could be fully relied upon. During his whole life, from the very nature of the circumstances which, surround him, the slave is trained in deception. If he did not learn to lie it would be exceedingly strange. It is my belief that the negroes are as truthful as could be expected from their education. White persons, under similar experience and training, would not be good examples for the young to imitate. The negroes tell many lies, but all negroes are not liars. Many white persons tell the truth, but I have met, in the course of my life, several men, of the Caucasian race, who never told the truth unless by accident.

I found in the plantation negroes a proneness to exaggeration, in cases where their fears or desires were concerned. One day, a negro from the back country came riding rapidly to our plantation, declaring that the woods, a mile distant, were "full of Rebels," and asking where the Yankee soldiers were. I questioned him for some time. When his fears were quieted, I ascertained that he had seen three mounted men, an hour before, but did not know what they were, or whether armed or not.

When I took the plantations, Mrs. B. told me there were twenty bales of cotton already picked; the negroes had told her so. When I surveyed the place on the first day of my occupation, the negroes called my attention to the picked cotton, of which they thought there were twenty or twenty-five bales. With my little experience in cotton, I felt certain there would be not more than seven bales of that lot. When it was passed through the gin and pressed, there were but five bales.

We wished to plant about fifty acres of corn on the larger plantation. There was a triangular patch in one corner that we estimated to contain thirty acres. The foreman of the plow-gang, who had lived twenty years on the place, thought there were about sixty acres. He was surprised when we found, by actual measurement, that the patch contained twenty-eight acres. Another spot, which he thought contained twenty acres, measured less than ten. Doubtless the man's judgment had been rarely called for, and its exercise, to any extent, was decidedly a new sensation.

Any thing to which the negroes were unaccustomed became the subject of amusing calculations. The "hog-minder" could estimate with considerable accuracy the weight of a hog, either live or dressed. When I asked him how much he supposed his own weight to be, he was entirely lost. On my demanding an answer, he thought it might be three hundred pounds. A hundred and sixty would not have been far from the real figure.

Incorrect judgment is just as prevalent among ignorant whites as among negroes, though with the latter there is generally a tendency to overestimate. Where negroes make wrong estimates, in three cases out of four they will be found excessive. With whites the variation will be diminutive as often as excessive. In judging of numbers of men, a column of troops, for example, both races are liable to exaggerate, the negro generally going beyond the pale-face. Fifty mounted men may ride past a plantation. The white inhabitants will tell you a hundred soldiers have gone by, while the negroes will think there were two or three hundred.

I was often surprised at the ability of the negroes to tell the names of the steamboats plying on the river. None of the negroes could read, but many of them would designate the different boats with great accuracy. They recognized the steamers as they would recognize the various trees of the forest. When a new boat made its appearance they inquired its name, and forgot it very rarely.

On one occasion a steamer came in sight, on her way up the river. Before she was near enough for me to make out the name on her side, one of the negroes declared it was the *Laurel Hill*. His statement proved correct. It was worthy of note that the boat had not passed that point for nearly a year previous to that day.

CHAPTER XLII
THE END OF THE EXPERIMENT

We did not look upon the post at Waterproof as a sure protection. There was no cavalry to make the promised patrol between Waterproof and the post next below it, or to hunt down any guerrillas that might come near. A few of the soldiers were mounted on mules and horses taken from the vicinity, but they were not effective for rapid movements. It was understood, and semi-officially announced, that the post was established for the protection of Government plantations. The commandant assured me he had no orders to that effect. He was placed there to defend the post, and nothing else. We were welcome to any protection his presence afforded, but he could not go outside the limits of the town to make any effort in our behalf.

There was a store at Waterproof which was doing a business of two thousand dollars daily. Every day the wives, brothers, or sisters of men known to belong to the marauding bands in the vicinity, would come to the town and make any purchases they pleased, frequently paying for them in money which the guerrillas had stolen. A gentleman, who was an intimate friend of General Thomas, was one of the proprietors of this store, and a son of that officer was currently reported to hold an interest in it. After a time the ownership was transferred to a single cotton speculator, but the trading went on without hinderance. This speculator told me the guerrilla leader had sent him a verbal promise that the post should not be disturbed or menaced so long as the store remained there. Similar scenes were enacted at nearly all the posts established for the "protection" of leased plantations. Trading stores were in full operation, and the amount of goods that reached the Rebels and their friends was enormous.

I have little doubt that this course served to prolong the resistance to our arms along the Mississippi River. If we had stopped all commercial intercourse with the inhabitants, we should have removed the inducement for Rebel troops to remain in our vicinity. As matters were managed, they kept close to our lines at all the military posts between Cairo and Baton Rouge, sometimes remaining respectfully quiet, and at others making occasional raids within a thousand yards of our pickets.

The absence of cavalry, and there being no prospect that any would arrive, led us to believe that we could not long remain unmolested. We were "in for it," however, and continued to plow and plant, trusting to good fortune in getting safely through. Our misfortune came at last, and brought our free-labor enterprise to an untimely end.

As I stated in the previous chapter, Colburn and myself made daily visits to the plantation, remaining there for dinner, and returning to Waterproof in the afternoon. On Monday, May 2d, we made our usual visit, and returned to the post. A steamer touched there, on its way to Natchez, just after our return, and we accepted the invitation of her captain to go to that place. Our journey to Natchez was purely from impulse, and without any real or ostensible business to call us away. It proved, personally, a very fortunate journey.

On Tuesday evening, a neighbor of ours reached Natchez, bringing news that the guerrillas had visited our plantation on that day. I hastened to Waterproof by the first boat, and found our worst fears were realized.

Thirty guerrillas had surrounded our house at the hour we were ordinarily at dinner. They called our names, and commanded us to come out and be shot. The house was empty, and as there was no compliance with the request, a half-dozen of the party, pistols in hand, searched the building, swearing they would kill us on the spot. Had we been there, I have no doubt the threat would have been carried out.

Failing to find us, they turned their attention to other matters. They caught our overseer as he was attempting to escape toward Waterproof. He was tied upon his horse, and guarded until the party was ready to move. The teams were plowing in the field at the time the robbers made their appearance. Some of the negroes unloosed the mules from the plows, mounted them, and fled to Waterproof. Others, who were slow in their movements, were captured with the animals. Such of the negroes as were not captured at once, fled to the woods or concealed themselves about the buildings.

Many of the negroes on the plantation were personally known to some of the guerrillas. In most cases these negroes were not disturbed. Others were gathered in front of the house, where they were drawn up in line and securely tied. Some of them were compelled to mount the captured mules and ride between their captors.

Several children were thrown upon the mules, or taken by the guerrillas on their own horses, where they were firmly held. No attention was paid to the cries of the children or the pleadings of their mothers. Some of the latter followed their children, as the guerrillas had, doubtless, expected. In others, the maternal instinct was less than the dread of captivity. Among those taken was an infant, little more than eight months old.

Delaying but a few moments, the captors and the captives moved away. Nineteen of our negroes were carried off, of whom ten were children under eleven years of age. Of the nineteen, five managed to make their escape within a few miles, and returned home during the night. One woman, sixty-five years old, who had not for a long time been able to do any work, was among those driven off. She fell exhausted before walking three miles, and was beaten by the guerrillas until she lay senseless by the roadside. It was not for several hours that she recovered sufficiently to return to the plantation and tell the story of barbarity.

From a plantation adjoining ours, thirty negroes were carried away at the same time. Of these, a half-dozen escaped and returned. The balance, joined to the party from our own plantation, formed a mournful procession. I heard of them at many points, from residents of the vicinity. These persons would not admit that the guerrillas were treating the negroes cruelly. Those who escaped had a frightful story to tell. They had been beaten most barbarously with whips, sticks, and frequently with the butts of pistols; two or three were left senseless by the roadside, and one old man had been shot, because he was too much exhausted to go further. I learned, a few days later, that the captured negroes were taken to Winnsboro; a small town in the interior, and there sold to a party of Texas traders.

From our plantation the guerrillas stole twenty-four mules at the time of their visit, and an equal number from our neighbors. These were sold to the same party of traders that purchased the negroes, and there was evidently as little compunction at speculating in the one "property" as in the other.

Our overseer, Mr. Owen, had been bound upon his horse and taken away. This I learned from the negroes remaining on the plantation. I made diligent inquiries of parties who arrived from the direction taken by the guerrillas, to ascertain, if possible, where he had been carried. One person assured me, positively, that he saw Mr. Owen, a prisoner, twenty miles away. Mrs.

Owen and five children were living at Waterproof, and, of course, were much alarmed on hearing of his capture.

It was on Thursday, two days after the raid, that I visited the plantation. Our lower plantation had not been disturbed, but many of the negroes were gone, and all work was suspended. It was of no use to attempt to prosecute the planting enterprise, and we immediately prepared to abandon the locality. The remaining negroes were set at work to shell the corn already gathered. As fast as shelled, it was taken to Waterproof for shipment to market. The plows were left rusting in the furrows, where they were standing at the moment the guerrillas appeared. The heaps of cotton-seed and the implements used by the planting-gang remained in *statu quo*. The cotton we planted was growing finely. To leave four hundred acres thus growing, and giving promise of a fine harvest, was to throw away much labor, but there was no alternative.

On Saturday, four days after the raid, the corporal of a scouting party came to our plantation and said the body of a white man had been found in the woods a short distance away. I rode with him to the spot he designated. The mystery concerning the fate of our overseer was cleared up. The man was murdered within a thousand yards of the house.

From the main road leading past our plantation, a path diverged into the forest. This path was taken by some of the guerrillas in their retreat. Following it two hundred yards, and then turning a short distance to the left, I found a small cypress-tree, not more than thirty feet high. One limb of this tree drooped as it left the trunk, and then turned upward. The lowest part of the bend of this limb was not much higher than a tall man's head.

It was just such a tree, and just such a limb, as a party bent on murder would select for hanging their victim. I thought, and still think, that the guerrillas turned aside with the design of using the rope as the instrument of death. Under this tree lay the remains of our overseer. The body was fast decomposing. A flock of buzzards was gathered around, and was driven away with difficulty. They had already begun their work, so that recognition under different circumstances would not have been easy. The skull was detached from the body, and lay with the face uppermost. A portion of the scalp adhered to it, on which a gray lock was visible. A bit of gray beard was clinging to the chin.

In the centre of the forehead there was a perforation, evidently made by a pistol-bullet. Death must have been instantaneous, the pistol doing the work which the murderers doubtless intended to accomplish by other means. The body had been stripped of all clothing, save a single under-garment. Within a dozen yards lay a pair of old shoes, and close by their side a tattered and misshapen hat. The shoes and hat were not those which our overseer had worn, but were evidently discarded by the guerrillas when they appropriated the apparel of their victim. I caused a grave to be dug, and the remains placed in a rude coffin and buried. If a head-stone had been obtainable, I would have given the locality a permanent designation. The particulars of the murder we were never able to ascertain.

Three days later we abandoned the plantation. We paid the negroes for the work they had done, and discharged them from further service.

Those that lived on the plantation previous to our going there, generally remained, as the guerrillas had assured them they would be unmolested if they cultivated no cotton. A few of them went to Natchez, to live near their "missus." Those whom we had hired from other localities scattered in various directions. Some went to the Contraband Home at Davis's Bend, others to the negro quarters at Natchez, others to plantations near Vidalia, and a few returned to their former homes. Our "family" of a hundred and sixty persons was thus broken up.

We removed the widow and children of our overseer to Natchez, and purchased for them the stock and goodwill of a boarding-house keeper. We sent a note to the leader of the guerrilla band that manifested such a desire to "go through" us, and informed him that we could be found in St. Louis or New York. Before the end of May we passed Vicksburg on our Journey Due North.

Most of the plantations in the vicinity of Natchez, Vicksburg, and Milliken's Bend were given up. Probably a dozen lessees were killed, and the same number carried to Texas. Near Vicksburg, the chivalric guerrillas captured two lessees, and tortured them most barbarously before putting them to death. They cut off the ears of one man, and broke his nose by a blow from a club. Thus mutilated, he was compelled to walk three or four miles. When he fell, fainting from loss of blood, he was tied to a tree, and the privilege of shooting him was sold at auction. They required his companion to witness these brutalities. Whenever he turned away his eyes, his captors pressed the point of a saber into his cheek. Finally, they compelled him to take a spade and dig his own grave. When it was finished, they stripped him of his clothing, and shot him as he stood by the brink of the newly-opened trench.

Blanchard and Robinson, two lessees near Natchez, both of them residents of Boston, were murdered with nearly the same fiendishness as exhibited in the preceding case. Their fate was for some time unknown. It was at length ascertained from a negro who was captured at the same time, but managed to escape. That "slavery makes barbarians" would seem to be well established by the conduct of these residents of Louisiana.

In the vicinity of Baton Rouge and New Orleans there were but few guerrillas, and the plantations generally escaped undisturbed. In all localities the "army-worm" made its appearance in July and August, and swept away almost the entire crop. Many plantations that were expected to yield a thousand bales did not yield a hundred, and some of them made less than ten. The appearance of this destructive worm was very sudden. On some plantations, where the cotton was growing finely and without a trace of blight, the fields, three days later, appeared as if swept by fire. There was consequently but little cotton made during the season.

The possibility of producing the great staples of the South by free labor was fully established. Beyond this there was little accomplished.

My four months of cotton-planting was an experience I shall never regret, though I have no desire to renew it under similar circumstances. Agriculture is generally considered a peaceful pursuit. To the best of my recollection I found it quite the reverse.

For the benefit of those who desire to know the process of cotton culture, from the planting season to the picking season, I give the following extract from an article written by Colonel T. B. Thorpe, of Louisiana, several years ago. After describing the process of preparing the ground and planting the seed, Colonel Thorpe says:--

> If the weather be favorable, the young plant is discovered making its way through in six or ten days, and "the scraping" of the crop, as it is termed, now begins. A light plow is again called into requisition, which is run along the drill, throwing the *earth away from the plant*; then come the laborers with their hoes, who dexterously cut away the superabundant shoots and the intruding weeds, and leave a single cotton-plant in little hills, generally two feet apart.
>
> Of all the labors of the field, the dexterity displayed by the negroes in "scraping cotton" is most calculated to call forth the admiration of the novice spectator. The hoe is a rude instrument, however well made and handled; the young cotton-plant is as delicate as vegetation can be, and springs up in lines of solid masses, composed of hundreds of plants. The field-hand, however, will single one delicate shoot from the surrounding multitude, and with his rude hoe he will trim away the remainder with all the boldness of touch of a master, leaving the incipient stalk unharmed and alone in its glory; and at nightfall you can look along the extending rows, and find the plants correct in line, and of the required distance of separation from each other.
>
> The planter, who can look over his field in early spring, and find his cotton "cleanly scraped" and his "stand" good, is fortunate; still, the vicissitudes attending the cultivation of the crop have only commenced. Many rows, from the operations of the "cut-worm," and from multitudinous causes unknown, have to be replanted, and an unusually

late frost may destroy all his labors, and compel him to commence again. But, if no untoward accident occurs, in two weeks after the "scraping," another hoeing takes place, at which time the plow throws the furrow *on to the roots* of the now strengthening plant, and the increasing heat of the sun also justifying the sinking of the roots deeper in the earth. The pleasant month of May is now drawing to a close, and vegetation of all kinds is struggling for precedence in the fields. Grasses and weeds of every variety, with vines and wild flowers, luxuriate in the newly-turned sod, and seem to be determined to choke out of existence the useful and still delicately-grown cotton.

It is a season of unusual industry on the cotton plantations, and woe to the planter who is outstripped in his labors, and finds himself "overtaken by the grass." The plow tears up the surplus vegetation, and the hoe tops it off in its luxuriance. The race is a hard one, but industry conquers; and when the third working-over of the crop takes place, the cotton-plant, so much cherished and favored, begins to overtop its rivals in the fields--begins to cast *a chilling shade of superiority* over its now intimidated groundlings, and commences to reign supreme.

Through the month of July, the crop is wrought over for the last time; the plant, heretofore of slow growth, now makes rapid advances toward perfection. The plow and hoe are still in requisition. The "water furrows" between the cotton-rows are deepened, leaving the cotton growing as it were upon à slight ridge; this accomplished, the crop is prepared for the "rainy season," should it ensue, and so far advanced that it is, under any circumstances, beyond the control of art. Nature must now have its sway.

The "cotton bloom," under the matured sun of July, begins to make its appearance. The announcement of the "first blossom" of the neighborhood is a matter of general interest; it is the unfailing sign of the approach of the busy season of fall; it is the evidence that soon the labor of man will, under a kind Providence, receive its reward.

It should perhaps here be remarked, that the color of cotton in its perfection is precisely that of the blossom--a beautiful light, but warm cream-color. In buying cotton cloth, the "bleached" and "unbleached" are perceptibly different qualities to the most casual observer; but the dark hues and harsh look of the "unbleached domestic" comes from the handling of the artisan and the soot of machinery. If cotton, pure as it looks in the field, could be wrought into fabrics, they would have a brilliancy and beauty never yet accorded to any other material in its natural or artificial state. There cannot be a doubt but that, in the robes of the ancient royal Mexicans and Peruvians, this brilliant and natural gloss of cotton was preserved, and hence the surpassing value it possessed in the eyes of cavaliers accustomed to the fabrics of the splendid court of Ferdinand and Isabella.

The cotton-blossom is exceedingly delicate in its organization. It is, if in perfection, as we have stated, of a beautiful cream-color. It unfolds in the night, remains in its glory through the morn--at meridian it has begun to decay. The day following its birth it has changed to a deep red, and ere the sun goes down, its petals have fallen to the earth, leaving inclosed in the capacious calyx a scarcely perceptible germ. This germ, in its incipient and early stages, is called "a form;" in its more perfected state, "a boll."

The cotton-plant, like the orange, has often on one stalk every possible growth; and often, on the same limb, may sometimes be seen the first-opened blossom, and the bolls, from their first development as "forms," through every size, until they have burst open and scattered their rich contents to the ripening winds.

The appearance of a well-cultivated cotton-field, if it has escaped the ravages of insects and the destruction of the elements, is of singular beauty. Although it may be a mile in extent, still it is as carefully wrought as is the mold of the limited garden of the coldest climate. The cotton-leaf is of a delicate green, large and luxuriant; the stalk indicates rapid growth, yet it has a healthy and firm look. Viewed from a distance, the perfecting plant has a warm and glowing expression. The size of the cotton-plant depends upon the accident of climate and soil. The cotton of Tennessee bears very little resemblance to the luxuriant growth of Alabama and Georgia; but even in those favored States the cotton-plant is not everywhere the same, for in the rich bottom-lands it grows to a commanding size, while in the more barren regions it is an humble shrub. In the rich alluvium of the Mississippi the cotton will tower beyond the reach of the tallest "picker," and a single plant will contain hundreds of perfect "bolls;" in the neighboring "piney-woods" it lifts its humble head scarcely above the knee, and is proportionably meager in its produce of fruit.

The growing cotton is particularly liable to accidents, and suffers immensely in "wet seasons" from the "rust" and "rot." The first named affects the leaves, giving them a brown and deadened tinge, and frequently causes them to crumble away. The "rot" attacks the "boll."

It commences by a black spot on the rind, which, increasing, seems to produce fermentation and decay. Worms find their way to the roots; the caterpillar eats into the "boll" and destroys the staple. It would be almost impossible to enumerate all the evils the cotton-plant is heir to, all of which, however, sink into nothingness compared with the scourge of the "army-worm."

The moth that indicates the advent of the army-worm has a Quaker-like simplicity in its light, chocolate-colored body and wings, and, from its harmless appearance, would never be taken for the destroyer of vast fields of luxuriant and useful vegetation.

The little, and, at first, scarcely to be perceived caterpillars that follow the appearance of these moths, can absolutely be seen to grow and swell beneath your eyes as they crawl from leaf to leaf. Day by day you can see the vegetation of vast fields becoming thinner and thinner, while the worm, constantly increasing in size, assumes at last an unctuous appearance most disgusting to behold. Arrived at maturity, a few hours only are necessary for these modern locusts to eat up all living vegetation that comes in their way. Leaving the localities of their birth, they will move from place to place, spreading a desolation as consuming as fire in their path.

All efforts to arrest their progress or annihilate them prove unavailing. They seem to spring out of the ground, and fall from the clouds; and the more they are tormented and destroyed, the more perceptible, seemingly, is their power. We once witnessed the invasion of the army-worm, as it attempted to pass from a desolated cotton-field to one untouched. Between these fields was a wide ditch, which had been deepened, to prove a barrier to the onward march of the worm. Down the perpendicular sides of the trench the caterpillars rolled in untold millions, until its bottom, for nearly a mile in extent, was a foot or two deep in a living mass of animal life. To an immense piece of unhewn timber was attached a yoke of oxen, and, as this heavy log was drawn through the ditch, it seemed absolutely to float on a crushed mass of vegetable corruption. The following day, under the heat of a tropical sun, the stench arising from this decaying mass was perceptible the country round, giving a strange and incomprehensible notion of the power and abundance of this destroyer of the cotton crop.

The change that has been effected by the result of the Rebellion, will not be confined to the social system alone. With the end of slavery there will be a destruction of many former applications of labor. Innovations have already been made, and their number will increase under the management of enterprising men.

In Louisiana several planters were using a "drill" for depositing the cotton-seed in the ground. The labor of planting is reduced more than one-half, and that of "scraping" is much diminished. The saving of seed is very great--the drill using about a tenth of the amount required under the old system.

One man is endeavoring to construct a machine that will pick cotton from the stalks, and is confident he will succeed. Should he do so, his patent will be of the greatest value. Owners of plantations have recently offered a present of ten thousand dollars to the first patentee of a successful machine of this character.

CHAPTER XLIII
THE MISSISSIPPI AND ITS PECULIARITIES

As railways are to the East, so are the rivers to the West. The Mississippi, with its tributaries, drains an immense region, traversed in all directions by steamboats. From the Gulf of Mexico one can travel, by water to the Rocky Mountains, or to the Alleghanies, at pleasure. It is estimated there are twenty thousand miles of navigable streams which find an outlet past the city of New Orleans. The Mississippi Valley contains nearly a million and a quarter square miles, and is one of the most fertile regions on the globe.

To a person born and reared in the East, the Mississippi presents many striking features. Above its junction with the Missouri, its water is clear and its banks are broken and picturesque. After it joins the Missouri the scene changes. The latter stream is of a chocolate hue, and its current is very rapid. All its characteristics are imparted to the combined stream. The Mississippi becomes a rapid, tortuous, seething torrent. It loses its blue, transparent water, and takes the complexion of the Missouri. Thus "it goes unvexed to the sea."

There is a story concerning the origin of the name given to the source of the Mississippi, which I do not remember to have seen in print. A certain lake, which had long been considered the head of the Great River, was ascertained by an exploring party to have no claim to that honor. A new and smaller lake was discovered, in which the Mississippi took its rise. The explorers wished to give it an appropriate name. An old *voyageur* suggested that they make a name, by coining a word.

"Will some of you learned ones tell me," said he, "what is the Latin word for *true*?"

"*Veritas*," was the response.

"Well, now, what is the Latin for *head*"

"*Caput*, of course."

"Now," suggested the *voyageur*, "write the two words together, by syllables."

A strip of birch bark was the tablet on which "*ver-i-tas-ca-put*" was traced.

"Read it out," was his next request.

The five syllables were read.

"Now, drop the first and last syllables, and you have a name for this lake."

In the Indian vernacular, "Mississippi" is said to signify "Great Water." "Missouri," according to some authorities, is the Indian for "Mud River," a most felicitous appellation. It should properly belong to the entire river from St. Louis to the Gulf, as that stream carries down many thousand tons of mud every year. During the many centuries that the Mississippi has been sweeping on its course, it has formed that long point of land known as the Delta, and shallowed the water in the Gulf of Mexico for more than two hundred miles.

Flowing from north to south, the river passes through all the varieties of climate. The furs from the Rocky Mountains and the cereals of Wisconsin and Minnesota are carried on its bosom to the great city which stands in the midst of orange groves and inhales the fragrance of the magnolia. From January to June the floods of its tributaries follow in regular succession, as the opening spring loosens the snows that line their banks.

The events of the war have made the Mississippi historic, and familiarized the public with some of its peculiarities. Its tortuosity is well known. The great bend opposite Vicksburg will be long remembered by thousands who have never seen it. This bend is eclipsed by many others. At "Terrapin Neck" the river flows twenty-one miles, and gains only three hundred yards. At "Raccourci Bend" was a peninsula twenty-eight miles around and only half a mile across. Several years ago a "cut-off" was made across this peninsula, for the purpose of shortening the course of the river. A small ditch was cut, and opened when the flood was highest.

An old steamboat-man once told me that he passed the upper end of this ditch just as the water was let in. Four hours later, as he passed the lower end, an immense torrent was rushing through the channel, and the tall trees were falling like stalks of grain before a sickle.

Within a week the new channel became the regular route for steamboats.

Similar "cut-offs" have been made at various points along the river, some of them by artificial aid, and others entirely by the action of the water. The channel of the Mississippi is the dividing line of the States between which it flows, and the action of the river often changes the location of real estate. There is sometimes a material difference in the laws of States that lie opposite each other. The transfer of property on account of a change in the channel occasionally makes serious work with titles.

I once heard of a case where the heirs to an estate lost their title, in consequence of the property being transferred from Mississippi to Louisiana, by reason of the course of the river being changed. In the former State they were heirs beyond dispute. In the latter their claim vanished into thin air.

Once, while passing up the Mississippi, above Cairo, a fellow-passenger called my attention to a fine plantation, situated on a peninsula in Missouri. The river, in its last flood, had broken across the neck of the peninsula. It was certain the next freshet would establish the channel in that locality, thus throwing the plantation into Illinois. Unless the negroes should be removed before this event they would become free.

"You see, sir," said my informant, "that this great river is an Abolitionist."

The alluvial soil through which the Mississippi runs easily yields to the action of the fierce current. The land worn away at one point is often deposited, in the form of a bar or tongue of land, in the concave of the next bend. The area thus added becomes the property of whoever owns the river front. Many a man has seen his plantation steadily falling into the Mississippi, year by year, while a plantation, a dozen miles below, would annually find its area increased. Real estate on the banks of the Mississippi, unless upon the bluffs, has no absolute certainty of permanence. In several places, the river now flows where there were fine plantations ten or twenty years ago.

Some of the towns along the Lower Mississippi are now, or soon will be, towns no more. At Waterproof, Louisiana, nearly the entire town-site, as originally laid out, has been washed away. In the four months I was in its vicinity, more than forty feet of its front disappeared. Eighteen hundred and seventy will probably find Waterproof at the bottom of the Mississippi. Napoleon, Arkansas, is following in the wake of Waterproof. If the distance between them were not so great, their sands might mingle. In view of the character Napoleon has long enjoyed, the friends of morality will hardly regret its loss.

The steamboat captains have a story that a quiet clergyman from New England landed at Napoleon, one morning, and made his way to the hotel. He found the proprietor superintending the efforts of a negro, who was sweeping the bar-room floor. Noticing several objects of a spherical form among the *débris* of the bar-room, the stranger asked their character.

"Them round things? them's *eyes*. The boys amused themselves a little last night. Reckon there's 'bout a pint-cup full of eyes this mornin'. Sometimes we gets a quart or so, when business is good."

Curious people were those natives of Arkansas, ten or twenty years ago. Schools were rare, and children grew up with little or no education. If there was a "barbarous civilization" anywhere in the United States, it was in Arkansas. In 1860, a man was hung at Napoleon for reading *The Tribune*. It is an open question whether the character of the paper or the man's ability to read was the reason for inflicting the death penalty.

The current of the Mississippi causes islands to be destroyed in some localities and formed in others. A large object settling at the bottom of the stream creates an eddy, in which the floating sand is deposited. Under favorable circumstances an island will form in such an eddy, sometimes of considerable extent.

About the year 1820, a steamboat, laden with lead, was sunk in mid-channel several miles below St. Louis. An island formed over this steamer, and a growth of cotton-wood trees soon covered it. These trees grew to a goodly size, and were cut for fuel. The island was cleared, and for several successive years produced fine crops of corn. About 1855, there was a change in the channel of the river, and the island disappeared. After much search the location of the sunken steamer was ascertained. By means of a diving-bell, its cargo of lead, which had been lying thirty-five years under earth and under water, was brought to light. The entire cargo was raised, together with a portion of the engines. The lead was uninjured, but the engines were utterly worthless after their long burial.

The numerous bends of the Mississippi are of service in rendering the river navigable. If the channel were a straight line from Cairo to New Orleans, the current would be so strong that no boat could stem it. In several instances, where "cut-offs" have been made, the current at their outlets is so greatly increased that the opposite banks are washed away. New bends are thus formed that may, in time, be as large as those overcome. Distances have been shortened by "cut-offs," but the Mississippi displays a decided unwillingness to have its length curtailed.

From St. Louis to the Red River the current of the Mississippi is about three miles an hour. It does not flow in a steady, unbroken volume. The surface is constantly ruffled by eddies and little whirlpools, caused by the inequalities of the bottom of the river, and the reflection of the current from the opposite banks. As one gazes upon the stream, it half appears as if heated by concealed fires, and ready to break into violent ebullition. The less the depth, the greater the disturbance of the current. So general is this rule, that the pilots judge of the amount of water by the appearance of the surface. Exceptions occur where the bottom, below the deep water, is particularly uneven.

From its source to the mouth of Red River, the Mississippi is fed by tributaries. Below that point, it throws off several streams that discharge no small portion of its waters into the Gulf of Mexico. These streams, or "bayous," are narrow and tortuous, but generally deep, and navigable for ordinary steamboats. The "Atchafalaya" is the first, and enters the Gulf of Mexico at the bay of the same name. At one time it was feared the Mississippi might leave its present bed, and follow the course of this bayou. Steps were taken to prevent such an occurrence. Bayou Plaquemine, Bayou Sara, Bayou La Fourche, Bayou Goula, and Bayou Teche, are among the streams that drain the great river.

These bayous form a wonderful net-work of navigable waters, throughout Western Louisiana. If we have reason to be thankful that "great rivers run near large cities in all parts of the world," the people of Louisiana should be especially grateful for the numerous natural canals in that State. These streams are as frequent and run in nearly as many directions as railways in Massachusetts.

During its lowest stages, the Mississippi is often forty feet "within its banks;" in other words, the surface is forty feet below the level of the land which borders the river. It rises with the freshets, and, when "bank full," is level with the surrounding lowland.

It does not always stop at this point; sometimes it rises two, four, six, or even ten feet above its banks. The levees, erected at immense cost, are designed to prevent the overflowing of the country on such occasions. When the levees become broken from any cause, immense areas of country are covered with water. Plantations, swamps, forests, all are submerged. During the present year (1865) thousands of square miles have been flooded, hundreds of houses swept away, and large amounts of property destroyed.

During the freshet of '63, General Grant opened the levee at Providence, Louisiana, in the hope of reaching Bayou Mason, and thence taking his boats to Red River. After the levee was cut an immense volume of water rushed through the break. Anywhere else it would have been a goodly-sized river, but it was of little moment by the side of the Mississippi. A steamboat was sent to explore the flooded region. I saw its captain soon after his return.

"I took my boat through the cut," said he, "without any trouble. We drew nearly three feet, but there was plenty of water. We ran two miles over a cotton-field, and could see the stalks as our wheels tore them up. Then I struck the plank road, and found a good stage of water for four miles, which took me to the bayou. I followed this several miles, until I was stopped by fallen trees, when I turned about and came back. Coming back, I tried a cornfield, but found it wasn't as good to steam in as the cotton-field."

A farmer in the Eastern or Middle States would, doubtless, be much astonished at seeing a steamboat paddling at will in his fields and along his roads. A similar occurrence in Louisiana does not astonish the natives. Steamers have repeatedly passed over regions where corn or cotton had been growing six months before. At St. Louis, in 1844, small boats found no difficulty in running from East St. Louis to Caseyville, nine miles distant. In making these excursions they passed over many excellent farms, and stopped at houses whose owners had been driven to the upper rooms by the water.

Above Cairo, the islands in the Mississippi are designated by names generally received from the early settlers. From Cairo to New Orleans the islands are numbered, the one nearest the former point being "One," and that nearest New Orleans "One Hundred and Thirty-one." Island Number Ten is historic, being the first and the last island in the great river that the Rebels attempted to fortify. Island Number Twenty-eight was the scene of several attacks by guerrillas upon unarmed transports. Other islands have an equally dishonorable reputation. Fifty years ago several islands were noted as the resorts of robbers, who conducted an extensive and systematic business. Island Number Sixty-five (if I remember correctly) was the rendezvous of the notorious John A. Murrell and his gang of desperadoes.

CHAPTER XLIV
STEAMBOATING ON THE MISSISSIPPI
IN PEACE AND WAR

No engineer has been able to dam the Mississippi, except by the easy process which John Phenix adopted on the Yuma River. General Pillow stretched a chain from Columbus, Kentucky, to the opposite shore, in order to prevent the passage of our gun-boats. The chain broke soon after being placed in position.

Near Forts Jackson and Philip, below New Orleans, the Rebels constructed a boom to oppose the progress of Farragut's fleet. A large number of heavy anchors, with the strongest cables, were fixed in the river. For a time the boom answered the desired purpose. But the river rose, drift-wood accumulated, and the boom at length went the way of all things Confederate. Farragut passed the forts, and appeared before New Orleans; "Picayune Butler came to town," and the great city of the South fell into the hands of the all-conquering Yankees.

Before steam power was applied to the propulsion of boats, the ascent of the Mississippi was very difficult.

From New Orleans to St. Louis, a boat consumed from two to four months' time. Sails, oars, poles, and ropes attached to trees, were the various means of stemming the powerful current. Long after steamboats were introduced, many flat-boats, loaded with products of the Northern States, floated down the river to a market. At New Orleans, boats and cargoes were sold, and the boatmen made their way home on foot. Until twenty years ago, the boatmen of the Mississippi were almost a distinct race. At present they are nearly extinct.

In the navigation of the Mississippi and its tributaries, the pilot is the man of greatest importance. He is supposed to be thoroughly familiar with the channel of the river in all its windings, and to know the exact location of every snag or other obstruction. He can generally judge of the depth of water by the appearance of the surface, and he is acquainted with every headland, forest, house, or tree-top, that marks the horizon and tells him how to keep his course at night. Professional skill is only acquired by a long and careful training.

Shortly after the occupation of Little Rock by General Steele, a dozen soldiers passed the lines, without authority, and captured a steamboat eighteen miles below the city. Steam was raised, when the men discovered they had no pilot. One of their number hit upon a plan as novel as it was successful.

The Arkansas was very low, having only three feet of water in the channel. Twenty-five able-bodied negroes were taken from a neighboring plantation, stretched in a line across the river, and ordered to wade against the current. By keeping their steamer, which drew only twenty inches, directly behind the negro who sank the deepest, the soldiers took their prize to Little Rock without difficulty.

For ten years previous to the outbreak of the Rebellion, steamboating on the Mississippi was in the height of its glory. Where expense of construction and management were of secondary consideration, the steamboats on the great river could offer challenge to the world. It was the boast of their officers that the tables of the great passenger-boats were better supplied than those of the best hotels in the South. On many steamers, claret, at dinner, was free to all. Fruit and ices were distributed in the evening, as well as choice cups of coffee and tea. On one line of boats, the cold meats on the supper-table were from carefully selected pieces, cooked and cooled expressly for the cenatory meal. Bands of music enlivened the hours of day, and afforded opportunity for dancing in the evening. Spacious cabins, unbroken by machinery; guards of great width, where cigars and small-talk were enjoyed; well-furnished and well-lighted state-rooms, and tables loaded with all luxuries of the place and season, rendered these steamers attractive to the traveler. Passengers were social, and partook of the gayety around them. Men talked, drank, smoked, and sometimes gambled, according to their desires. The ladies practiced no frigid reserve toward each other, but established cordial relations in the first few hours of each journey.

Among the many fine and fast steamers on the Western waters, there was necessarily much competition in speed. Every new boat of the first class was obliged to give an example of her abilities soon after her appearance. Every owner of a steamboat contends that *his* boat is the best afloat. I have rarely been on board a Mississippi steamer of any pretensions whose captain has not assured me, "She is the fastest thing afloat, sir. Nothing can pass her. We have beaten the--, and the--, and the--, in a fair race, sir." To a stranger, seeking correct information, the multiplicity of these statements is perplexing.

In 1853 there was a race from New Orleans to Louisville, between the steamers *Eclipse* and *A.L. Shotwell*, on which seventy thousand dollars were staked by the owners of the boats. An equal amount was invested in "private bets" among outside parties. The two boats were literally "stripped for the race." They were loaded to the depth that would give them the greatest speed, and their arrangements for taking fuel were as complete as possible. Barges were filled with wood at stated points along the river, and dropped out to midstream as the steamers approached. They were taken alongside, and their loads of wood transferred without any stoppage of the engines of the boats.

At the end of the first twenty-four hours the *Eclipse* and *Shotwell* were side by side, three hundred and sixty miles from New Orleans. The race was understood to be won by the *Eclipse*, but was so close that the stakes were never paid.

In the palmy days of steamboating, the charges for way-travel were varied according to the locality. Below Memphis it was the rule to take no single fare less than five dollars, even if the passenger were going but a half-dozen miles. Along Red River the steamboat clerks graduated the fare according to the parish where the passenger came on board. The more fertile and wealthy the region, the higher was the price of passage. Travelers from the cotton country paid more than those from the tobacco country. Those from the sugar country paid more than any other class. With few exceptions, there was no "ticket" system. Passengers paid their fare at any hour of their journey that best suited them. Every man was considered honest until he gave proof to the contrary. There was an occasional Jeremy Diddler, but his operations were very limited.

When the Rebellion began, the old customs on the Mississippi were swept away. The most rigid "pay-on-entering" system was adopted, and the man who could evade it must be very shrewd. The wealth along the Great River melted into thin air. The *bonhommie* of travel disappeared, and was succeeded by the most thorough selfishness in collective and individual bodies. Scrambles for the first choice of state-rooms, the first seat at table, and the first drink at the bar, became a part of the new *régime*. The ladies were little regarded in the hurly-burly of steamboat life. Men would take possession of ladies' chairs at table, and pay no heed to remonstrances.

I have seen an officer in blue uniform place his muddy boots on the center-table in a cabin full of ladies, and proceed to light a cigar. The captain of the boat suggested that the officer's conduct was in violation of the rules of propriety, and received the answer:

"I have fought to help open the Mississippi, and, by ----, I am going to enjoy it."

The careless display of the butt of a revolver, while he gave this answer, left the pleasure-seeker master of the situation. I am sorry to say that occurrences of a similar character were very frequent in the past three years. With the end of the war it is to be hoped that the character of Mississippi travel will be improved.

In May, 1861, the Rebels blockaded the Mississippi at Memphis. In the same month the National forces established a blockade at Cairo. In July, '63, the capture of Vicksburg and Port Hudson removed the last Rebel obstruction. The *Imperial* was the first passenger boat to descend the river, after the reopening of navigation.

Up to within a few months of the close of the Rebellion, steamers plying on the river were in constant, danger of destruction by Rebel batteries. The Rebel Secretary of War ordered these batteries placed along the Mississippi, in the hope of stopping all travel by that route. His plan was unsuccessful. Equally so was the barbarous practice of burning passenger steamboats while in motion between landing-places. On transports fired upon by guerrillas (or Rebels), about a hundred persons were killed and as many wounded. A due proportion of these were women and children. On steamboats burned by Rebel incendiaries, probably a hundred and fifty lives were lost. This does not include the dead by the terrible disaster to the *Sultana*. It is supposed that this boat was blown up by a Rebel torpedo in her coal.

It was my fortune to be a passenger on the steamer *Von Phul*, which left New Orleans for St. Louis on the evening of December 7th, 1863. I had been for some time traveling up and down the Mississippi, and running the gauntlet between Rebel batteries on either shore. There was some risk attending my travels, but up to that time I escaped unharmed.

On the afternoon of the 8th, when the boat was about eight miles above Bayou Sara, I experienced a new sensation.

Seated at a table in the cabin, and busily engaged in writing, I heard a heavy crash over my head, almost instantly followed by another. My first thought was that the chimneys or some part of the pilot-house had fallen, and I half looked to see the roof of the cabin tumbling in. I saw the passengers running from the cabin, and heard some one shout:

"The guerrillas are firing on us."

I collected my writing materials and sought my state-room, where I had left Mr. Colburn, my traveling companion, soundly asleep a few minutes before.

He was sitting on the edge of his berth, and wondering what all the row was about. The crash that startled me had awakened him. He thought the occurrence was of little moment, and assented to my suggestion, that we were just as safe there as anywhere else on the boat.

Gallantry prevented our remaining quiet. There were several ladies on board, and it behooved us to extend them what protection we could. We sought them, and "protected" them to the best of our united ability. Their place of refuge was between the cabin and the wheel-house, opposite the battery's position. A sheet of wet paper would afford as much resistance to a paving-stone as the walls of a steamboat cabin to a six-pound shot. As we stood among the ladies, two shells passed through the side of the cabin, within a few inches of our heads.

The shots grew fewer in number, and some of them dropped in the river behind us. Just as we thought all alarm was over, we saw smoke issuing from the cabin gangway. Then, some one shouted, "*The boat is on fire!*"

Dropping a lady who evinced a disposition to faint, I entered the cabin. A half-dozen men were there before me, and seeking the locality of the fire. I was first to discover it.

A shell, in passing through a state-room, entered a pillow, and scattered the feathers through the cabin. A considerable quantity of these feathers fell upon a hot stove, and the smoke and odor of their burning caused the alarm.

The ladies concluded not to faint. Three minutes after the affair was over, they were as calm as ever.

The Rebels opened fire when we were abreast of their position, and did not cease until we were out of range. We were fifteen minutes within reach of their guns.

Our wheels seemed to turn very slowly. No one can express in words the anxiety with which we listened, after each shot, for the puffing of the engines. So long as the machinery was uninjured, there was no danger of our falling into Rebel hands. But with our engines disabled, our chances for capture would be very good.

As the last shot fell astern of the boat and sent up a column of spray, we looked about the cabin and saw that no one had been injured. A moment later came the announcement from the pilot-house:

"Captain Gorman is killed!"

I ascended to the hurricane deck, and thence to the pilot-house. The pilot, with his hat thrown aside and his hair streaming in the wind, stood at his post, carefully guiding the boat on her course. The body of the captain was lying at his feet. Another man lay dying, close by the opening in which the wheel revolved. The floor was covered with blood, splinters, glass, and the fragments of a shattered stove. One side of the little room was broken in, and the other side was perforated where the projectiles made their exit.

The first gun from the Rebels threw a shell which entered the side of the pilot-house, and struck the captain, who was sitting just behind the pilot. Death must have been instantaneous. A moment later, a "spherical-case shot" followed the shell. It exploded as it struck the wood-work, and a portion of the contents entered the side of the bar-keeper of the boat. In falling to the floor he fell against the wheel. The pilot, steering the boat with one hand, pulled the dying man from the wheel with the other, and placed him by the side of the dead captain.

Though, apparently, the pilot was as cool and undisturbed as ever, his face was whiter than usual. He said the most trying moment of all was soon after the first shots were fired. Wishing to "round the bend" as speedily as possible, he rang the bell as a signal to the engineer to check the speed of one of the wheels. The signal was not obeyed, the engineers having fled to places of safety. He rang the bell once more. He shouted down the speaking-tube, to enforce compliance with his order.

There was no answer. The engines were caring for themselves. The boat must be controlled by the rudder alone. With a dead man and a dying man at his feet, with the Rebel shot and shell every moment perforating the boat or falling near it, and with no help from those who should control the machinery, he felt that his position was a painful one.

We were out of danger. An hour later we found the gun-boat *Neosho*, at anchor, eight miles further up the stream. Thinking we might again be attacked, the commander of the *Neosho* offered to convoy us to Red River. We accepted his offer. As soon as the *Neosho* raised sufficient steam to enable her to move, we proceeded on our course.

Order was restored on the *Von Phul*. Most of the passengers gathered in little groups, and talked about the recent occurrence. I returned to my writing, and Colburn gave his attention to a book. With the gun-boat at our side, no one supposed there was danger of another attack.

A half-hour after starting under convoy of the gun-boat, the Rebels once more opened fire. They paid no attention to the *Neosho*, but threw all their projectiles at the *Von Phul*. The first shell passed through the cabin, wounding a person near me, and grazing a post against which Colburn and myself were resting our chairs. This shell was followed by others in quick succession, most of them passing through the cabin. One exploded under the portion of the cabin directly beneath my position. The explosion uplifted the boards with such force as to overturn my table and disturb the steadiness of my chair.

I dreaded splinters far more than I feared the pitiless iron. I left the cabin, through which the shells were pouring, and descended to the lower deck. It was no better there than above. We were increasing the distance between ourselves and the Rebels, and the shot began to strike lower down. Nearly every shot raked the lower deck.

A loose plank on which I stood was split for more than half its length, by a shot which struck my foot when its force was nearly spent. Though the skin was not abraded, and no bones were broken, I felt the effect of the blow for several weeks.

I lay down upon the deck. A moment after I had taken my horizontal position, two men who lay against me were mortally wounded by a shell. The right leg of one was completely severed below the knee. This shell was the last projectile that struck the forward portion of the boat.

With a handkerchief loosely tied and twisted with a stick, I endeavored to stop the flow of blood from the leg of the wounded man. I was partially successful, but the stoppage of blood could not save the man's life. He died within the hour.

Forty-two shot and shell struck the boat. The escape-pipe was severed where it passed between two state-rooms, and filled the cabin with steam. The safe in the captain's office was perforated as if it had been made of wood. A trunk was broken by a shell, and its contents were scattered upon the floor. Splinters had fallen in the cabin, and were spread thickly upon the carpet. Every person who escaped uninjured had his own list of incidents to narrate.

Out of about fifty persons on board the *Von Phul* at the time of this occurrence, twelve were killed or wounded. One of the last projectiles that struck the boat, injured a boiler sufficiently to allow the escape of steam. In ten minutes our engines moved very feebly. We were forced to "tie up" to the eastern bank of the river. We were by this time out of range of the Rebel battery. The *Neosho* had opened fire, and by the time we made fast to the bank, the Rebels were in retreat.

The *Neosho* ceased firing and moved to our relief. Before she reached us, the steamer *Atlantic* came in sight, descending the river. We hailed her, and she came alongside. Immediately on learning our condition, her captain offered to tow the *Von Phul* to Red River, twenty miles distant. There we could lie, under protection of the gun-boats, and repair the damages to our machinery. We accepted his offer at once.

I can hardly imagine a situation of greater helplessness, than a place on board a Western passenger-steamer under the guns of a hostile battery. A battle-field is no comparison. On solid earth the principal danger is from projectiles. You can fight, or, under some circumstances, can run away. On a Mississippi transport, you are equally in danger of being shot. Added to this, you may be struck by splinters, scalded by steam, burned by fire, or drowned in the water. You cannot fight, you cannot run away, and you cannot find shelter. With no power for resistance or escape, the sense of danger and helplessness cannot be set aside.

A few weeks after the occurrence just narrated, the steamer *Brazil*, on her way from Vicksburg to Natchez, was fired upon by a Rebel battery near Rodney, Mississippi. The boat was struck a half-dozen times by shot and shell. More than a hundred rifle-bullets were thrown on board. Three persons were killed and as many wounded.

Among those killed on the *Brazil*, was a young woman who had engaged to take charge of a school for negro children at Natchez. The Rebel sympathizers at Natchez displayed much gratification at her death. On several occasions I heard some of the more pious among them declare that the hand of God directed the fatal missile. They prophesied violent or sudden deaths to all who came to the South on a similar mission.

The steamer *Black Hawk* was fired upon by a Rebel battery at the mouth of Red River. The boat ran aground in range of the enemy's guns. A shell set her pilot-house on fire, and several persons were killed in the cabin.

Strange to say, though aground and on fire under a Rebel battery, the *Black Hawk* was saved. By great exertions on the part of officers and crew, the fire was extinguished after the pilot-house was burned away. A temporary steering apparatus was rigged, and the boat moved from the shoal where she had grounded. She was a full half hour within range of the Rebel guns.

CHAPTER XLV
THE ARMY CORRESPONDENT

Having lain aside my pen while engaged in planting cotton and entertaining guerrillas, I resumed it on coming North, after that experiment was finished. Setting aside my capture in New Hampshire, narrated in the first chapter, my adventures in the field commenced in Missouri in the earliest campaign. Singularly enough, they terminated on our Northern border. In the earlier days of the Rebellion, it was the jest of the correspondents, that they would, some time, find occasion to write war-letters from the Northern cities. The jest became a reality in the siege of Cincinnati. During that siege we wondered whether it would be possible to extend our labors to Detroit or Mackinaw.

In September, 1864, the famous "Lake Erie Piracy" occurred. I was in Cleveland when the news of the seizure of the *Philo Parsons* was announced by telegraph, and at once proceeded to Detroit. The capture of the *Parsons* was a very absurd movement on the part of the Rebels, who had taken refuge in Canada. The original design was, doubtless, the capture of the gun-boat *Michigan*, and the release of the prisoners on Johnson's Island. The captors of the *Parsons* had confederates in Sandusky, who endeavored to have the *Michigan* in a half-disabled condition when the *Parsons* arrived. This was not accomplished, and the scheme fell completely through. The two small steamers, the *Parsons* and *Island Queen*, were abandoned after being in Rebel hands only a few hours.

The officers of the *Parsons* told an interesting story of their seizure. Mr. Ashley, the clerk, said the boat left Detroit for Sandusky at her usual hour. She had a few passengers from Detroit, and received others at various landings. The last party that came on board brought an old trunk bound with ropes. The different parties did not recognize each other, not even when drinking at the bar. When near Kelly's Island in Lake Erie, the various officers of the steamer were suddenly seized. The ropes on the trunk were cut, the lid flew open, and a quantity of revolvers and hatchets was brought to light.

The pirates declared they were acting in the interest of the "Confederacy." They relieved Mr. Ashley of his pocket-book and contents, and appropriated the money they found in the safe. Those of the passengers who were not "in the ring," were compelled to contribute to the representatives of the Rebel Government. This little affair was claimed to be "belligerent" throughout. At Kelly's Island the passengers and crew were liberated on parole not to take up arms against the Confederacy until properly exchanged.

After cruising in front of Sandusky, and failing to receive signals which they expected, the pirates returned to Canada with their prize. One of their "belligerent" acts was to throw overboard the cargo of the *Parsons*, together with most of her furniture. At Sandwich, near Detroit, they left the boat, after taking ashore a piano and other articles. Her Majesty's officer of customs took possession of this stolen property, on the ground that it was brought into Canada without the proper permits from the custom-house. It was subsequently recovered by its owners.

The St. Albans raid, which occurred a few months later, was a similar act of belligerency. It created more excitement than the Lake Erie piracy, but the questions involved were practically the same. That the Rebels had a right of asylum in Canada no one could deny, but there was a difference of opinion respecting the proper limits to those rights. The Rebels hoped to involve us in a controversy with England, that should result in the recognition of the Confederacy. This was frequently avowed by some of the indiscreet refugees.

After the capture of the *Parsons* and the raid upon St. Albans, the Canadian authorities sent a strong force of militia to watch the frontier. A battalion of British regulars was stationed at Windsor, opposite Detroit, early in 1864, but was removed to the interior before the raids occurred. The authorities assigned as a reason for this removal, the desire to concentrate their forces at some central point. The real reason was the rapid desertion of their men, allured by the high pay and opportunity of active service in our army. In two months the battalion at Windsor was reduced fifteen per cent, by desertions alone.

Shortly after the St. Albans raid, a paper in Rochester announced a visit to that city by a cricket-club from Toronto. The paragraph was written somewhat obscurely, and jestingly spoke of the Toronto men as "raiders." The paper reached New York, and so alarmed the authorities that troops were at once ordered to Rochester and other points on the frontier. The misapprehension was discovered in season to prevent the actual moving of the troops.

With the suppression of the Rebellion the mission of the war correspondent was ended. Let us all hope that his services will not again be required, in this country, at least, during the present century. The publication of the reports of battles, written on the field, and frequently during the heat of an engagement, was a marked feature of the late war. "Our Special Correspondent" is not, however, an invention belonging to this important era of our history.

His existence dates from the days of the Greeks and Romans. If Homer had witnessed the battles which he described, he would, doubtless, be recognized as the earliest war correspondent. Xenophon was the first regular correspondent of which we have any record. He achieved an enduring fame, which is a just tribute to the man and his profession.

During the Middle Ages, the Crusades afforded fine opportunities for the war correspondents to display their abilities. The prevailing ignorance of those times is shown in the absence of any reliable accounts of the Holy Wars, written by journalists on the field. There was no daily press, and the mail communications were very unreliable. Down to the nineteenth century, Xenophon had no formidable competitors for the honors which attached to his name.

The elder Napoleon always acted as his own "Special." His bulletins, by rapid post to Paris, were generally the first tidings of his brilliant marches and victories. His example was thought worthy of imitation by several military officials during the late Rebellion. Rear-Admiral Porter essayed to excel Napoleon in sending early reports of battles for public perusal. "I have the honor to inform the Department," is a formula with which most editors and printers became intimately acquainted. The admiral's veracity was not as conspicuous as his eagerness to push his reports in print.

At Waterloo there was no regular correspondent of the London press. Several volunteer writers furnished accounts of the battle for publication, whose accuracy has been called in question. Wellington's official dispatches were outstripped by the enterprise of a London banking-house. The Rothschilds knew the result of the battle eight hours before Wellington's courier arrived.

Carrier pigeons were used to convey the intelligence. During the Rebellion, Wall Street speculators endeavored to imitate the policy of the Rothschilds, but were only partially successful.

In the war between Mexico and the United States, "Our Special" was actively, though not extensively, employed. On one occasion, *The Herald* obtained its news in advance of the official dispatches to the Government. The magnetic telegraph was then unknown. Horse-flesh and steam were the only means of transmitting intelligence. If we except the New Orleans *Picayune*, *The Herald* was the only paper represented in Mexico during the campaigns of Scott and Taylor.

During the conflict between France and England on the one hand, and Russia on the other, the journals of London and Paris sent their representatives to the Crimea. The London *Times*, the foremost paper of Europe, gave Russell a reputation he will long retain. The "Thunderer's" letters from the camp before Sebastopol became known throughout the civilized world. A few years later, the East Indian rebellion once more called the London specials to the field. In giving the history of the campaigns in India, *The Times* and its representative overshadowed all the rest.

Just before the commencement of hostilities in the late Rebellion, the leading journals of New York were well represented in the South. Each day these papers gave their readers full details of all important events that transpired in the South. The correspondents that witnessed the firing of the Southern heart had many adventures. Some of them narrowly escaped with their lives.

At Richmond, a crowd visited the Spottswood House, with the avowed intention of hanging a *Herald* correspondent, who managed to escape through a back door of the building. A representative of *The Tribune* was summoned before the authorities at Charleston, on the charge of being a Federal spy. He was cleared of the charge, but advised to proceed North as early as possible. When he departed, Governor Pickens requested him, as a particular favor, to ascertain the name of *The Tribune* correspondent, on arrival in New York, and inform him by letter. He promised to do so. On reaching the North, he kindly told Governor Pickens who *The Tribune* correspondent was.

A *Times* correspondent, passing through Harper's Ferry, found himself in the hands of "the Chivalry," who proposed to hang him on the general charge of being an Abolitionist. He was finally released without injury, but at one time the chances of his escape were small.

The New Orleans correspondent of *The Tribune* came North on the last passenger-train from Richmond to Aquia Creek. One of *The Herald's* representatives was thrown into prison by Jeff. Davis, but released through the influence of Pope Walker, the Rebel Secretary of War. Another remained in the South until all regular communication was cut off. He reached the North in safety by the line of the "underground railway."

When the Rebellion was fairly inaugurated, the various points of interest were at once visited by the correspondents of the press. Wherever our armies operated, the principal dailies of New York and other cities were represented. Washington was the center of gravity around which the Eastern correspondents revolved. As the army advanced into Virginia, every movement was carefully chronicled. The competition between the different journals was very great.

In the West the field was broader, and the competition, though active, was less bitter than along the Potomac. In the early days, St. Louis, Cairo, and Louisville were the principal Western points where correspondents were stationed. As our armies extended their operations, the journalists found their field of labor enlarged. St. Louis lost its importance when the Rebels were driven from Missouri. For a long time Cairo was the principal rendezvous of the journalists, but it became less noted as our armies pressed forward along the Mississippi.

Every war-correspondent has his story of experiences in the field. Gathering the details of a battle in the midst of its dangers; sharing the privations of the camp and the fatigues of the march; riding with scouts, and visiting the skirmishers on the extreme front; journeying to the rear through regions infested by the enemy's cavalry, or running the gauntlet of Rebel batteries, his life was far from monotonous. Frequently the correspondents acted as volunteer aids to generals during engagements, and rendered important service. They often took the muskets of fallen soldiers and used them to advantage. On the water, as on land, they sustained their reputation, and proved that the hand which wielded the pen was able to wield the sword. They contributed their proportion of killed, wounded, and captured to the casualties of the war. Some of them accepted commissions in the army and navy.

During the campaign of General Lyon in Missouri, the journalists who accompanied that army were in the habit of riding outside the lines to find comfortable quarters for the night. Frequently they went two or three miles ahead of the entire column, in order to make sure of a good dinner before the soldiers could overtake them. One night two of them slept at a house three miles from the road which the army was following. The inmates of the mansion were unaware of the vicinity of armed "Yankees," and entertained the strangers without question. Though a dozen Rebel scouts called at the house before daylight, the correspondents were undisturbed. After that occasion they were more cautious in their movements.

In Kentucky, during the advance of Kirby Smith upon Cincinnati, the correspondents of *The Gazette* and *The Commercial* were captured by the advance-guard of Rebel cavalry. Their baggage, money, and watches became the property of their captors. The correspondents were released, and obliged to walk about eighty miles in an August sun. A short time later,

Mr. Shanks and Mr. Westfall, correspondents of *The Herald*, were made acquainted with John Morgan, in one of the raids of that famous guerrilla. The acquaintance resulted in a thorough depletion of the wardrobes of the captured gentlemen.

In Virginia, Mr. Cadwallader and Mr. Fitzpatrick, of *The Herald*, and Mr. Crounse, of *The Times*, were captured by Mosby, and liberated after a brief detention and a complete relief of every thing portable and valuable, down to their vests and pantaloons. Even their dispatches were taken from them and forwarded to Richmond. A portion of these reports found their way into the Richmond papers. Stonewall Jackson and Stuart were also fortunate enough to capture some of the representatives of the Press. At one time there were five correspondents of *The Herald* in the hands of the Rebels. One of them, Mr. Anderson, was held more than a year. He was kept for ten days in an iron dungeon, where no ray of light could penetrate.

I have elsewhere alluded to the capture of Messrs. Richardson and Browne, of *The Tribune*, and Mr. Colburn, of *The World*, in front of Vicksburg. The story of the captivity and perilous escape of these representatives of *The Tribune* reveals a patience, a fortitude, a daring, and a fertility of resource not often excelled.

Some of the most graphic battle-accounts of the war were written very hastily. During the three days' battle at Gettysburg, *The Herald* published each morning the details of the fighting of the previous day, down to the setting of the sun. This was accomplished by having a correspondent with each corps, and one at head-quarters to forward the accounts to the nearest telegraph office. At Antietam, *The Tribune* correspondent viewed the battle by day, and then hurried from the field, writing the most of his account on a railway train. From Fort Donelson the correspondents of *The World* and *The Tribune* went to Cairo, on a hospital boat crowded with wounded. Their accounts were written amid dead and suffering men, but when published they bore little evidence of their hasty preparation.

I once wrote a portion of a letter at the end of a medium-sized table. At the other end of the table a party of gamblers, with twenty or thirty spectators, were indulging in "Chuck-a-Luck." I have known dispatches to be written on horseback, but they were very brief, and utterly illegible to any except the writer. Much of the press correspondence during the war was written in railway cars and on steamboats, and much on camp-chests, stumps, or other substitutes for tables. I have seen a half-dozen correspondents busily engaged with their letters at the same moment, each of them resting his port-folio on his knee, or standing upright, with no support whatever. On one occasion a fellow-journalist assured me that the broad chest of a slumbering *confrere* made an excellent table, the undulations caused by the sleeper's breathing being the only objectionable feature.

Sometimes a correspondent reached the end of a long ride so exhausted as to be unable to hold a pen for ten consecutive minutes. In such case a short-hand writer was employed, when accessible, to take down from rapid dictation the story of our victory or defeat.

Under all the disadvantages of time, place, and circumstances, of physical exhaustion and mental anxiety, it is greatly to the correspondents' credit that they wrote so well. Battle-accounts were frequently published that would be no mean comparison to the studied pen-pictures of the famous writers of this or any other age. They were extensively copied by the press of England and the Continent, and received high praise for their vivid portrayal of the battle-field and its scenes. Apart from the graphic accounts of great battles, they furnished materials from which the historians will write the enduring records of the war. With files of the New York dailies at his side, an industrious writer could compile a history of the Rebellion, complete in all its details.

It was a general complaint of the correspondents that their profession was never officially recognized so as to give them an established position in the army. They received passes from head-quarters, and could generally go where they willed, but there were many officers who chose to throw petty but annoying restrictions around them. As they were generally situated throughout the army, they were, to some extent, dependent upon official courtesies. Of course, this dependence was injurious to free narration or criticism when any officer had conducted improperly.

If there is ever another occasion for the services of the war correspondent on our soil, it is to be hoped Congress will pass a law establishing a position for the journalists, fixing their status in the field, surrounding them with all necessary restrictions, and authorizing them to purchase supplies and forage from the proper departments. During the Crimean war, the correspondents of the French and English papers had a recognized position, where they were subject to the same rules, and entitled to the same privileges, as the officers they accompanied. When Sir George Brown, at Eupatoria, forbade any officer appearing in public with unshaven chin, he made no distinction in favor of the members of the Press.

Notwithstanding their fierce competition in serving the journals they represented, the correspondents with our army were generally on the most friendly terms with each other. Perhaps this was less the case in the East than in the West, where the rivalry was not so intense and continuous. In the armies in the Mississippi Valley, the representatives of competing journals frequently slept, ate, traveled, and smoked together, and not unfrequently drank from the same flask with equal relish. In the early days, "Room 45," in the St. Charles Hotel at Cairo, was the resort of all the correspondents at that point. There they laid aside their professional jealousies, and passed their idle hours in efforts for mutual amusement. On some occasions the floor of the room would be covered, in the morning, with a confused mass of boots, hats, coats, and other articles of masculine wear, out of which the earliest riser would array himself in whatever suited his fancy, without the slightest regard to the owner. "Forty-five" was the neutral ground where the correspondents planned campaigns for all the armies of the Union, arranged the downfall of the Rebellion, expressed their views of military measures and military men, exulted over successes, mourned over defeats, and toasted in full glasses the flag that our soldiers upheld.

Since the close of the war, many of the correspondents have taken positions in the offices of the journals they represented in the field. Some have established papers of their own in the South, and a few have retired to other civil pursuits. Some are making professional tours of the Southern States and recording the status of the people lately in rebellion. *The Herald* has sent several of its *attachés* to the European capitals, and promises to chronicle in detail the next great war in the Old World.

CHAPTER XLVI
THE PRESENT CONDITION OF THE SOUTH

The suppression of the Rebellion, and the restoration of peace throughout the entire South, have opened a large field for emigration. The white population of the Southern States, never as dense as that of the North, has been greatly diminished in consequence of the war. In many localities more than half the able-bodied male inhabitants have been swept away, and everywhere the loss of men is severely felt. The breaking up of the former system of labor in the cotton and sugar States will hinder the progress of agriculture for a considerable time, but there can be little doubt of its beneficial effect in the end. The desolation that was spread in the track of our armies will be apparent for many years. The South will ultimately recover from all her calamities, but she will need the energy and capital of the Northern States to assist her.

During the progress of the war, as our armies penetrated the fertile portions of the "Confederacy," many of our soldiers cast longing eyes at the prospective wealth around them. "When the war is over we will come here to live, and show these people something they never dreamed of," was a frequent remark. Men born and reared in the extreme North, were amazed at the luxuriance of Southern verdure, and wondered that the richness of the soil had not been turned to greater advantage. It is often said in New England that no man who has once visited the fertile West ever returns to make his residence in the Eastern States. Many who have explored the South, and obtained a knowledge of its resources, will be equally reluctant to dwell in the regions where their boyhood days were passed.

While the war was in progress many Northern men purchased plantations on the islands along the Southern coast, and announced their determination to remain there permanently. After the capture of New Orleans, business in that city passed into the hands of Northerners, much to the chagrin of the older inhabitants. When the disposition of our army and the topography of the country made the lower portion of Louisiana secure against Rebel raids, many plantations in that locality were purchased outright by Northern speculators. I have elsewhere shown how the cotton culture was extensively carried on by "Yankees," and that failure was not due to their inability to conduct the details of the enterprise.

Ten years ago, emigration to Kansas was highly popular. Aid Societies were organized in various localities, and the Territory was rapidly filled. Political influences had much to do with this emigration from both North and South, and many implements carried by the emigrants were not altogether agricultural in their character. The soil of Kansas was known to be fertile, and its climate excellent. The Territory presented attractions to settlers, apart from political considerations. But in going thither the emigrants crossed a region equally fertile, and possessing superior advantages in its proximity to a market. No State in the Union could boast of greater possibilities than Missouri, yet few travelers in search of a home ventured to settle within her limits.

The reason was apparent. Missouri was a slave State, though bounded on three sides by free soil. Few Northern emigrants desired to settle in the midst of slavery. The distinction between the ruling and laboring classes was not as great as in the cotton States, but there was a distinction beyond dispute. Whatever his blood or complexion, the man who labored with his hands was on a level, or nearly so, with the slave. Thousands passed up the Missouri River, or crossed the northern portion of the State, to settle in the new Territory of Kansas. When political influences ceased, the result was still the same. The Hannibal and St. Joseph Railway threw its valuable lands into the market, but with little success.

With the suppression of the late Rebellion, and the abolition of slavery in Missouri, the situation is materially changed. From Illinois, Ohio, and Indiana, there is a large emigration to Missouri. I was recently informed that forty families from a single county in Ohio had sent a delegation to Missouri to look out suitable locations, either of wild land or of farms under cultivation. There is every prospect that the State will be rapidly filled with a population that believes in freedom and in the dignity of labor. She has an advantage over the other ex-slave States, in lying west of the populous regions of the North. Hitherto, emigration has generally followed the great isothermal lines, as can be readily seen when we study the population of the Western States. Northern Ohio is more New Englandish than Southern Ohio, and the parallel holds good in Northern and Southern Illinois. There will undoubtedly be a large emigration to Missouri in preference to the other Southern States, but our whole migratory element will not find accommodation in her limits. The entire South will be overrun by settlers from the North.

Long ago, *Punch* gave advice to persons about to marry. It was all comprised in the single word, "DON'T." Whoever is in haste to emigrate to the South, would do well to consider, for a time, this brief, but emphatic counsel. No one should think of leaving the Northern States, until he has fairly considered the advantages and disadvantages of the movement. If he departs with the expectation of finding every thing to his liking, he will be greatly disappointed at the result.

There will be many difficulties to overcome. The people now residing in the late rebellious States are generally impoverished. They have little money, and, in many cases, their stock and valuables of all kinds have been swept away. Their farms are often without fences, and their farming-tools worn out, disabled, or destroyed. Their system of labor is broken up. The negro is a slave no longer, and the transition from bondage to freedom will affect, for a time, the producing interests of the South.

Though the Rebellion is suppressed, the spirit of discontent still remains in many localities, and will retard the process of reconstruction. The teachings of slavery have made the men of the South bitterly hostile to those of the North. This hostility was carefully nurtured by the insurgent leaders during the Rebellion, and much of it still exists. In many sections of the South, efforts will be made to prevent immigration from the North, through a fear that the old inhabitants will lose their political rights.

At the time I am writing, the owners of property in Richmond are holding it at such high rates as to repel Northern purchasers. Letters from that city say, the residents have determined to sell no property to Northern men, when they can possibly avoid it. No encouragement is likely to be given to Northern farmers and artisans to migrate thither. A scheme for taking a large number of European emigrants directly from foreign ports to Richmond, and thence to scatter them throughout Virginia, is being considered by the Virginia politicians. The wealthy men in the Old Dominion, who were Secessionists for the sake of secession, and who gave every assistance to the Rebel cause, are opposed to the admission of Northern settlers. They may be unable to prevent it, but they will be none the less earnest in their efforts.

This feeling extends throughout a large portion of Virginia, and exists in the other States of the South. Its intensity varies in different localities, according to the extent of the slave population in the days before the war, and the influence that the Radical men of the South have exercised. While Virginia is unwilling to receive strangers, North Carolina is manifesting a desire to fill her territory with Northern capital and men. She is already endeavoring to encourage emigration, and has offered large quantities of land on liberal terms. In Newbern, Wilmington, and Raleigh, the Northern element is large. Newbern is "Yankeeized" as much as New Orleans. Wilmington bids fair to have intimate relations with New York and Boston. An agency has been established at Raleigh, under the sanction of the Governor of the State, to secure the immediate occupation of farming and mining lands, mills, manufactories, and all other kinds of real estate. Northern capital and sinew is already on its way to that region. The great majority of the North Carolinians approve the movement, but there are many persons in the State who equal the Virginians in their hostility to innovations.

In South Carolina, few beside the negroes will welcome the Northerner with open arms. The State that hatched the secession egg, and proclaimed herself at all times first and foremost for the perpetuation of slavery, will not exult at the change which circumstances have wrought. Her Barnwells, her McGraths, her Rhetts, and her Hamptons declared they would perish in the last ditch, rather than submit. Some of them have perished, but many still remain. Having been life-long opponents of Northern policy, Northern industry, and Northern enterprise, they will hardly change their opinions until taught by the logic of events.

Means of transportation are limited. On the railways the tracks are nearly worn out, and must be newly laid before they can be used with their old facility. Rolling stock is disabled or destroyed. Much of it must be wholly replaced, and that which now remains must undergo extensive repairs. Depots and machine-shops have been burned, and many bridges are bridges no longer. On the smaller rivers but few steamboats are running, and these are generally of a poor class. Wagons are far from abundant, and mules and horses are very scarce. The wants of the armies have been supplied with little regard to the inconvenience of the people.

Corn-mills, saw-mills, gins, and factories have fed the flames. Wherever our armies penetrated they spread devastation in their track. Many portions of the South were not visited by a hostile force, but they did not escape the effects of war. Southern Georgia and Florida suffered little from the presence of the Northern armies, but the scarcity of provisions and the destitution of the people are nearly as great in that region as elsewhere.

Until the present indignation at their defeat is passed away, many of the Southern people will not be inclined to give any countenance to the employment of freed negroes. They believe slavery is the proper condition for the negro, and declare that any system based on free labor will prove a failure. This feeling will not be general among the Southern people, and will doubtless be removed in time.

The transition from slavery to freedom will cause some irregularities on the part of the colored race. I do not apprehend serious trouble in controlling the negro, and believe his work will be fully available throughout the South. It is natural that he should desire a little holiday with his release from bondage. For a time many negroes will be idle, and so will many white men who have returned from the Rebel armies. According to present indications, the African race displays far more industry than the Caucasian throughout the Southern States. Letters from the South say the negroes are at work in some localities, but the whites are everywhere idle.

Those who go to the South for purposes of traffic may or may not be favored with large profits. All the products of the mechanic arts are very scarce in the interior, while in the larger towns trade is generally overdone. Large stocks of goods were taken to all places accessible by water as soon as the ports were opened. The supply exceeded the demand, and many dealers suffered heavy loss. From Richmond and other points considerable quantities of goods have been reshipped to New York, or sold for less than cost. Doubtless the trade with the South will ultimately be very large, but it cannot spring up in a day. Money is needed before speculation can be active. A year or two, at the least, will be needed to fill the Southern pocket.

So much for the dark side of the picture. Emigrants are apt to listen to favorable accounts of the region whither they are bound, while they close their ears to all stories of an unfavorable character. To insure a hearing of both sides of the question under discussion, I have given the discouraging arguments in advance of all others. Already those who desire to stimulate travel to the South, are relating wonderful stories of its fertility and its great advantages to settlers. No doubt they are telling much that is true, but they do not tell all the truth. Every one has heard the statement, circulated in Ireland many years since, that America abounded in roasted pigs that ran about the streets, carrying knives and forks in their mouths, and making vocal requests to be devoured. Notwithstanding the absurdity of the story, it is reported to have received credit.

The history of every emigration scheme abounds in narratives of a brilliant, though piscatorial, character. The interior portions of all the Western States are of wonderful fertility, and no inhabitant of that region has any hesitation in announcing the above fact. But not one in a hundred will state frankly his distance from market, and the value of wheat and corn at the points of their production. In too many cases the bright side of the story is sufficient for the listener.

I once traveled in a railway car where there were a dozen emigrants from the New England States, seeking a home in the West. An agent of a county in

Iowa was endeavoring to call their attention to the great advantages which his region afforded. He told them of the fertility of the soil, the amount of corn and wheat that could be produced to the acre, the extent of labor needed for the production of a specified quantity of cereals, the abundance of timber, and the propinquity of fine streams, with many other brilliant and seductive stories. The emigrants listened in admiration of the Promised Land, and were on the point of consenting to follow the orator.

I ventured to ask the distance from those lands to a market where the products could be sold, and the probable cost of transportation.

The answer was an evasive one, but was sufficient to awaken the suspicions of the emigrants. My question destroyed the beautiful picture which the voluble agent had drawn.

Those who desire to seek their homes in the South will do well to remember that baked pigs are not likely to exist in abundance in the regions traversed by the National armies.

CHAPTER XLVII
HOW DISADVANTAGES MAY BE OVERCOME

The hinderances I have mentioned in the way of Southern emigration are of a temporary character. The opposition of the hostile portion of the Southern people can be overcome in time. When they see there is no possible hope for them to control the National policy, when they fully realize that slavery is ended, and ended forever, when they discover that the negro will work as a free man with advantage to his employer, they will become more amiable in disposition. Much of their present feeling arises from a hope of compelling a return to the old relation of master and slave. When this hope is completely destroyed, we shall have accomplished a great step toward reconstruction. A practical knowledge of Northern industry and enterprise will convince the people of the South, unless their hearts are thoroughly hardened, that some good can come out of Nazareth. They may never establish relations of great intimacy with their new neighbors, but their hostility will be diminished to insignificance.

Some of the advocates of the "last ditch" theory, who have sworn never to live in the United States, will, doubtless, depart to foreign lands, or follow the example of the Virginia gentleman who committed suicide on ascertaining the hopelessness of the Rebellion. Failing to do either of these things, they must finally acquiesce in the supremacy of National authority.

The Southern railways will be repaired, their rolling stock replaced, and the routes of travel restored to the old status. All cannot be done at once, as the destruction and damage have been very extensive, and many of the companies are utterly impoverished. From two to five years will elapse before passengers and freight can be transported with the same facility, in all directions, as before the war.

Under a more liberal policy new lines will be opened, and the various portions of the Southern States become accessible. During the war two railways were constructed under the auspices of the Rebel Government, that will prove of great advantage in coming years. These are the lines from Meridian, Mississippi, to Selma, Alabama, and from Danville, Virginia, to

Greensborough, North Carolina. A glance at a railway map of the Southern States will show their importance.

On many of the smaller rivers boats are being improvised by adding wheels and motive power to ordinary scows. In a half-dozen years, at the furthest, we will, doubtless, see the rivers of the Southern States traversed by as many steamers as before the war. On the Mississippi and its tributaries the destruction of steamboat property was very great, but the loss is rapidly being made good. Since 1862 many fine boats have been constructed, some of them larger and more costly than any that existed during the most prosperous days before the Rebellion. On the Alabama and other rivers, efforts are being made to restore the steamboat fleets to their former magnitude.

Horses, mules, machinery, and farming implements must and will be supplied out of the abundance in the North. The want of mules will be severely felt for some years. No Yankee has yet been able to invent a machine that will create serviceable mules to order. We must wait for their production by the ordinary means, and it will be a considerable time before the supply is equal to the demand. Those who turn their attention to stock-raising, during the next ten or twenty years, can always be certain of finding a ready and remunerative market.

The Southern soil is as fertile as ever. Cotton, rice, corn, sugar, wheat, and tobacco can be produced in their former abundance. Along the Mississippi the levees must be restored, to protect the plantations from floods. This will be a work of considerable magnitude, and, without extraordinary effort, cannot be accomplished for several years. Everywhere fences must be rebuilt, and many buildings necessary in preparing products for market must be restored. Time, capital, energy, and patience will be needed to develop anew the resources of the South. Properly applied, they will be richly rewarded.

No person should be hasty in his departure, nor rush blindly to the promised land. Thousands went to California, in '49 and '50, with the impression that the gold mines lay within an hour's walk of San Francisco. In '59, many persons landed at Leavenworth, on their way to Pike's Peak, under the belief that the auriferous mountain was only a day's journey from their landing-place. Thousands have gone "West" from New York and New England, believing that Chicago was very near the frontier. Those who start with no well-defined ideas of their destination are generally disappointed. The war has given the public a pretty accurate knowledge of the geography of the South, so that the old mistakes of emigrants to California and

Colorado are in slight danger of repetition, but there is a possibility of too little deliberation in setting out.

Before starting, the emigrant should obtain all accessible information about the region he intends to visit. Geographies, gazetteers, census returns, and works of a similar character will be of great advantage. Much can be obtained from persons who traveled in the rebellious States during the progress of the war. The leading papers throughout the country are now publishing letters from their special correspondents, relative to the state of affairs in the South. These letters are of great value, and deserve a careful study.

Information from interested parties should be received with caution. Those who have traveled in the far West know how difficult it is to obtain correct statements relative to the prosperity or advantages of any specified locality. Every man assures you that the town or the county where he resides, or where he is interested, is the best and the richest within a hundred miles. To an impartial observer, lying appears to be the only personal accomplishment in a new country. I presume those who wish to encourage Southern migration will be ready to set forth all the advantages (but none of the disadvantages) of their own localities.

Having fully determined where to go and what to do, having selected his route of travel, and ascertained, as near as possible, what will be needed on the journey, the emigrant will next consider his financial policy. No general rule can be given. In most cases it is better not to take a large amount of money at starting. To many this advice will be superfluous. Bills of exchange are much safer to carry than ready cash, and nearly as convenient for commercial transactions. Beyond an amount double the estimated expenses of his journey, the traveler will usually carry very little cash.

For the present, few persons should take their wives and children to the interior South, and none should do so on their first visit. Many houses have been burned or stripped of their furniture, provisions are scarce and costly, and the general facilities for domestic happiness are far from abundant. The conveniences for locomotion in that region are very poor, and will continue so for a considerable time. A man can "rough it" anywhere, but he can hardly expect his family to travel on flat cars, or on steamboats that have neither cabins nor decks, and subsist on the scanty and badly-cooked provisions that the Sunny South affords. By all means, I would counsel any young man on his way to the South not to elope with his neighbor's wife. In view of the condition of the country beyond Mason and Dixon's line, an elopement would prove his mistake of a lifetime.

I have already referred to the resources of Missouri. The State possesses greater mineral wealth than any other State of the Union, east of the Rocky Mountains. Her lead mines are extensive, easily worked, very productive, and practically inexhaustible. The same may be said of her iron mines. Pilot Knob and Iron Mountain are nearly solid masses of ore, the latter being a thousand feet in height. Copper mines have been opened and worked, and tin has been found in several localities. The soil of the Northern portion of Missouri can boast of a fertility equal to that of Kansas or Illinois. In the Southern portion the country is more broken, but it contains large areas of rich lands. The productions of Missouri are similar to those of the Northern States in the same latitude. More hemp is raised in Missouri than in any other State except Kentucky. Much of this article was used during the Rebellion, in efforts to break up the numerous guerrilla bands that infested the State. Tobacco is an important product, and its culture is highly remunerative. At Hermann, Booneville, and other points, the manufacture of wine from the Catawba grape is extensively carried on. In location and resources, Missouri is without a rival among the States that formerly maintained the system of slave labor.

CHAPTER XLVIII
THE RESOURCES OF THE SOUTHERN STATES

Compared with the North, the Southern States have been strictly an agricultural region. Their few manufactures were conducted on a small scale, and could not compete with those of the colder latitudes. They gave some attention to stock-raising in a few localities, but did not attach to it any great importance. Cotton was the product which fed, clothed, sheltered, and regaled the people. Even with the immense profits they received from its culture, they did not appear to understand the art of enjoyment. They generally lived on large and comfortless tracts of land, and had very few cities away from the sea-coast. They thought less of personal comfort than of the acquisition of more land, mules, and negroes.

In the greatest portion of the South, the people lived poorer than many Northern mechanics have lived in the past twenty years. The property in slaves, to the extent of four hundred millions of dollars, was their heaviest item of wealth, but they seemed unable to turn this wealth to the greatest advantage. With the climate and soil in their favor, they paid little attention to the cheaper luxuries of rational living, but surrounded themselves with much that was expensive, though utterly useless. On plantations where the owners resided, a visiter would find the women adorned with diamonds and laces that cost many thousand dollars, and feast his eyes upon parlor furniture and ornaments of the most elaborate character. But the dinner-table would present a repast far below that of a New England farmer or mechanic in ordinary circumstances, and the sleeping-rooms would give evidence that genuine comfort was a secondary consideration. Outside of New Orleans and Charleston, where they are conducted by foreigners, the South has no such market gardens, or such abundance and variety of wholesome fruits and vegetables, as the more sterile North can boast of everywhere. So of a thousand other marks of advancing civilization.

Virginia, "the mother of Presidents," is rich in minerals of the more useful sort, and some of the precious metals. Her list of mineral treasures includes gold, copper, iron, lead, plumbago, coal, and salt. The gold mines are not available except to capitalists, and it is not yet fully settled whether the yield is sufficient to warrant large investments. The gold is extracted from an auriferous region, extending from the Rappahannock to the Coosa River, in Alabama. The coal-beds in the State are easy of access, and said to be inexhaustible. The Kanawha salt-works are well known, and the petroleum regions of West Virginia are attracting much attention.

Virginia presents many varieties of soil, and, with a better system of cultivation, her productions can be greatly increased. (The same may be said of all the Southern States, from the Atlantic to the Rio Grande.) Her soil is favorable to all the products of the Northern States. The wheat and corn of Virginia have a high reputation. In the culture of tobacco she has always surpassed every other State of the Union, and was also the first State in which it was practiced by civilized man to any extent. Washington pronounced the central counties of Virginia the finest agricultural district in the United States, as he knew them. Daniel Webster declared, in a public speech in the Shenandoah Valley, that he had seen no finer farming land in his European travel than in that valley.

Until 1860, the people of Virginia paid considerable attention to the raising of negroes for the Southern market. For some reason this trade has greatly declined within the past five years, the stock becoming unsalable, and its production being interrupted. I would advise no person to contemplate moving to Virginia with a view to raising negroes for sale. The business was formerly conducted by the "First Families," and if it should be revived, they will doubtless claim an exclusive privilege.

North Carolina abounds in minerals, especially in gold, copper, iron, and coal. The fields of the latter are very extensive. The gold mines of North Carolina have been profitably worked for many years. A correspondent of *The World*, in a recent letter from Charlotte, North Carolina, says:

> In these times of mining excitement it should he more widely known that North Carolina is a competitor with California, Idaho, and Nebraska. Gold is found in paying quantities in the State, and in the northern parts of South Carolina and Georgia. For a hundred miles west and southwest of Charlotte, all the streams contain more or less gold-dust. Nuggets of a few ounces have been frequently found, and there is one well-authenticated case of a solid nugget weighing twenty-eight pounds, which was purchased from its ignorant owner for three dollars, and afterward sold at the Mint. Report says a still larger lump was found and cut up by the guard at one of the mines. Both at Greensboro, Salisbury, and here, the most reliable residents concur in pointing to certain farms where the owners procure large

sums of gold. One German is said to have taken more than a million of dollars from his farm, and refuses to sell his land for any price. Negroes are and have been accustomed to go out to the creeks and wash on Saturdays, frequently bringing in two or three dollars' worth, and not unfrequently negroes come to town with little nuggets of the pure ore to trade.

The iron and copper mines were developed only to a limited extent before the war. The necessities of the case led the Southern authorities, however, after the outbreak, to turn their attention to them, and considerable quantities of the ore were secured. This was more especially true of iron.

North Carolina is adapted to all the agricultural products of both North and South, with the exception of cane sugar. The marshes on the coast make excellent rice plantations, and, when drained, are very fertile in cotton. Much of the low, sandy section, extending sixty miles from the coast, is covered with extensive forests of pitch-pine, that furnish large quantities of lumber, tar, turpentine, and resin, for export to Northern cities. When cleared and cultivated, this region proves quite fertile, but Southern energy has thus far been content to give it very little improvement. Much of the land in the interior is very rich and productive. With the exception of Missouri, North Carolina is foremost, since the close of the war, in encouraging immigration. As soon as the first steps were taken toward reconstruction, the "North Carolina Land Agency" was opened at Raleigh, under the recommendation of the Governor of the State. This agency is under the management of Messrs. Heck, Battle & Co., citizens of Raleigh, and is now (August, 1865) establishing offices in the Northern cities for the purpose of representing the advantages that North Carolina possesses.

The auriferous region of North Carolina extends into South Carolina and Georgia. In South Carolina the agricultural facilities are extensive. According to Ruffin and Tuomey (the agricultural surveyors of the State), there are six varieties of soil: 1. Tide swamp, devoted to the culture of rice. 2. Inland swamp, devoted to rice, cotton, corn, wheat, etc. 3. Salt marsh, devoted to long cotton. 4. Oak and pine regions, devoted to long cotton, corn, and wheat. 5. Oak and hickory regions, where cotton and corn flourish. 6. Pine barrens, adapted to fruit and vegetables.

The famous "sea-island cotton" comes from the islands along the coast, where large numbers of the freed negroes of South Carolina have been recently located. South Carolina can produce, side by side, the corn, wheat, and tobacco of the North, and the cotton, rice, and sugar-cane of the South, though the latter article is not profitably cultivated.

Notwithstanding the prophecies of the South Carolinians to the contrary, the free-labor scheme along the Atlantic coast has proved successful. The following paragraph is from a letter written by a prominent journalist at Savannah:--

> The condition of the islands along this coast is now of the greatest interest to the world at large, and to the people of the South in particular. Upon careful inquiry, I find that there are over two hundred thousand acres of land under cultivation by free labor. The enterprises are mostly by Northern men, although there are natives working their negroes under the new system, and negroes who are working land on their own account. This is the third year of the trial, and every year has been a success more and more complete. The profits of some of the laborers amount to five hundred, and in some cases five thousand dollars a year. The amount of money deposited in bank by the negroes of these islands is a hundred and forty thousand dollars. One joint, subscription to the seven-thirty loan amounted to eighty thousand dollars. Notwithstanding the fact that the troops which landed on the islands robbed, indiscriminately, the negroes of their money, mules, and supplies, the negroes went back to work again. General Saxton, who has chief charge of this enterprise, has his head-quarters at Beaufort. If these facts, and the actual prosperity of these islands could be generally known throughout the South, it would do more to induce the whites to take hold of the freed-labor system than all the general orders and arbitrary commands that General Hatch has issued.

The resources of Georgia are similar to those of South Carolina, and the climate differs but little from that of the latter State. The rice-swamps are unhealthy, and the malaria which arises from them is said to be fatal to whites. Many of the planters express a fear that the abolition of slavery has ended the culture of rice. They argue that the labor is so difficult and exhaustive, that the negroes will never perform it excepting under the lash. Cruel modes of punishment being forbidden, the planters look upon the rice-lands as valueless. Time will show whether these fears are to be realized or not. If it should really happen that the negroes refuse to labor where their lives are of comparatively short duration, the country must consent to restore slavery to its former status, or purchase its rice in foreign countries. As rice is produced in India without slave labor, it is possible that some plan may be invented for its cultivation here.

Georgia has a better system of railways than any other Southern State, and she is fortunate in possessing several navigable rivers. The people are not as hostile to Northerners as the inhabitants of South Carolina, but they do not display the desire to encourage immigration that is manifested in North Carolina. In the interior of Georgia, at the time I am writing, there is much suffering on account of a scarcity of food. Many cases of actual starvation are reported.

Florida has few attractions to settlers. It is said there is no spot of land in the State three hundred feet above the sea-level. Men born with fins and webbed feet might enjoy themselves in the lakes and swamps, which form a considerable portion of Florida. Those whose tastes are favorable to timber-cutting, can find a profitable employment in preparing live-oak and other timbers for market. The climate is very healthy, and has been found highly beneficial to invalids. The vegetable productions of the State are of similar character to those of Georgia, but their amount is not large.

In the Indian tongue, Alabama signifies "Here we rest." The traveler who rests in the State of that name, finds an excellent agricultural region. He finds that cotton is king with the Alabamians, and that the State has fifteen hundred miles of navigable rivers and a good railway system. He finds that Alabama suffered less by the visits of our armies than either Georgia or South Carolina. The people extend him the same welcome that he received in Georgia. They were too deeply interested in the perpetuation of slavery to do otherwise than mourn the failure to establish the Confederacy.

Elsewhere I have spoken of the region bordering the lower portion of the Great River of the West, which includes Louisiana and Mississippi. In the former State, sugar and cotton are the great products. In the latter, cotton is the chief object of attention. It is quite probable that the change from slavery to freedom may necessitate the division of the large plantations into farms of suitable size for cultivation by persons of moderate capital. If this should be done, there will be a great demand for Northern immigrants, and the commerce of these States will be largely increased.

Early in July, of the present year, after the dispersal of the Rebel armies, a meeting was held at Shreveport, Louisiana, at which resolutions were passed favoring the encouragement of Northern migration to the Red River valley. The resolutions set forth, that the pineries of that region would amply repay development, in view of the large market for lumber along Red River and the Mississippi. They further declared, that the cotton and sugar plantations of West Louisiana offered great attractions, and were worthy the attention of Northern men. The passage of these resolutions indicates a better spirit than has been manifested by the inhabitants of other portions of the Pelican State. Many of the people in the Red River region profess to have been loyal to the United States throughout the days of the Rebellion.

The Red River is most appropriately named. It flows through a region where the soil has a reddish tinge, that is imparted to the water of the river. The sugar produced there has the same peculiarity, and can be readily distinguished from the sugar of other localities.

Arkansas is quite rich in minerals, though far less so than Missouri. Gold abounds in some localities, and lead, iron, and zinc exist in large quantities. The saltpeter caves along the White River can furnish sufficient saltpeter for the entire Southwest. Along the rivers the soil is fertile, but there are many sterile regions in the interior. The agricultural products are similar to those of Missouri, with the addition of cotton. With the exception of the wealthier inhabitants, the people of Arkansas are desirous of stimulating emigration. They suffered so greatly from the tyranny of the Rebel leaders that they cheerfully accept the overthrow of slavery. Arkansas possesses less advantages than most other Southern States, being far behind her sisters in matters of education and internal improvement. It is to be hoped that her people have discovered their mistake, and will make earnest efforts to correct it at an early day.

A story is told of a party of strolling players that landed at a town in Arkansas, and advertised a performance of "Hamlet." A delegation waited upon the manager, and ordered him to "move on." The spokesman of the delegation is reported to have said:

"That thar Shakspeare's play of yourn, stranger, may do for New York or New Orleans, but we want you to understand that Shakspeare in Arkansas is pretty ---- well played out."

Persons who wish to give attention to mining matters, will find attractions in Tennessee, in the deposits of iron, copper, and other ores. Coal is found in immense quantities among the Cumberland Mountains, and lead exists in certain localities. Though Tennessee can boast of considerable mineral wealth, her advantages are not equal to those of Missouri or North Carolina. In agriculture she stands well, though she has no soil of unusual fertility, except in the western portion of the State. Cotton, corn, and tobacco are the great staples, and considerable quantities of wheat are produced. Stock-raising has received considerable attention. More mules were formerly raised in Tennessee than in any other State of the Union. A large portion of the State is admirably adapted to grazing.

Military operations in Tennessee, during the Rebellion, were very extensive, and there was great destruction of property in consequence. Large numbers of houses and other buildings were burned, and many farms laid waste. It will require much time, capital, and energy to obliterate the traces of war.

The inhabitants of Kentucky believe that their State cannot be surpassed in fertility. They make the famous "Blue Grass Region," around Lexington, the subject of especial boast. The soil of this section is very rich, and the grass has a peculiar bluish tinge, from which its name is derived. One writer says the following of the Blue Grass Region:--

> View the country round from the heads of the Licking, the Ohio, the Kentucky, Dick's, and down the Green River, and you have a hundred miles square of the most extraordinary country on which the sun has ever shone.

Farms in this region command the highest prices, and there are very few owners who have any desire to sell their property. Nearly all the soil of the State is adapted to cultivation. Its staple products are the same as those of Missouri. It produces more flax and hemp than any other State, and is second only to Virginia in the quality and quantity of its tobacco. Its yield of corn is next to that of Ohio. Like Tennessee, it has a large stock-raising interest, principally in mules and hogs, for which there is always a ready market.

Kentucky suffered severely during the campaigns of the Rebel army in that State, and from the various raids of John Morgan. A parody on "My Maryland" was published in Louisville soon after one of Morgan's visits, of which the first stanza was as follows:--

> John Morgan's foot is on thy shore,
> Kentucky! O Kentucky!
>
> His hand is on thy stable door,
> Kentucky! O Kentucky!
>
> He'll take thy horse he spared before,
>
> And ride him till his back is sore,
>
> And leave him at some stranger's door,
> Kentucky! O Kentucky!

Last, and greatest, of the lately rebellious States, is Texas. Every variety of soil can be found there, from the richest alluvial deposits along the river bottoms, down to the deserts in the northwestern part of the State, where a wolf could not make an honest living. All the grains of the Northern States can be produced. Cotton, tobacco, and sugar-cane are raised in large quantities, and the agricultural capabilities of Texas are very great. Being a new State, its system of internal communications is not good. Texas has the reputation of being the finest grazing region in the Southwest. Immense droves of horses, cattle, and sheep cover its prairies, and form the wealth of many of the inhabitants. Owing to the distance from market, these animals are generally held at very low prices.

Shortly after its annexation to the United States, Texas became a resort for outcasts from civilized society. In some parts of the Union, the story goes that sheriffs, and their deputies dropped the phrase *"non est inventus"* for one more expressive. Whenever they discovered that parties for whom they held writs had decamped, they returned the documents with the indorsement "G.T.T." (gone to Texas). Some writer records that the State derived its name from the last words of a couplet which runaway individuals were supposed to repeat on their arrival:--

> When every other land rejects us,
> This is the land that freely takes us.

Since 1850, the character of the population of Texas has greatly improved, though it does not yet bear favorable comparison to that of Quaker villages, or of rural districts of Massachusetts or Connecticut. There is a large German element in Texas, which displayed devoted loyalty to the Union during the days of the Rebellion.

An unknown philosopher says the world is peopled by two great classes, those who have money, and those who haven't--the latter being most numerous. Migratory Americans are subject to the same distinction. Of those who have emigrated to points further West during the last thirty years, a very large majority were in a condition of impecuniosity. Many persons emigrate on account of financial embarrassments, leaving behind them debts of varied magnitude. In some cases, Territories and States that desired to induce settlers to come within their limits, have passed laws providing that no debt contracted elsewhere, previous to emigration, could be collected by any legal process. To a man laboring under difficulties of a pecuniary character, the new Territories and States offer as safe a retreat as the Cities of Refuge afforded to criminals in the days of the ancients.

Formerly, the West was the only field to which emigrants could direct their steps. There was an abundance of land, and a great need of human sinew to make it lucrative. When land could be occupied by a settler and held under his pre-emption title, giving him opportunity to pay for his possession from the products of his own industry and the fertility of the soil, there was comparatively little need of capital. The operations of speculators frequently tended to retard settlement rather than to stimulate it, as they shut out large areas from cultivation or occupation, in order to hold them for an advance. In many of the Territories a dozen able-bodied men, accustomed to farm labor and willing to toil, were considered a greater acquisition than a speculator with twenty thousand dollars of hard cash. Labor was of more importance than capital.

To a certain extent this is still the case. Laboring men are greatly needed on the broad acres of the far-Western States. No one who has not traveled in that region can appreciate the sacrifice made by Minnesota, Iowa, and Kansas, when they sent their regiments of stalwart men to the war. Every arm that carried a musket from those States, was a certain integral portion of their wealth and prosperity. The great cities of the seaboard could spare a thousand men with far less loss than would accrue to any of the States I have mentioned, by the subtraction of a hundred. There is now a great demand for men to fill the vacancy caused by deaths in the field, and to occupy the extensive areas that are still uncultivated. Emigrants without capital will seek the West, where their stout arms will make them welcome and secure them comfortable homes.

In the South the situation is different. For the present there is a sufficiency of labor. Doubtless there will be a scarcity several years hence, but there is no reason to fear it immediately. Capital and direction are needed. The South is impoverished. Its money is expended, and it has no present source of revenue. There is nothing wherewith to purchase the necessary stock, supplies, and implements for prosecuting agricultural enterprise. The planters are generally helpless. Capital to supply the want must come from the rich North.

Direction is no less needed than capital. A majority of Southern men declare the negroes will be worthless to them, now that slavery is abolished. "We have," say they, "lived among these negroes all our days. We know them in no other light than as slaves. We command them to do what we wish, and we punish them as we see fit for disobedience. We cannot manage them in any other way."

No doubt this is the declaration of their honest belief. A Northern man can give them an answer appealing to their reason, if not to their conviction. He can say, "You are accustomed to dealing with slaves, and you doubtless tell the truth when declaring you cannot manage the negroes under the new system. We are accustomed to dealing with freemen, and do not know how to control slaves. The negroes being free, our knowledge of freemen will enable us to manage them without difficulty."

Every thing is favorable to the man of small or large capital, who desires to emigrate to the South. In consideration of the impoverishment of the people and their distrust of the freed negroes as laborers, lands in the best districts can be purchased very cheaply. Plantations can be bought, many of them with all the buildings and fences still remaining, though somewhat out of repair, at prices ranging from three to ten dollars an acre. A few hundred dollars will do far more toward securing a home for the settler in the South than in the West. Labor is abundant, and the laborers can be easily controlled by Northern brains. The land is already broken, and its capabilities are fully known. Capital, if judiciously invested and under proper direction, whether in large or moderate amounts, will be reasonably certain of an ample return.